Scholars and Their Kin

Scholars and Their Kin

Historical Explorations, Literary Experiments

EDITED BY STÉPHANE GERSON

The University of Chicago Press
Chicago and London

The University of Chicago Press, Chicago 60637
The University of Chicago Press, Ltd., London
© 2025 by The University of Chicago
Published 2025
Printed in the United States of America

34 33 32 31 30 29 28 27 26 25   1 2 3 4 5

ISBN-13: 978-0-226-82081-1 (cloth)
ISBN-13: 978-0-226-82083-5 (paper)
ISBN-13: 978-0-226-82082-8 (e-book)
DOI: https://doi.org/10.7208/chicago/9780226820828.001.0001

Library of Congress Cataloging-in-Publication Data

Names: Gerson, Stéphane, editor.
Title: Scholars and their kin : historical explorations, literary experiments /
    edited by Stéphane Gerson.
Description: Chicago : The University of Chicago Press, 2025. |
    Includes bibliographical references.
Identifiers: LCCN 2024024469 | ISBN 9780226820811 (cloth) |
    ISBN 9780226820835 (paperback) | ISBN 9780226820828 (ebook)
Subjects: LCSH: Families—History. | Families—Historiography. | Genealogy. |
    Scholars—Family relationships—History—20th century. | Scholars—Family
    relationships—History—21st century. | Scholars—Genealogy—History. |
    Racially mixed families.
Classification: LCC HQ519 .S368 2025 | DDC 306.8509—dc23/eng/20240611
LC record available at https://lccn.loc.gov/2024024469
♾ This paper meets the requirements of ANSI/NISO Z39.48-1992 (Permanence of Paper).

Contents

Introduction: Recoveries, Excavations, Recastings

STÉPHANE GERSON

At sixteen, LaToya Ruby Frazier began photographing her family life in Brad-dock, Pennsylvania, a steel mill suburb of Pittsburgh. For fourteen years, she took photographs of her mother Cynthia and her grandma Ruby, sometimes with Frazier herself: images of women and men in empty rooms, women and men afflicted by disease, women and men comforting one another. In 2005, Frazier asked her mother and her mother's boyfriend, Mr. Art, to pose to-gether. In one photograph, Cynthia sits behind Mr. Art, her chin resting on his left shoulder, her arms wrapping around his naked chest. Mr. Art looks to the side, "detached and numb," Frazier writes; he is too spent from his menial wage job to sustain her gaze. Cynthia holds her companion while staring into the camera and creating a trace of this fugitive moment. *Mom Holding Mr. Art* shows love and endurance and solidarity—weighed down by pain and the emotional depletion that afflicts those who, like Frazier and her kin, "strug-gle to survive environmental racism."[1]

I first encountered this photograph series, *The Notion of Family*, at the Brooklyn Museum in 2013. Though moved and intrigued, I knew too little about the history of documentary photography to grasp the radical nature of Frazier's project. Walker Evans and Lewis Hine had also photographed mid-western mills, but from the outside; Dorothea Lange made iconic portraits of Dust Bowl refugees, but without naming migrant mothers such as Florence Owens Thompson. Frazier, in contrast, positioned herself *within* a family that happened to be hers and, from that location, she gave voice to individual lives afflicted by systemic violence. "Each of us are markers along a larger historical timeline," she writes of her closest relatives.[2] Her photographs, sliv-ers of "Braddock's black steel experience," limn the critical edges of this time-line: labor exploitation and segregated housing, pollution infesting human organisms, political neglect and failing health care systems. Frazier's photographs link "the private, domestic, steeply gendered, and multilayered world inside her home to the collective public history of her town, county, state, and nation."[3]

For a long time, I believed that such engagement with family and history was closed off to historians. Born in Brussels in 1967, I grew up in a Jewish family that, like others, lived in the shadow of the Holocaust. The family story I heard throughout my childhood, the only story my grandmother Zosia told at home, revolved around her wartime survival between Belgium and France. This story nourished my historical vocation, and yet, as a doctoral student in the 1990s, I selected an altogether different dissertation topic: local memory in nineteenth-century France. I was not alone in choosing what French historian Claire Zalc calls avoidance. "My departed relatives dwell on the edge," she writes. "I've kept dodging them."[4] She has done so by tracing the trajectories of other Jewish immigrants to France, immigrants whose voices both veiled and channeled those of her ancestors. My avoidance followed a different route: In 1994, I returned to Brussels to videotape Zosia as she told her story once again; afterward, I allowed this tape to sit in a drawer. The personal and the professional, the familial and the scholarly would remain separate.

This was partly because the matter felt too close, too fraught, too embedded in my grandmother's own story. How could a witness and a historian coexist within the same family? Beyond this, the expectation of analytical distance I internalized as a doctoral student prevented me from contemplating family history as a line of research. "History disembodied from the historian has a long and rich tradition in this country," writes Charles Dew, a scholar of the American South who waited until late in his career before writing about racism in his Florida family. "It is what I was taught in graduate school. We should try to be scientists. . . . Strip the personal out of our scholarship."[5] Like others, I took it as fact that this familial domain resided outside the boundaries of legitimate historical investigation.

While this belief pervaded the US and European academic worlds, fissures have appeared. Long compelled to suppress their family histories in the name of professional acceptance and "objectivity," some African American historians have embraced autobiography, memoir, and family histories because, Carla Peterson explained in 2011, "too often, African Americans are seen in the aggregate as a problem." Peterson chose to write about her kin to fulfill "a sense of obligation to the dead, to give a face to those left faceless by acts of trauma and erasure" enacted in histories, archives, and genealogies.[6] Some feminist historians have sought to recover within their families the intimate experiences and political activities of ordinary women—Black, white,

Chicano, and other. Seeking to understand the ways in which gender and class take form in specific households and familial situations, seeking also to fashion a politics of embodiment, Carolyn Steedman thus explored the stories her mother shared about "the terrible unfairness of things, the subterranean culture of longing for that which one can never have."[7]

Such family histories, like those of other scholars in American studies, comparative literature, or anthropology, largely escaped my attention in the mid-1990s. This was partly because I did not search for such works and partly because it was not that difficult to miss them at the time. This would soon change. Since the 2000s, and even more so the 2010s, a growing number of scholars have blended the scholarly and the personal in family histories that cut "against the grain" of the historical profession. Some of them have approached their families as social and affective spaces, institutions, sets of power dynamics, "barometer[s] for the society, tracing and reflecting the atmospherics of social life and social change."[8] Through this prism, scholars of migration and labor have apprehended social trajectories, interpersonal dynamics, and quotidian expressions of solidarity and suffering.[9] Historians of colonialism and colonized societies have studied violent dynamics of debt and dependence, experiences of domination and exile, complicated relationships to assimilation.[10] Scholars of Holocaust history and memory have traced emblematic trajectories of survival or exile, or sought out ancestors who vanished with nary a trace—*the lost* to whom they bore vicarious witness.[11] Personal family history thus has a history of its own, as Marianne Hirsch and Leo Spitzer make clear in their afterword to this volume, a history very much in the making given the current stream of books,[12] articles, online forums, workshops, and collective research projects in various parts of the world.[13]

A few years ago, I retrieved the recording of Zosia's war story, a memorial artifact I am now turning into a source for a history of survival, aid, postwar storytelling, and familial remembrance. In doing so, I am encountering other scholars who are investigating families that happen to be theirs. While drawing from personal memoir, they are nonetheless venturing beyond self-writing, embracing the methods and commitments of their intellectual disciplines to capture the experiences of relatives and kin whose lives unfolded against specific historical horizons. As Christine J. Walley explains in her book about her working-class family in Chicago, writing in this vein "means not only looking inward but also turning the self outward and tracing the links and relationships that shape and define . . . the broader social worlds of which we are a part."[14] Like Frazier, these scholars are unveiling "more complexity, more depth, more intimacy"—and critical edges as well—within worlds that are both near and remote, both theirs in a collective sense and populated by distant and hence unknown actors.[15]

This critical mass makes the present moment a rich, stimulating one. Still, few of the scholars I have encountered were necessarily aware of the colleagues who had embarked on similar projects in other fields and countries. There is still little interface, little common experimentation or consideration of what the genre makes possible in terms of historical knowledge. Nor is there universal acceptance of this mode of writing. A decade or two ago, personal family historians were commonly told that their research did not fit within categories of legitimate scholarship. Atina Grossmann, a US-based historian of Germany, found it "both perilous and rewarding" to delve into her family archive; she encountered resistance among some editors. In France, Martine Sonnet likewise received eighteen rejections before a small publisher accepted her "unclassifiable" manuscript about her father, a blacksmith at the Renault ironworks, and his family.[16]

While this suspicion has softened, it persists. In the eyes of some, studying familial subjects produces biases; it precludes the surprise, the strangeness on which scholarly analysis relies. Others deem the genre presentist and too individualistic ("neoliberal") to apprehend broader collective forces. It may even mark a retreat, "an evasion of the challenges of social and political reform."[17] Women and members of underrepresented ethnic and racial minorities are sometimes accused of writing "narrow, me-search" that too closely shadows their objects of study.[18] Junior scholars who experiment with such writing sometimes encounter resistance as well, a particularly ominous result as they face the greatest professional risk in doing so.[19] One such scholar told me not long ago that her dissertation committee praised the chapter she devoted to her family, but also advised her not to publish it any time soon. "Students often ask me for permission or the license to write freely and authoritatively about their family histories," Tao Leigh Goffe tells us in her essay. Securing this license is not always straightforward for scholars either.[20]

This collection thus begins with a paradox: a growing number of personal family historians coupled with a sense of isolation for many of them. It also begins with frictions: a yearning for experimentation coupled with unease in some quarters, a lingering belief that this turn toward family may close off analytical and political opportunities. In March 2020, I invited nine scholars who had launched personal family histories to address these intellectual, institutional, and political questions while sharing their works in progress. This symposium, held at New York University, drew so many faculty, graduate students, and nonacademics that we had to close registration.[21] One attendee, a historian, emailed me afterward that she had "never seen so many scholars, in a public setting, feel comfortable enough with each other to share their vulnerability while discussing serious methodological issues." The historian Kendra T. Field, a respondent that day, declared that conversations such as these are just beginning.

The present volume stretches this beginning toward a deeper grasp of the genre's present and future possibilities.[22] A collection of essays loosely based on the symposium papers, *Scholars and Their Kin* is imagined as rigorous and exploratory, alive and contentious, critical and self-critical, creative and comfortable with its own inner tensions. It maps a genre's multiple strands; freezes a specific moment in scholarly writing; opens a window into quotidian histories that leave few traces; and creates a space in which contributors and readers alike may imagine new forms of writing about the past, the dead, and the contours of scholarly investigations. As Christine Détrez asks in her essay, "What instruments, taken from the social sciences and literature, can we use to darn the holes of history and memory?"

The collection seeks to capture some of the voices, perspectives, and positions within personal family history, and to foster cross-pollination across disciplines, generations, and geographical boundaries. Slightly more than half the contributors are historians, specialists of the nineteenth and twentieth centuries who approach their families with tools in legal, gender, social, cultural, and political history. Others are sociologists, anthropologists, critics, and specialists in sexuality, race and diaspora, and African American studies. This disciplinary, temporal, and geographical breadth—far from exhaustive, but encompassing the Caribbean and Asia, Tunisia, England, France, Belgium, and various US regions—makes it possible to trace filiations and allows for comparisons. While most of the contributors hold tenured positions in US and European research universities—evidence of the symbolic capital often required to experiment in this fashion—two of them, Tao Leigh Goffe and Amy Moran-Thomas, wrote about their families before going up for tenure. Regardless of rank, all the contributors framed their essays as they saw fit. Altogether, they offer diverse templates and sources of inspiration for future experimentation.

In a recent book on his grandparents' exile from Eastern Europe to South America, Claudio Lomnitz wrote that "we are no longer governed by tradition, so we can't simply rely on a collective past. For this reason, family history is again relevant. It is no longer an aristocratic incantation of the glories of a lineage, but very simply our precondition: a matrix of past decisions that made us possible. And we stretch back to those decisions in moments of danger."[23] Danger constitutes the horizon against which the genre has recently blossomed: the 2008 subprime crisis and growing social inequalities, racist police violence, the COVID-19 pandemic, the growth of anti-democratic forces, global warming, all of them embedded within what Siegfried Krakauer calls "the tiny catastrophes which make up daily life."[24] Not unlike genealogy, whose relationship to the historical discipline is notoriously fraught, some personal family historians are turning to the local and the familial as loci of meaning and self-identification, or even refuges which bear tactile traces of a grounded, collective past, resisting the ravages of time. "In the midst of general distress," philosopher Simone Weil wrote in 1949, "the almost irresistible force of attraction" of family provides "a little living warmth against the icy cold which all of a sudden ha[s] descended."[25]

The personal family histories offered in this collection are immersed in such pursuits, but not consumed by them. They stand at a slight remove, just under the surface of their own undertakings, attentive to the methodological, political, and ethical ramifications of their choices. From this critical position, they both acknowledge and question the force of attraction that Weil describes, the visible and imperceptible longings that lead us to see certain things though not others in our archives and writing. There is, of course, a politics to these longings and delineations of family, a politics to our genealogical lines and narratives of origin, belonging, or rupture. Instead of retreating, the essays that follow reckon with this politics and engage with broader worlds within and beyond our families. They do so through three operations that surface across the volume: recovery, excavation, and recasting.

Access to experiences, reminiscences, personal papers, photographs, physical spaces, and oral stories enables the contributors to provide histories from within an expanse that often eludes researchers. Blending temporalities, cutting across the periodizations, the geographical divides, the categories that structure and at times constrain scholarly inquiry, they uncover subtle, sometimes more acrid, sometimes more inclusive histories of ordinary people and familial relations. The volume's first register is thus one of *recovery* of past lives and relationships. By "reestablish[ing] the flesh and blood of [her] mother's body," Christine Détrez contributes to a history that grants "the ordinary dead" depth and density. This personal family history produces specific forms of knowledge, open to intimate domains as well as the familial and societal norms that determine what can be shown or shared.[26] It also participates in a broader reconfiguration of Western relationships to death and grieving: an invention of new public and private forms of mourning, all the more necessary when collective affiliations weaken and, as Détrez writes, "our familial inheritance consists of silence and loneliness."[27]

Like other contributors, Détrez embraces a microhistorical perspective that aims its gaze not at the state or totalizing mechanisms alone, but at interactions between ordinary people and broader forces that shape but do not flatten their worlds. Among the some 150 passengers and 10 crew aboard TWA flight 741, hijacked between Tel Aviv and New York in 1970, were two unaccompanied minors, Martha Hodes and her sister. Half a century later, Hodes traces the emotional and memorial ramifications of this world-historical event within her nuclear family. In this essay, as in others, the family is the locale in which historical crises—wars, genocides, structural racism, deindustrialization, ecological destruction—are felt and experienced, filtered and refracted. Within these crises, the contributors uncover spaces in which men and women made choices that had lasting consequences. Moving beyond a "post-ironic" stance that subsumes individuals within discourses and typologies, Marnix Beyen connects the life experiences of his Flemish grandfather August to, first, the older man's collaboration during World War II and, second, the complicated aftermath of his actions within his family. Leslie Harris unearths complexity by recovering the calculus that surrounded relationships to race and class within her African American family. Expecting to write a history of social ascent into New Orleans's middle class, she came across more unexpected choices, starting with her great-grandmother Zulime's rejection of a Creole ancestry that could confer higher status but also—in Zulime's view—leave her descendants vulnerable to jealousy and discrimination. "My ancestors' lives and choices show that the costs of upward mobility are sometimes measured against the possibility of personal, even intimate, anguish or satisfaction."[28]

Some contributors hence recover pain, affection, and care giving within the texture of families. Christine Bard's essay captures the love that her father Jack, a school teacher and poet from northern France, gave and received. "At its core: fatherly love, daughterly love," anchored in the familial solidarity of a "modest middle class . . . underrepresented in non-fiction and literature." Along the edges of family life, Bard also maps the secret "geography" of a closeted homosexual man who found freedom, escape, and self-discovery in collages of dried flowers and furtive trysts along the ramparts of the town of Maubeuge. My own essay recovers the layers of a wartime relationship in which attraction, friendship, and care were interlaced with deference, class difference, abandonment, and humanitarian politics that proved impossible to acknowledge after the war. This relationship both connected and separated my grandmother from the French woman who helped her in Nice between 1942 and 1944 and then all but vanished from familial memory.

Like LaToya Ruby Frazier, the contributors understand that violence, too, can lodge itself within the texture of family life. This violence often evades the eye in official archives and gets erased from public stories, out of revulsion or shame. In the familial realm, it is felt, perceptible, recalled, embodied, and occasionally said or shown. This violence requires its own intimate and critical history, a series of *excavations* that constitute the volume's second register.[29]

Sometimes, the violence originates outside the family. The "overseas intimacies" Tao Leigh Goffe retrieves in her grandparents' transoceanic itineraries, between the Black Pacific and the Chinese Atlantic, involved men and women who cared for one another within "the racial formations and the political economy of the Caribbean plantation." Some of these relatives, the inheritors, are pictured in Goffe's family albums while others, the disinherited, usually darker skinned, are missing. Focusing on bureaucratic and embodied forms of violence, Martha S. Jones considers the laws and regulations, agents and paperwork that, in Harlem and then Port Washington, New York, constrained the lives of her interracial family, leaving indelible marks on those who, like Jones, "remained among the monstrous, the mongrel, the fatally misplaced." In other situations, violence implicates the people it affects. Inspired by W. G. Sebald's unfinished last book on his family's complicities at a remove, Amy Moran-Thomas excavates the trajectory of her white working- and middle-class family across the Pennsylvania Salient, their lives "bound up with the origins of oil" on land taken from others, mined for carbon, and then depleted.[30] Elsewhere, buried harms show a very different face as "obscured" forms of violence surface within the family itself. Clare Hemmings excavates the sexual abuse of great-uncle Charles and the "banal brutality" of grandfather Reg in the English coastal city of Brighton. While grandpa's beatings and humiliations may have reflected wartime trauma or class socialization, he "beat his son because he could. Because he liked it; he was good at it; it was his due."

Hemmings writes about familial violence she observed, violence spoken about at home, and violence left out of family stories that "gestured and buried as well as revealed." The stories that are told and heard, retold and reformulated, effaced and recollected constitute prime sites of excavation, between the past and the present. "Family history asks who we are, how we came to be," writes Jones. "Sometimes the answers are revealed in matters of flesh, of blood, of color, texture, and timber. They may be of girth and pace, grace and stillness. Still, they are also always stories." Jones's parents "didn't have an experience, a vocabulary, or an analysis that placed us in another light," but they had "their own story, one about how they, as two people of different races, troubled law, culture, and the very idea of family." The texture of families is woven out of stories that endow the world with meaning without necessarily conforming to broader norms—or even coalescing into a notion of family that all relatives make their own. Fashioned, heard, and experienced by family members, these stories sometimes foreground what Hemmings calls "the subjective and desiring nature of *adjudication*—which story one settles with or embellishes." At other times, they reveal what has been left out because it is too acute, too painful, too dangerous. Martha Hodes writes eloquently about the journal she kept as a twelve-year-old in the Jordan desert: "My determination to craft a story about the hijacking that erased fear was impelled by the thought of my father awaiting—desperately hoping for—the return of his daughters."

The scholar's familial position thus opens yet other histories that seldom leave traces: silences and erasures, the unknown and the unacknowledged, sites of forgetting rather than sites of memory. We still know more about the collective memory of wars or genocides, to name but these, than we do about their afterlives within homes, transmitted (or not) from one generation to the next through words and omissions, gestures and bodily stances, papers and photographs. "The presence of a historian within a family . . . makes it somewhat possible to foil the law of silence, to resist the gravitational pull of the unsaid," writes Christine Bard. "It permits us to ask questions and listen to answers."[31] Indeed, something about personal family history engages our senses and vulnerabilities, allowing us to think more precisely and expansively about absences and secrets.

By excavating the myths that have obscured relationships to class and race within her family, Leslie Harris enables us to grasp "the loss" of historical actors in familial memory as well as broader historical processes: "what has been covered up because it does not fit with the triumphal narratives of US history, . . . what has been lost because some ancestors believed that histories of slavery and racism were too painful to retell." Christine Détrez excavates the gendered silence that, in her family, turned her mother's death into a secret. My ethnography of my grandmother's war story follows the same two-pronged approach. I both recover the rescuer whose name was never uttered and make this silence an object of study, with its political afterlives in postwar Belgium: "the interactions and sentiments my relatives and I could not imagine, the gestures we could not emulate, the appreciation we could not express."

Moving past debunking, such personal family history approaches myth making and silencing as quotidian, collective processes. As she explores what her relatives did not say (or know) about violence in the Pennsylvania Salient, Amy Moran-Thomas unveils the multiple layers of what, at the symposium, she called "deep forgetting." Her tender yet critical history encompasses familial "origin myths" that elide participation in the oil boom; larger

entwinements of geological and racial tropes that legitimate white seizure of
Seneca land; an environmental destruction no one wanted to see; as well as
toy trains and souvenir railroad spikes bearing testament within the home
to "violent land dispossessions." Moran-Thomas delineates what is done but
not said, the emotions embedded in that silence, and the scholar's attempts to
excavate "the tension between knowing and not knowing the grounds of an
American family history."

Exploring the known and the unknown, the familiar and the foreign, the intimate and the historically distant can destabilize us as scholars. At the same
time, it reconfigures our relationships to historical actors and archival traces,
opening up a third register, a *recasting* that makes us notice what our histories
owe to our own fears and desires. In 1986, Carolyn Steedman already tapped
the emotions that traversed her relationship with her mother to fashion an
embodied knowledge that rejected gendered notions of scientific neutrality. In
the decades that followed, scholars across the disciplines have shown that what
speaks to us may also be what moves us, that what we think and what we feel
can enrich one another. They have fashioned lines of inquiry shaped by doubt,
desire, regret, shame, guilt, and other facets of what Renato Rosaldo calls "the
whole self."[32] The COVID-19 pandemic accentuated this: "The range of emotions that field researchers are feeling now—fear, sadness, nostalgia, longing
for connection"—contribute in important ways to human understanding.[33]
Emotions become vectors of a tactile, sensorial, experiential knowledge and a
hermeneutical relationship with actors whose lives personal family historians
touch and feel and try to understand. This volume is suffused with loss and
love (Bard mentions both explicitly, but they surface in most essays), encounters with traces of pain, difficulties grieving in the face of silence (Détrez), and
yearnings that are not only intellectual. Marnix Beyen comes to grasp the grip
family history holds on descendants who are also scholars: what he once believed about his grandfather's actions, the "pattern of justification" in his own
version of the familial past, his "horizon of expectations." Clare Hemmings
likewise reflects on the narratives she needs about her grandparents: narratives
of ambivalence, guilty pleasures, disappointment, and violence, all of them
"shot through with my own queer feminist desires."
  Such self-reflexivity is both an epistemological move, seeking fuller forms
of knowledge, and an ethical one that protects historical actors by acknowledging all scholars project upon the past. Writing about individuals whom
they know personally, the contributors wrestle with the "ethics of care" that
governs their relationships with their subjects. Ethnographers have argued
that these relationships, or "negotiations for control," are "exposed in raw

form . . . , more up front, more honest" when the latter are relatives.[34] Amy Moran-Thomas hence speaks of a tug between competing urges, "a realization of the need to acknowledge, and a deep human fear of learning something poisonous" about relatives for whom she feels responsible. Other contributors lay bare their discomfort when piercing lives that are private and yet, by their own doing, now public as well. How, as empathetic scholars, do we avoid overwhelming our subjects, appropriating their stories, speaking in their place, turning them into heroic figures of suffering or victims alone? Do we have the right to publish, without authorization, the life stories of people who may have cherished their privacy?[35] "An ethical question surfaced: What do I do with Jack's secret?" asks Christine Bard regarding her father's sexuality and the character—"my gay father, my queer father"—she finds herself molding on the page. Her answer: renounce the tropes of investigation and revelation, embrace Jack Bard's fog (his own metaphor), "accept what remains unsaid and realize that I cannot say everything I know."

Acknowledging what cannot be articulated or completely known, acknowledging "the irrevocable impossibility of making the dead speak" (Détrez), these scholars recast their scholarly stances. The relationships they uncover within their families are shaped by gaps, withholding, and absence. The home opens intimate encounters with what is within reach and yet just out of reach, discernible but not always visible or documented. "The ethical terrain of writing about family, of seeking a path requires humility," writes Tao Leigh Goffe. "An acceptance of uncertainty and intergenerational trust is crucial."

Many of the contributors approach the known and the unknown by tapping family papers. Most of the personal family histories written in recent years likewise rest on such sources, but they often sit unquestioned, dehistoricized, and dematerialized (this is less true of family photographs). Enduring disciplinary norms may generate unease about such documents, deemed less legitimate than state archives; familial empathy may also make it difficult to critique such sources. And yet, the latter are mementos, traces of relationships, political stakes, forms of gendered labor, interfaces with bureaucratic or legal regimes, and artifacts whose lives within the home require their own histories. "With this sort of writing, it seems important to distrust the material, even to make distrust itself the material," Patrick McGuinness writes in his book about his family in Bouillon, Belgium. In this spirit, Martha Hodes's essay can be read as an intricate decrypting of family papers—her girlhood diary, her father's "Hijack" file folder—that are less transparent than she had initially surmised. Like others, her essay invites us to think critically about the production, preservation, selection, organization, and transmission of family archives, whether they were given this name at home or not.[36]

Another future direction: How do we *write* from and about these archives and histories? At the symposium, Hodes wondered how to "narrate layers and versions of memories, and the motivations and justifications behind those layers and versions, without sacrificing narrative flow." How can scholars write the family and its world—relationships and circulations, silences and absences, emotional resonances and political gestures—in all of their complexity and uncertainty? How, in other words, can we marshal form, genre, and rhetoric to produce new forms of knowledge from within?

These questions carry urgency. To some extent, we still live with the notion that professional legitimacy requires a remote, neutral, explicatory stance, or more bluntly that we must "sacrifice our voices." Some anthropologists likewise regret that "radical possibilities for experimentation with ethnographic writing remain unexplored."[37] This said, scholars such as Kate Brown, Arlette Farge, and Nicole Lapierre invite us to invent new languages to grasp historical and social experiences, languages that bend "words to the rhythm of the surprises experienced when in dialogue with the archives."[38] Growing numbers of scholars are joining them by writing memoirs, first-person narrations, hybrid forms of nonfiction, blends of verse and prose, and other literary forms.[39] Still, much remains to be invented at the interface of scholarly inquiry and aesthetics. To make historical voices audible; to convey multiple relationships to the past, the dead, and archival silence; to reach readers within and beyond academia, personal family historians inhabit a space in which "the arts of showing" infuse "the science of knowing."[40] Shifting between voices, the contributors to this volume trouble boundaries of genre.

For Amy Moran-Thomas, literary recasting takes the form of fragmented structure, a collage of texts and photographs that captures the pulse of fossil fuel meaning, its unpredictable violence, the clay veins of memory and experience across time and space. For Christine Détrez, it is a recourse to the materiality of archives, documents included in full within the text to outline a presence and an absence while protecting the author and her readers from pathos. For Clare Hemmings, it is a play with genre, a string of juxtapositions and interruptions that "refuse singular histories, singular affects, and singular modes of reading." In conversation with other scholars who experiment with verse, she also pens fictional "interventions" to characterize "how we spin yarns of our own to find ways of living with the past."[41] For Christine Bard, finally, recasting entails a "distinctive poetics": words that "evoke and suggest rather than describe and explain," questions lost along the way, tenderness toward her sources and especially Jack's poems, his verses interlaced with her own words, neither voice overwhelming the other.

"Between my background and my foreground, I am not sure where I stand."[42]

LaToya Ruby Frazier's words capture the exploratory stance of scholars who recover, excavate, and recast their family histories without codifying a genre, launching a school, or suggesting that all or even most of us ought to undertake such explorations. Those who have done so are likely to move on to terrains and forms of writing in which, beyond the recent past, men and women exist in their strangeness rather than their proximity.[43] Scholars can lead multiple lives at once, in flux and even in tension. Still, the methodological, ethical, and political questions we confront while writing about our kin expand and sharpen our craft. Christine Bard says so explicitly. Not only does this historian of women and gender now think in new ways about sexual identities, but she also grasps how much, over the decades, she has censored herself while writing about historical actors to whom she is not related.

The composition of *Mom Holding Mr. Art*, its lighting, its black and gray tones are Frazier's. *The Notion of Family* "is my testimony and my fight for justice," she says of her series.[44] And yet, she is not in the frame of this photograph, and she does not know where exactly she stands at the very moment she seems to tell us where she stands. Though Frazier is present, the project is not fundamentally about her. The same is true of the contributors to this volume. Personal experiences reveal human and physical histories that are the authors', but not only theirs. The double entendre in Moran-Thomas's chapter title—"Mine"—makes a broader point: Family histories can be personal without becoming proprietary.

Still, who among us is permitted to write such histories, and who is rewarded for doing so? What authority do we obtain within the family while writing about our kin, and at whose expense? What authority do we relinquish when our history is rooted in what novelist Nathalie Léger calls "the queasy fear of family life"?[45] What do we include, reframe, or leave out when it comes to secrets that, in our eyes or those of relatives, may sully the family name or generate disappointment, shame, even disgust? And how do we guard against the exclusionary potential of genealogical investigations?

This question opens a history of familial obligations and norms that are sometimes embraced and sometimes subverted. Some of these histories are necessarily rooted in the dynamics of nuclear or extended biological families: heredity, transmission, genetics.[46] Others hold expansive, playful understandings of family, along lines outlined by critic Angelika Bammer several years ago: "It is the relationship between these two—the families to whom we are born and the communities to which we are joined by choice, tradition, or force of historical necessity—that shape our sense not only of who we are but of our location as subjects of/in history."[47] These are histories of connection, attachment, and adoption, histories of shared commitments and elective affiliations, histories that, by bringing kin and others into proximity, illuminate the interactions that shape and curtail the possibilities open to all.

Marnix Beyen's essay on his grandfather morphs into a history of wartime human experiences in the village of Wijgmaal outside Brussels, a history that connects him "intimately" with neighbors who are more than strangers. Beyond blood ties and "the logic of inheritance" of plantation economies, Tao Leigh Goffe traces capacious, unruly genealogies that include extended kin, "putative fathers" of children born to mothers who are not their wives, and fellow members of what she calls "Afro-Asian feminist genealogies." My ethnography of my grandmother's war story reaches beyond the boundaries of our family toward a woman who was a friend, a helper, a godmother—a kin—and a stranger whose experiences must be grasped on their own terms. Christine Détrez's search for her mother leads her toward her mother's classmates, young women who navigated new social and institutional universes in the 1950s. They become part of her family history, and not only in compensation for her mother's absence. By situating families within broader collective worlds, by outlining a multiplicity of "familial" relationships and frameworks, always in flux, these histories provide distinctive, critical perspectives on "the constructed nature of family history, lineage, and pedigree."[48] They inhabit the open-ended space between our backgrounds and our foregrounds.

LaToya Ruby Frazier credits her mother and grandmother as coauthors of their own histories in Braddock. From Pennsylvania, Frazier made her way to Flint, Michigan, where in 2016 she spent five months with Shea S. Cobb, a poet and school bus driver, Cobb's mother Ms. Renée, and her daughter Zion. They took photographs; they wrote about lives in Flint. Inspired by Gordon Park's photo essay, *A Harlem Family 1967*, the four of them told a story of intergenerational solidarity among relatives and fellow citizens who, in "a collective act of trust," provided water when the authorities failed to do so. The Cobbs and Frazier are not biological relatives but "kindred creative spirits" in a photographic and poetic venture that draws from a "common lineage and shared experiences."[49] The book they fashioned together is entitled *Flint Is Family in Three Acts*.

Whose family history? Whose notion of family? Like Frazier's photographs, the essays in this volume impel us to seek answers in dialogue with our historical subjects. "In a speculative mode, family history can be a source of power," Tao Leigh Goffe writes. "It is choice. It is an act of taking the permission to imagine the intimacies that official archives cannot contain."

What's in a Name? Defining Race and Class in a New Orleans Family

LESLIE M. HARRIS

Shortly after the 2005 hurricane season devastated my hometown of New Orleans, I began to construct a book project that would explore the city's history
of race and class through my own and my family's experiences in the late
twentieth century. I sought to complicate the vision of African Americans
that was depicted in the days, weeks, and months after Hurricane Katrina
flooded 80 percent of the city and led to the relocation of just under half a
million residents, two-thirds of whom were Black. With significant exceptions such as Spike Lee's masterful *When the Levees Broke*, most accounts
appeared narrowed to fit immediate political arguments of blame for the col-
lapse of the levees; the failure of federal, state, and local governments to evacuate all residents before the storm; and even the fact that people continued
to live in such a fragile environment.[1] Many of these discussions bore only
partial relationship to the complex world of my family's experience and history there, not to mention the complicated emotional and cultural decision-
making that still informs commitments to remain in New Orleans, even now
amid the realities of climate change.

I started with the idea that my family's experiences were best encapsulated
in a post–civil rights, upwardly mobile trajectory that justified Black people's
decisions to remain in the city with which they identified. In charting the
American dream success story I knew best, I hoped to put to rest simplistic
criticism of those who lived in New Orleans, a place that had been environ-
mentally fragile from its founding. I was born in 1965, amid the greatest expansion in civil rights for African Americans since Reconstruction. We lived
into the opportunities that became available in the 1970s and 1980s: higher
education, professional status, and comfortable middle-class and upper-
middle-class lives. My parents, my sisters, and I secured places in an educated

Black professional class within New Orleans and beyond.[2] All of this occurred amid a more general post–World War II belief, reinforced by the Cold War, that American science could improve our lives and keep us safe. For New Orleans, this meant that the levees constructed by the Army Corps of Engineers after Hurricane Betsy in 1965 and maintained by local and state governments would protect us from future hurricanes. For forty years, until the 2005 hurricane season, those beliefs in safety from a hurricane remained untested.

As I began to research my book, I imagined that my family and I belonged to the first generation to have the opportunity to secure middle-class status—the fulfillment, following a popular African American saying, of the dreams of our ancestors. But as I delved into my family's histories and stories—even some that I thought I knew—I gleaned a more complex understanding of upward mobility and even racial identity. Although I am an experienced scholar of pre–Civil War African American history, part of a generation of historians who have recovered histories long believed to be unknowable, I began my own project convinced that I would be unable to discover much about my family's specific history. Yet I have learned more about this history—from the nineteenth century on—than I initially thought possible.

My family's history challenges a simplistic narrative of intergenerational progress as a marker of success. The possibility of upward mobility is deeply rooted in the American psyche. Numerous structural issues rooted in white supremacy—enslavement, racial terrorism, restrictions on voting and political participation, redlining—have limited the ability of African Americans to achieve and retain wealth and status. At the same time, the fact that wealth creation is often rooted in white supremacist practices—owning enslaved people, only serving white people when one owns a business, being submissive to whites—led some Blacks to disengage from traditional definitions of status and success. My exploration of my family has deepened my understanding of how individuals make these choices, sometimes at great cost. Some family members pushed back against economic, political, and social practices they viewed as egregious. Sometimes they also rewrote their family histories while rewriting their own lives, leading to remembering and forgetting within individual families and sometimes societies as a whole.

Growing up in New Orleans in the 1970s and early 1980s, there was one thing I thought I knew for certain about my parents and their ancestors: My mother's family was Creole, and my father's family was not. "Creole" in New Orleans is an important, historically complex, layered term and source of identity that has changed over time, in response to different racial regimes, and often with a rootedness in ancestry, but also in a somewhat mythic past.

Initially, the term referred to those born in lower Louisiana, of partial or full French and/or Spanish ancestry. In the nineteenth century, when "Creole" emerged with the most power as a unique identity for those in New Orleans and lower Louisiana, the term encompassed white, African-descended, and mixed-race (African, white, and Native) people who identified with French language and culture, including Catholic religion, foodways, music, and literature. It became a way for Blacks and whites to claim Louisiana as culturally and politically theirs, even as it became incorporated into the United States via the Louisiana Purchase. Louisiana's history encompasses numerous Native American cultures, French colonization in the eighteenth century, Spanish rule between 1762 and 1801, and then American rule following the 1803 Louisiana Purchase. But French culture in Louisiana drew renewed strength from the influx of white and African-descended immigrants fleeing the Haitian Revolution (1791–1804). In New Orleans, the Francophone population of African descent dramatically increased by 1810. For the remainder of the nineteenth century, residents, observers, and later historians focused largely on the ways in which Francophone, Anglo-American, and African cultures blended to create lower Louisiana's politics and culture.[3]

In African-descended New Orleans communities before the Civil War, Creole could refer to both enslaved and free people. French language and culture combined with African cultural practices in antebellum New Orleans. This is not to say that there were no divisions between enslaved and free people of African descent. Free Blacks, known in New Orleans as *gens des couleur libres*, self-consciously maintained their freedom by aligning with enslavers when necessary. They offered their military labor to put down slave rebellions and served in the Revolutionary War and the War of 1812; some owned enslaved people. White men also entered into sexually intimate relationships with women of African descent. The children of these relationships sometimes received an economic foundation from their fathers in the form of property, money, or business connections that also helped them to maintain their freedom.

These practices differ in degree, not kind, from the experiences of free Black people throughout the South.[4] But in New Orleans, as Emily Clark has argued, white travelers as well as non-Creole residents opposed "French" practices to "American" practices. They created the idea that most "free people of color" in pre–Civil War New Orleans were descended of interracial sexual relationships, known as *plaçage* relationships, in which women of African descent were "placed" by their African-descended mothers in intimate relationships with men of European descent. They created the idea of "quadroon balls" that exaggerated the sexualized beauty of free women of color and, in these myths, largely ignored the existence of free Black men within that community. Certainly there were numerous interracial relationships in New Orleans. French and American laws explicitly outlawed legal marriages between Blacks and whites. Similarly, Spanish law stated that those below the age of twenty-five who sought to marry someone of "'substantial social inequality,'" which was understood to mean of a lesser racial status, had to get the permission of their parents. Thus, these relationships could carry an air of illegality and immorality with them. But over time, the lived experience and variety of those relationships became ensnared in a romanticized idea of *plaçage* that narrowed our understanding of the history of free Blacks, race, and slavery in New Orleans. The mythical aspects of New Orleans as a center of interracial sexual relationships also elided the existence of these relationships elsewhere.[5]

By the 1830s, several myths or stereotypes about people of African descent and interracial relationships led to a narrow view of Creoles of African descent. Mixed-race, light-skinned Creole women became the most obvious symbol of these Creoles, and they were assumed to be in *plaçage* or concubinage relationships with wealthy white men. Kenneth Aslakson shows that in fact most of the white men in interracial relationships were of middling status, and the women were not all young, mixed-race, or light-skinned. And Emily Clark argues that the overemphasis on interracial relationships has overshadowed the strength of intimate relationships and family ties among free people of color themselves.[6]

Free people of color in antebellum New Orleans owned the most property as a group of any antebellum free Black community in the United States, North or South.[7] If one examines the web of antebellum laws and practices in Louisiana that limited Blacks' access to property, and then notes the high rate of property ownership among Creole women of African descent, one might assume that Creole women were living off the largesse of wealthy white men. Free women of African descent outnumbered free men of African descent in New Orleans; and free women of African descent owned more real estate than free men of African descent. These facts have led to an overemphasis on Black women's sexuality as a path to wealth for New Orleans' antebellum free Black community.

But throughout the South, being free and of African descent required a positive relationship with whites, be they intimate partners, family members, business associates, or customers. More broadly, free Blacks had to stay on the right side of the white power structure and the ways that power in the South was rooted in the protection of slavery. Connections to the white community, even intimate ones, were only a start. Freedom alone did not guarantee wealth. In her study of the first large expansion of the free Black population during Spanish rule, Kimberly Hanger observes that becoming "well-to-do" sometimes consolidated after two or three generations of freedom. In other words, most of those who gained freedom were not economically supported by their former enslavers or other whites. Rather, maintaining freedom and establishing economic stability, much less wealth, entailed hard work and business acumen.[8] Free Black women and men occupied particular economic and political niches that enabled their success in New Orleans. Some of these positions parallel patterns in other antebellum southern free Black communities. The majority of enslaved people who gained freedom in the Spanish period were perceived by enslavers to be useful as artisans in slave societies. The New Orleans community proved this after several fires in the late eighteenth century, when rebuilding the city rested on their skills.[9] Similarly, free Black men occupied a range of skilled positions in other southern cities, partly because slavery itself meant that whites were accustomed to Black men performing all kinds of labor and partly because white men sought to become enslavers, merchants, and plantation owners, ceding other forms of artisan labor to Black men. For free Black women, occupations as cooks, seamstresses, vendors, and domestic workers were more widespread in cities, and enabled them to earn money more easily than Black men. Women provided a labor for which there was an economic need whereas Black men could find better jobs and perhaps more money outside urban areas—either as sailors, the highest-paying job overall that Black men held in the antebellum era, or as agricultural laborers and perhaps landowners in rural areas. This led to a gender imbalance not only in New Orleans, but in every city in the antebellum North and South.[10]

Even as free Blacks created a variety of paths to relative economic independence, New Orleans' free Black population was not famous throughout the nation for its material wealth or military contributions. Rather, the seed of truth that the freedom and wealth of free Blacks depended on relationships with whites, including intimate relationships for some, overwhelmed the larger reality that hard work and a perilous middle status between slavery and freedom sustained all they achieved.[11] Although their highly skilled labor and entrepreneurship were a hallmark of Black Creoles down through the twentieth century, by the 1840s whites within and outside New Orleans promulgated the belief that the primary social and economic value of the city's antebellum free Blacks was rooted in the sexual availability of the community's women. Such projections paralleled long-held beliefs among enslavers that people of African descent were uniquely lascivious and immoral.[12]

Within communities of African descent, the significance of Creole identity went through complex changes. In the nineteenth century, the fact that

economic success for free people of color was tied to the white power structure meant that some free people hewed to practices rooted in white supremacy: They owned enslaved people or helped put down slave rebellions. After
the Civil War, some Creoles defined themselves and their ancestors as "free"
to indicate their distinct history from "freedpeople" who had been enslaved
until the Thirteenth Amendment in 1865. By the end of the nineteenth century, white supremacist laws began compressing all people of African descent
into a largely undifferentiated group of second-class citizens via racial clas-
sifications and Jim Crow segregation. New Orleans Blacks, both Creole and
non-Creole, continued to fight against these unfair laws as they built their
own institutions and community practices, most famously via the court case
of Homer Plessy, a fair-skinned Creole of African ancestry who could pass for
white. He used his appearance to bring a court case against racial segregation
on street cars. His loss in the Supreme Court case *Plessy v. Ferguson* in 1896
enshrined the legality of "separate but equal" segregation.[13]

As white supremacy pressed Black Creoles into an undifferentiated legal
status with all people of African descent, some began to focus on physical traits
as a way to distinguish themselves. Physical appearance was only one element
of Black Creole identity, and it was not very important, depending on the context. Alignment with particular Catholic churches and schools, as well as ancestry, occupations, and other cultural practices were just as significant. But
accounts of clubs that admitted only people with skin "lighter than a paper bag"
or hair through which a comb could easily pass marked the rise in importance
of physical appearance, especially as other markers such as French language
receded. Not until the Black Power movement of the 1960s did a large number
of African American Creoles reject this term as meaningful in opposition to
Blackness. But the advantages of Creole status remained active in the life of the
city. The first Black mayors were of Creole ancestry; Black Creole businesses
continued to flourish. In other words, ancestral wealth and cultural knowledge
still mattered socially and economically, with far-reaching consequences.[14]

As a child in late twentieth-century New Orleans, I first understood Creole
identity by observing physical differences, and then hearing stories about
those physical differences that connected to family histories. Although my
parents told stories about their families, we didn't often explicitly discuss
"Creoles" or "Blacks." In fact, we only self-identified as Black when I was
growing up. Much later, I would come to realize that my mother in particular
had a very complicated relationship to her family's Creole heritage, rooted
in her and her mother's exclusion from the family. My mother was a classic
Creole beauty: not bright white, but light-skinned, with the thick hair—not

straight, but strong, dark, curly, long, unruly—that impressed me as the unreachable goal of so many little Black girls in New Orleans. Given her almond eyes and smooth, light-brown skin, many white people asked her if she was Mexican or even Chinese. It was too dangerous for them to ask the more logical question in a city that had been at the center of the fancy trade, in which white men traveled across the South to purchase enslaved Black women as concubines. To ask "Who was the white man in your family tree?" would raise matters of slavery, illicit sex, real estate ownership, and inheritances misdirected from children with mothers of African descent

As I grew older, I began to understand that this beauty came from interracial relationships often rooted in slavery. Part of this knowledge came from my mother's research into her family's history in the late 1970s, in preparation for a family reunion. Her family was from Reserve, Louisiana, one of a line of small towns along the Mississippi River, about forty miles west of New Orleans. Her great-grandmother, Elodie Robinet, gave birth to seven children who had the last name of Perrilloux, including my mother's grandfather Louis. This was the same last name, except for the extra "r," as Marcellin Periloux, a white landowner in the nearby town of Lions who was listed on Elodie's children's marriage certificates as their father. Marcellin may have given Elodie the money that she and her brother Leo used to purchase a large plot of land on Valentine's Day in 1873. My mother's family still lives on that land. But my mother spent most of her childhood in New Orleans, where she attended St. Mary's Academy, founded in the antebellum period by the Sisters of the Holy Family. Henriette Delille, Juliette Gaudin, and Josephine Charles, daughters of Black women and white men, founded the order and embraced the celibacy of Catholic religious women in order to avoid *plaçage* relationships with white men. St. Mary's Academy was an institution deeply rooted in Creole New Orleans. To me, this further confirmed my mother's Creole identity. Her 1959 yearbook provided a visual depiction of the range of New Orleans Creoles.[15]

Beyond slavery, my mother's complicated relationship to her family was rooted in the fact that her mother Madonia's half-siblings had rejected her. Madonia's father Louis consolidated his land with some of the land that one of his brothers owned, land on which he employed tenant farmers. Madonia was his "natural" child by Therese, a woman who had been abused by her husband, one of the tenant farmers. Louis chased the husband off his land and then entered a common law relationship with Therese. Louis's children with his first wife, who had died, never welcomed Therese or Madonia into the family. And neither she nor my mother had any legal claim to the land, even though we often visited my mother's relatives in Reserve—more often than we visited my father's family in New Orleans.

My mother's beauty, the most visible sign of her Creole identity, posed a different kind of challenge for my high-achieving parents. They had four girls, and light skin and good hair—or really, physical beauty of any kind—were not to be valued above education. My mother graduated as salutatorian of her high school class at St. Mary's Academy, and although she had also been a cheerleader and a member of the homecoming court for St. Augustine High School, St. Mary's male counterpart, it was always clear to me which achievement was more important. The emphasis on education was a good thing for me: I was smart, wore glasses, and I believe I looked nothing like her when I was growing up—I felt awkward and too tall. All of those things got me into trouble with my classmates, though not the adults in my life. But my sisters were real beauties. Jennifer, closest in age to me, was the spitting image of my mother, but in chocolate brown. Regina was as fair as my mother's mother—everyone said she "took after" her. Born a decade after Regina, my youngest sister Rachel resembled her in coloring but had my mother's and Jennifer's facial features and eyes.

I always felt that I took after my father's family, which firmly believed it had no Creole heritage. As far as we knew, they had never owned land or property. My father's mother was petite, dark-skinned; my grandfather large, pecan-brown. My mother did not think it was a problem that I did not look like her side of the family. "You have keen features, like your grandmother"—my father's mother. Indeed, I have her pointy chin and small, thin-lipped mouth. And I was tall and lean like many of my paternal cousins. But I knew lots of people with brown skin and nappy hair like mine, and none of us were considered beautiful—just ordinary. I often wondered what it would feel like to look like my mother's family, to have my mother's hair and her easy, recognizable beauty.

My limited ideas about physical appearances and their relationship to Creole identity paralleled my ideas about which parts of my family history were recoverable and which were not. A narrow idea of "Creole" limited my view of how free Black people could be in antebellum New Orleans. I wasn't alone in this view. White enslavers in the early decades of the nineteenth century were more likely to free the children they had with enslaved women, and then to provide these children with small amounts of money and skills to set themselves up in business. These free Black individuals were more likely to leave traces in the archives, in the form of property ownership, probated wills of their own, legal records, and church records.[16] As I learned this history as a doctoral student in the late 1980s and early 1990s, I unconsciously adopted the idea that my mother may have been able to uncover her family history because her relatives had been free before the Civil War (although I still haven't found any evidence of that) and because they were Creole. When I was a child, her family story was, in my mind, so rooted in "Creole" and the purchase of the land that I assumed they had been free Blacks before the Civil War and acquired land in the antebellum era. My maternal family's references to their pre–Civil War history trails off in references to their arrival in Louisiana from "the islands"—perhaps Haiti? We just don't know.

I assumed that my father's non-Creole family history was rooted in slavery and thus unknowable. Before 1850, enslaved African Americans were enumerated in the federal census, not listed by name. Only if one knew one's ancestor's enslavers, and only if those enslavers had left some other record— probated wills, financial records, baptismal records, diaries, letters, or other papers with details of the people they possessed—might it be possible to transform those numbers into people. When it came to my paternal ancestors, it seemed an insurmountable task. In third grade, my teacher told us to ask an elder about their parents or grandparents. I vaguely remember asking my father's mother about her mother or perhaps grandmother. I remember that Walker was her mother's or grandmother's last name, and that it referred to her walk from Virginia to Louisiana. My grandmother passed away decades before I understood the significance of those words—a description perhaps of movement in the early nineteenth century as part of a slave coffle, with a slave trader, or with her own enslaver.

When I began this research, my mother shared materials and suggestions. I didn't want to ignore the work she had done. But my mother's family and life experiences had always had a bigger presence in our family than my father's. For this reason, I decided to focus on the latter half of the twentieth century for both families. In this way, my mother's and my father's family histories would occupy more equal knowledge bases. In 2010, I conducted an oral history with my father, focusing on his family knowledge and youth. I collected the full names of his mother and father and eleven brothers and sisters. I asked about their educational backgrounds, his father's and his mother's occupations. I also asked about his grandparents.

"Here," he said, pointing to a framed photograph on the side table near us. "This is Zulime, my grandmother." His grandmother looked like my maternal grandmother in terms of skin color, something I had never considered although I had seen the photograph for years.

"Zulime? Could you spell that?" I asked, "What kind of name is that?"

"I don't know—I think it's Indian. . . ."

Native American ancestry is the default answer for so many uncomfortable truths about race, not only among African Americans but also among whites in the United States. The notion that my grandmother Zulime was part Indian fit in with another piece of history my father imparted for the first time that day. He told me that his father, my grandfather, had been what is called a Mardi Gras Indian. Mardi Gras Indian tribes are composed of people of African and perhaps Native descent as well, who parade in New Orleans on Mardi Gras Day and on St. Joseph's Day. Their incredible costumes combine twentieth-century fantasies about Native Americans with the actual historic collaboration between enslaved people and Native Americans against European oppressors in eighteenth- and nineteenth-century Louisiana and beyond. Enslaved people would sometimes run to Native settlements in search of freedom.[17] Whether Native groups welcomed them depended on their own political strategies as they, too, battled European incursions on their land and sought self-determination. People of African descent also fought, unwillingly and willingly, against Native people throughout the nation.

Scholars of Native Americans have stated that the seeming embrace of Native people as ancestors often occurs most strongly in the places where Native people have undergone removal. For example, many southerners claim Cherokee ancestry, although the violent removal of Cherokee people via the Trail of Tears between 1830 and 1850 makes that unlikely.[18] Still, hearing that Zulime might refer to Native ancestry made me wonder whether it were possible to link Mardi Gras Indians to actual Native identities. Could my family history provide a new understanding of the city's intermingled racial histories? I was under no illusion, however, that uncovering Native ancestry would be simpler than uncovering the names of my enslaved ancestors.

My grandfather would have paraded before World War II. Mardi Gras Indian tribes warred—literally—in the streets of New Orleans until the 1960s, when Big Chief Allison "Tootie" Montana convinced the groups to limit their competitions to dances and elaborate costumes rather than physical combat. My father told me that an elderly cousin who now lived in California, Agnes Williams Dixon, had sewn my grandfather's costumes. We made plans to visit her and other relatives who had moved to California as part of the Great Migration. In the meantime, I searched online for "Zulime," expecting to find a Native American connection. Random court cases came up, from New Orleans and France. My French was not good enough to decipher the cases, and I could not figure out why the name Zulime appeared in nineteenth-century French documents. Was this a Native American woman caught up in the French court system?

That summer, my father and I journeyed to Vallejo, California, north of Oakland. Agnes and her family had moved there during the World War II era. I was excited to meet the oldest living relative in my dad's family. Agnes had known people who had lived through Reconstruction in New Orleans and possibly earlier—people who had survived slavery. She was slightly deaf. "Did your mother or father ever talk to you about slavery?" I yelled. "Slavery?" she replied. "Why, yes, they owned slaves."

Owned slaves? I thought she had misunderstood my question.

"What about slaves?" I asked again.

"Yes, we owned slaves. My grandmother told me that we owned slaves—a little girl."

I was speechless. This was not the family story! If anyone in my family had owned slaves, surely it would be on my mother's side—the Creoles.

Suddenly, the pieces of family history began to change shape. My father and his family had disdained Creole identity all their lives, but were they descended from slave-owning free Blacks—Creoles? I later learned that Zulime was a French name, not a Native American one. And whether the Native American ancestry I had been seeking existed or not, my father's invocations now seemed part of a larger family narrative that sought to avoid Creole identity.

Indeed, this is what Zulime herself had sought to do. According to Agnes, Zulime partnered with at least three men during her lifetime, one of whom may have been white. By the time she married the last, my great-grandfather William Harris, she had turned her back on the Creole ancestry that most of her family had embraced in the nineteenth and twentieth centuries. Agnes says that Zulime, who was fair enough to pass for white, wanted to avoid confusion about her racial identity and her children's. They would be Black. Although no pictures have surfaced of William, he was apparently of clear African descent.

The exact details of Zulime's relationships to her family, her intimate partners, and her racial identity are lost. But a woman of her generation, Alice Moore Dunbar Nelson, wrote of the difficulties of mixed ancestry in the late nineteenth and early twentieth centuries. Born in 1875 to a mother of African descent and an absentee white father she never met, Alice Moore attended a segregated Black public school where darker students bullied her for being a "light nigger, with straight hair" and "half white." Within her family, Dunbar Nelson writes in an unpublished essay, "we never spoke of [skin and hair color]. Indian browns and café au laits were mingled with pale bronze and blond yellows all in one group of cousins and uncles and aunts and brothers and sisters." Outside her family, however, her appearance made her a target for Blacks who throughout her life assumed that her white ancestry gave her advantages. At the same time, whites who perceived her as white refused to hire her for jobs held by Black women, nor would they allow her to remain in the Jim Crow cars of trains. Some Blacks suggested that she pass for white, but that would have alienated her from her family and required an alliance with white supremacy that she refused. Although Zulime may not have experienced all of this, Dunbar Nelson's essay provides an unparalleled account of the struggles of mixed-race people who did not have the wealth or numbers to create or participate in the elite society most associate with Creole New Orleans.[19]

Still, Zulime's Creole ancestry was also more complex than it first appeared. As I completed my interview with Agnes, one of her nieces, Barbara Ann Williams Trapps, said, "You need to meet my grandson. He has researched all the family history, and he knows all kinds of things about it." Darius Alexander Trapps-Chabala, a high school junior, had researched our family history since the age of thirteen, interning in the Mormon archives near his home in Sacramento. At sixteen, he became the youngest registered genealogist in the United States and began to undertake genealogical work for people across the country.

Alex had contacted numerous members of our family, requesting digital family pictures that he posted on a Facebook site. He had searched Ances try.com and created a family tree. But the most important thing he revealed was the identity of our founding ancestor in New Orleans. For months, I refused to believe it. My father was not simply a descendant of enslaved and then working-class New Orleanians, who had not owned anything until our generation. Rather, he was a direct descendant of Jordan Bankston Noble— the famed Drummer Boy of the Battle of New Orleans. Noble was known throughout New Orleans in the nineteenth century for having kept time on the battlefield throughout the final battle of the War of 1812 under Andrew Jackson, future president of the United States.

As my cousin and I began to collaborate on our family research, we learned that Jordan Bankston Noble was born in Augusta, Georgia, around 1800. Both he and his mother, Judith, were enslaved by the Bankston family, who migrated to Louisiana with them. By 1813, Jordan and his mother were living in the Spanish Barracks just outside New Orleans. Apparently, the Bankston family had sold Jordan and his mother to John Brandt, who sold them in the fall of 1813 to the French slave trader J. G. Chaumette. Judith and Jordan were sold yet again in the summer of 1814, this time to John Noble, a lieutenant of the Seventh US Regiment of the Garrison of New Orleans. Noble retained ownership of the pair for just under a year before selling them in May 1815 to Captain Alexander White of the same regiment. It's unclear when Jordan learned to drum or why he retained the names Bankston and Noble, even though he was owned by several other enslavers after Bankston and Noble. But while owned by Noble, he performed the feat that would earn him glory as the Drummer Boy of the Battle of New Orleans: He maintained the drum roll until Jackson's US forces defeated the British in the final battle of the War of 1812.

Jordan was lauded for his wartime service by Jackson and others, but he was not granted freedom. His final enslaver, François Toulouse, provided for the freedom of all his enslaved people upon his death in 1837. By then, Jordan had "married" Pauline Evariste, also owned by Toulouse. Descended of enslaved great-grandparents who resided in New Orleans in the eighteenth century, Pauline would have been considered a Louisiana Creole. Jordan and Pauline were the parents of five children—Jordan Bankston Noble Jr., Valery, Juliette, Marianne, and Desiree—who also gained their freedom. After Pauline's death in 1849, Jordan entered into a relationship with Juliette Moran, a woman originally from Haiti. Of Jordan's children with Pauline, only Valery, Juliette, and Marianne survived to adulthood. Both Alex and I are descendants of Valery and his wife, Jeanette Aiken Noble, who are Zulime's parents.

Jordan is described in numerous accounts as a mulatto. His self-description on his applications for military pensions details his hazel eyes.[20] But Jordan's birth in Georgia, as opposed to Louisiana, Saint Domingue, or other French Caribbean colonies, would have excluded him from Louisiana's Creole class. In *Nos hommes et notre histoire* (*Our People and Our History*), published in 1911, Rodolphe Desdunes, a chronicler of the nineteenth-century Creole community, centers Louisiana French language and culture, along with fair skin, as constitutive of Creole identity. In the eyes of Desdunes, Jordan's white parentage, marriage to a Louisiana Creole and then to a Haitian woman, and his fame in the New Orleans community, especially after his enslavement ended, did not overcome his lack of French culture. Desdunes does not mention him in his chapter on the War of 1812, the politics of the Civil War and Reconstruction, or musicians in New Orleans.[21] At the same time, Jordan's wives, and especially his children, with conspicuously French first names, may have been French speakers and may have been more easily accepted into Creole society if they wanted to be.

Still, Jordan was the only person of African descent included in the Creole Exposition of 1884–85. This was a celebration of Louisiana Creole life that accompanied New Orleans' World's Industrial and Cotton Centennial Exposition. White Creoles created the exhibition at the exact moment they were working to exclude people of African descent from any connection to the word "Creole," to Louisiana French language and culture, and certainly to connections with white families. As a light-skinned person of African descent, Jordan claimed the most obvious physical markers of Creole status. Yet, he was born in Georgia, far from New Orleans or Haiti, the traditional foundation for Creole identity. He may not have spoken French fluently, if at all, which further separated him from an important marker of Creole status for Blacks and whites. Why would he have been included?

Highlighting the Battle of New Orleans may have reinforced Louisiana's place in the United States in a less complicated way than the recent Union occupation of Louisiana by federal troops during the Civil War and Reconstruction. And by holding up Jordan for his participation in the Battle of New Orleans, whites elided the participation of two battalions of free Black men as well as numerous others who served in the War of 1812.[22] Focusing on the War of 1812 also avoided the fact that Blacks fighting on the side of the United States in the Civil War were part of the conquering forces. But erasing the military service performed by Black Louisianans may not have been the most important "problem" that concerned French-descended whites. Rather, had the men who carried arms in the War of 1812 been included in the exhibition, many of their last names may have paralleled those of white families. The rapidly evolving project of racial segregation, which relied on a clear division between Blacks and whites, would have been revealed for the hypocrisy that undergirded it. As a "drummer boy" who did not carry weapons, and whose last name did not obviously connect to any of the French families in New Orleans, Jordan would neither valorize Black military prowess nor impugn the reputations of white Creole families by suggesting illicit antebellum relationships with women of African descent.

The loss of Jordan Noble in my own family remains a puzzle. The relatives I knew best carry no history or memory of him. When I returned to California the year after my initial visit, and Alex and I showed Agnes the photographs and materials we had gathered about Jordan and his children, she did not recognize him or know anything about his history. Although my father had been taking care of the gravesite of Jordan's son Valery—the same grave in which his own parents are buried—the name "Valery" meant nothing to him, even though he was Zulime's father.

How could someone so famous during his lifetime vanish from view within his own family? When Jordan's granddaughter Zulime turned her back on Creole and mixed-race ancestry, she also reinforced those ideas for at least one of her children—my grandfather Henry. Following his mother's lead, Henry married a dark-skinned woman, Dorothy. According to family lore, this cut him off from the light-skinned part of the family, who were trading more successfully on their elite identity, whether because of their Creole status or as descendants of Jordan Noble. In rejecting this status, my grandfather was choosing a life with my grandmother, but also accepting one of manual labor. Most of his relatives appear to have subtly but firmly ostracized him and his children. My family never met that part of the family. Henry worked as a moving man and Dorothy as a domestic servant, and they raised my father and their other ten children (except two who died young) in the public housing projects of New Orleans.

My father's family reveals the complicated calculus that surrounds the decisions made at different life moments to embrace particular race and class identities, for oneself and one's children. Much of the historiography has assumed that men and women who passed for another racial identity would choose whiteness or a racial identity as close to whiteness as possible. As Allyson Hobbs writes in her history of racial passing, many scholars have assumed that embracing whiteness was self-evidently better: "To be called black was to be defamed, insulted, and slandered. No injury was incurred when one was called white."[23] In New Orleans, holding onto Creole identity was another option, although increasingly one that carried more meaning within the Black community than for whites or the legal system. My great-grandmother's choice of Blackness signals a different path, taken for personal reasons, or political ones, or both. Zulime's choice and her son Henry's may have narrowed their economic opportunities as well as their children's, but they also rejected a vision of success rooted in closeness to whiteness and white supremacy. These choices signaled a moral choice that, in their eyes, carried greater importance than economic success.

My family history challenges the idea of a simplistic upward trajectory calculated through property ownership, education, and intergenerational transfer of wealth and social capital. To some degree, the lack of an upward trajectory can be attributed to racism. But what happens when some family members choose to step off, or are pushed off, the ladder of upward mobility because of character, personal values, or shifts in historic context? The narrative of inevitable upward mobility has served as a marker of success for the United States but also a moral judgment against Black people who failed to achieve it. That narrative is now being challenged in the aftermath of decades of economic turmoil, the more immediate disruptions of the COVID-19 pandemic, and the growth of anti-democratic forces. Upward class mobility is revealed to be an elusive and unpredictable combination of personality, opportunity, reaction to positive and negative social change, and cultural standards imposed from without and within communities. My ancestors' lives and choices show that the costs of upward mobility are sometimes measured against the possibility of personal, even intimate, anguish or satisfaction.

My academic training has informed my understanding of my family history and my understanding of the history of the city. For many, the distinctiveness of New Orleans has been rooted in an understanding of its free Black community as one that became wealthy because of its unique practices of sexual intimacy with whites. In reality, good relationships with whites, and not just sexual relationships, were necessary for Blacks to remain safe as well as to attain wealth in all parts of the South—not just in New Orleans. Blacks were wealthy in New Orleans because the city was the slave trade capital of the South—the wealthiest southern city—and antebellum free Blacks retained access to a wide range of skills and businesses that allowed them to siphon off part of that wealth for themselves, as long as they did not challenge the system of slavery and race.

An ending refrain in Toni Morrison's book *Beloved* stays with me: "It was not a story to pass on."[24] This response to trauma runs through my work, which seeks to recover lives and experiences in the face of actual or perceived loss. What has been covered up because it does not fit with the triumphal narratives of US history: The forced migration of the slave trade or Native American removal versus immigration? Slavery versus freedom? Entrenched poverty versus upward mobility? What has been lost because African Americans did not have the financial or institutional stability to build and maintain archives? And what has been lost because some ancestors believed that histories of slavery and racism were too painful to retell? As a graduate student, I accepted the challenge of recovering these histories without thinking about how difficult it might be to write about African American lives in the pre–Civil War era, without knowing what it would take to balance the rigor of writing academic history with the challenges of African American history. I continue to salvage my family's history and the history of New Orleans in the wake of Hurricane Katrina and the encroachment of climate change—I continue without knowing what future generations will make of this place and these histories once New Orleans vanishes beneath the sea.

What Did I Do with the One I Lost?

CHRISTINE DÉTREZ

"What do you do with your dead?" Such is the question artist Sophie Calle asked visitors to her 2017 exhibit at the Musée de la chasse et de la nature in Paris. Guestbooks were interspersed among the stuffed animals. So, then: What do people do with their dead? "Cross-outs in a datebook." "Passwords: MARGOT 3006." "I scatter the ashes little by little on each of my trips because I want him by my side." "When she dies, my mother wants my sisters and me to cremate her and then eat her with yogurt." "I symbolically designate them a part of my body. My brother has my left hand." "I ask them to make storms on my birthday. I watch for clouds." "For a long time, I read summaries of *Santa Barbara* episodes at my grandmother's grave because she loved that show. Now, the show has ended, it's sad." "From time to time, I go into a perfume store just to smell a small bottle of Chanel No. 5. That was my grandmother's smell." "I am twenty years old, this question seems to be written in another language." "I put him here, in this book. Antoine. I slip him between these pages so that a little bit of him remains somewhere. Antoine, Antoine, Antoine, Antoine, Antoine, Antoine, Antoine, Antoine, Antoine, Antoine."[1]

These are all undoubtedly ways of taming absence, of countering the silence in which death plunges the lost. For even in the most faithful and conservative families, memory of the dead dims and fades away after two, three, or at most four generations. But some of the dead are more silent than others. First, the ordinary dead, the unremarkable, all the "tiny" lives, the "weak" lives, the "forgotten" lives.[2] Then, the dead on whom weigh secrecy and taboos, those we are not allowed to speak about because they have been silenced. This is the silence I want to explore, the specific, familial silence that fell upon an equally specific woman: Christiane, an unknown woman who happened to be my mother. Hers, too, was an ordinary life, the life of an ordinary woman, distinctive only in its ending, at age twenty-six, in a car accident in Tunisia. A railroad crossing without a gate. A train. Christiane in the all-too-well-named death seat.

But the point in telling the story of a mother I hardly knew—I do not have a single memory of her—is to ask broader questions. How, at the turn of the twenty-first century, can we still erase the life of a woman? What do family secrets tell us about relationships of power and domination so tightly woven into daily life that we can no longer see their patterns? What instruments, taken from the social sciences and literature, can we use to darn the holes of history and memory? Is it possible for a sociologist to turn her own family stories and memories into objects of research?[3] Would this resolve their mysteries?[4] Reading the collective into the private is entirely consistent with my definition of the sociologist's craft: to meticulously deconstruct broad questions and concepts, to test them on the most ordinary situations, anchored in details and daily practices.

A First Project: Christiane in Huguette's Shadow

Let's begin with the facts. My mother, Christiane, died in a car accident: the car crashed into a train. I was two and a half; we were in Sfax, Tunisia, where my father was a *coopérant*.[5] Those are the only pieces of information I knew growing up, even though Tunisia was ever present in my childhood. My father used a few Arabic words (*fissa* for quickly, *barakalofik* for thank you), pieces of pottery and statuettes were displayed in the living room cabinets, my bedroom had a colorful rug, we owned shopping baskets woven from rush, a copper mortar and pestle, a birdcage in finely wrought metal, and an amphora on a forged iron pedestal—the objects that made up the childhoods of a whole generation of *coopérants'* children, born in Tunisia, Algeria, Morocco, or, like me, during summer vacation in France. In our photo album were pictures of the house, our dog, and me as a baby with my father and brother. But not a single photo of Christiane.

To learn more about a loss so close to me, the most obvious path would have been to ask my father questions. But a child does not need an unequivocal refusal to know that she cannot ask such questions. In her documentary *History of a Secret* (2007), the director Mariana Otero searches for the truth about her deceased mother and makes a similar observation: While she and her sister had been told the young woman left them to become an artist, they learned through their investigation that their mother had died from an illegal abortion.[6] Otero questions her father, who retorts that he never forbade them from asking questions. They only had to ask. In *Plot 35* (2017), the filmmaker

Eric Caravaca likewise notes this impossibility of asking questions, something that, like others, he later regretted, when the people who could have answered were no longer alive.[7] For a long time, I did not ask questions either. When I was fifteen or so, my father angrily flung out a sentence that closed any possibility of dialogue: "She wanted to leave me. She had a lover and when I told her, 'what about the kids?' she replied, 'I don't care, you can keep them.'" I was not a sociologist at the time; I was not exploring the multiple demands that weighed on women, such as be a good mother. It is easy to imagine the impact that my father's reply had on his teenage daughter. And so I took his side, the side of silence. The bad mother had simply gotten what she deserved. The lid of silence fell down once again.

Two encounters launched my investigation. Karine Bastide was in the audience when I spoke about one of my books. She told me about the "archives" left by her own mother, Huguette, who had died from cancer. Huguette Bastide had published a book and corresponded with Simone de Beauvoir. Karine had this correspondence, along with many readers' letters sparked by her book, a trunk of rejected manuscripts, love letters between her mother and a New Wave journalist, her mother's school records, the "feminist" section of her book collection, and countless other documents. Born in 1942, Huguette had taught at a primary school. My father's birthdate and profession suggested that Christiane had been her contemporary; she had likely been a primary school teacher as well. I thought I would never know anything about Christiane, that there was nothing to uncover, nothing for which to search. Her parents and younger brother had died, and I knew neither her older brother, my uncle, nor my cousins. I told myself that the excess of information about one woman could illuminate the dearth of information about the other. Along with Karine, I thus dove into her mother's archives.

We first presented our work at a 2017 symposium at the University of Réunion Island. All the documents we shared that day came from Karine's sleeves of paper, suitcase full of manuscripts, and binders of letters. When I mentioned the dearth of documents about my mother, the sociologist Jacques Walter told me that bureaucracies always keep traces. I took note, and then began reading investigations about the lost—by the historian Ivan Jablonka, the writer and classicist Daniel Mendelsohn, the lawyer Philippe Sands, all of them in search of grandparents, great-uncles, wives, and daughters who had been killed by the Nazis and, until their heirs launched these investigations, existed only in the silences and discomfort of those who remained.[8] There can of course be no comparison between the murdered people of history and those forgotten by time's relentless passage. Still, all of these stories conveyed the same message: Bureaucracies keep traces.

I decided to break this unusual, intense silence in my own family. But this raised another question: Why, after so many years, should we know? The writer Marguerite Yourcenar is unequivocal as she retraces the short life of her mother Fernande, who died a few days after her birth: "I take issue with the common assertion that the premature death of a mother is always a disaster, or that a child deprived of its mother feels a lifelong sense of loss and a yearning for the deceased," she writes in *Dear Departed*. "In my case, at least, things turned out otherwise."[9] Yourcenar explains that her "maid" Barbara did not only "replace" but "*was*" her mother. I likewise grew up with, and give thanks to, my second mother, Danielle. It was therefore something else entirely that swung me into motion: an interest for "ordinary" lives and what they say about social issues, especially when these ordinary lives belong to women.

I redirected my inquiry. Instead of projecting Christiane's life in the shadow of Huguette's, I would search for whatever information I could find about Christiane's. I had to start at the beginning, with an administrative document, and determine the dates that, at the moments of birth and death, bookended her life. I knew only two dates in her biography: my brother's birthday and my own. August 25, 1969, in Denain (northern France); October 14, 1970, in Sfax. I had to collect, discover, and invent the tiny traces that each individual does indeed leave in bureaucracies, in archives.

I requested the *copie intégrale* of my birth certificate.[10] It included my mother's birth date and town: July 2, 1945, in Halluin (northern France). After several steps (the file was nowhere to be found at first), I received a copy of Christiane's birth certificate, with marginal notes recording her wedding and death dates, irreversible and irrevocable: July 2, 1945; July 28, 1966; December 28, 1971. This woman who until then had neither a height nor a weight—people told me she was tall—became a series of archival call numbers, as in those science fiction movies where columns of numbers delineate a silhouette. It was a virtual frame, hung with flesh and skin. Numbers and a few letters, black symbols that proclaimed magical words: open sesame. In the Halluin town hall: document 100417–10042017143322. At the Archives Départementales du Nord: call numbers 1895 W 92, 1919 W 329, 1913 W 361, 1077 W 11. At the Archives Diplomatiques de la Courneuve: 2162INVA, box 320. In the Archives Diplomatiques de Nantes: SFAX_634PO3_49.

At the Archives Départementales du Nord in Lille, I was given access to Christiane's academic file thanks to an exemption. Since the most recent document dated from 1971, I would have had to wait several more years, until the end of the fifty-year restriction. Box 1077 W 11 contained documents from her short career as a teacher. It confirmed that she had passed the entrance exam to the École Normale des Filles de Douai (northern France).[11] I knew that my father, a primary school teacher, had also followed the career path of the Écoles Normales des Garçons, for young men, but he had never told me that he had met his future wife at the neighboring school for girls. And yet, in addition to the commitment Christiane signed to work in the education system for a decade (*engagement décennal*), I found a primary school inspector's preliminary report. It spoke of Christiane's "good" intellectual abilities, "sharp" intelligence, and "good, sometimes very good" work. There were more personal details too: "Impulsive nature, sensitive," or "Distracted student, immature personality, but can improve." And this last evaluation: "Intelligent and sensitive student whose results will improve once she acquires a little more maturity."

The administrative paperwork, paradoxically, brought her to life.

At the time, the school system separated students. Even today, equality of opportunity is a utopia more than a reality, but, until the creation of vocational middle schools in 1959, academic fates were determined at birth.[12] After primary school, an additional year of studies (*le cours complémentaire*) was possible for working-class students, whose education was meant to be short. Students from privileged backgrounds entered high school beginning in sixth grade; they were meant to continue until the national baccalaureate exam at the end of their senior year. But it was also possible for good students like Christiane to escape factory or home life after their additional year of studies by taking the École Normale's competitive entrance exam. After ninth grade, girls who had been flagged as promising candidates took a year of preparatory classes. If they passed the entrance exam, they signed a decade-long commitment to teach in public schools, and spent four years, usually as boarders, studying in their region's École Normale. Later, after taking the baccalaureate exam, they became primary school teachers. Christiane was the only one of her siblings to pass the baccalaureate, and, as her older brother Raymond told me when I met him later, "of the three, George was the resourceful one, I was good with my hands, and your mother was the intellectual."[13]

From Literature to Sociology: Searching for One's Mother, Uncovering a Cohort

In the archives of Christiane's École Normale, an "individual record" contained all of her report cards, with grade averages, class ranks, and teachers' comments: "Muddled mind. Poor work habits. We wish Christiane would be calmer and more thoughtful." "Some progress. Christiane must learn to control herself, to remain calm and attentive." "Christiane has certainly made efforts. She is capable of succeeding, but she has poor control over her learning. It would be good to consult a neurologist. The boarding school and her studies could be accentuating her difficulties" (tenth grade). "Conscientious, consistent, and disciplined effort is necessary. [Christiane] carries and presents herself better, but she must manage her behavior in class." "Her work has improved a bit, but Christiane is much too childish for her age. She uses crude language that is not suitable for the occupation she seeks." "It is necessary to read and reflect. You waste too much time. Christiane must make efforts to organize her thoughts. Much too impulsive" (eleventh grade). And finally, in twelfth grade, "Much too childish for this level of study. Her work lacks organization. Christiane may well fail if she does not force herself to make a more *conscientious* effort." "Still fidgety, little aware of exam requirements." "Effort made, but serious shortcomings remain."

It is possible that these comments, this portrait of an agitated and impulsive young woman, reframed my investigation. Daniel Mendelsohn noted the same reorientation in his foundational inquiry about "his" dead relatives. Searching for his great-uncle Shmiel, his wife, and their four daughters, whose inevitable end he knew all too well, he realized that the central question resided not in the details of their deaths but in the texture of their existence—the tiny details that brought them back to life. In addition, the terms employed in Christiane's report cards caused me to wonder whether they were meant to portray a specific person, this young woman who would later become my mother, or whether they revealed categories of academic and social judgment that I could uncover elsewhere. To find out, I requested all the student files from the class of 1965. I tabulated every profession (miner, lathe operator, gardener, railroad worker, factory worker, small farmer. . . . Some were teachers' daughters, but the majority of the girls came from the working class) and every teacher's comment. Christiane was not the only one to endure criticism. My inquiry was shifting from the individual to the collective.

The stakes were important: to turn worthy working-class girls into primary school teachers, a profession that mattered at the time. The girls had to be educated, capable of teaching, and at the same time toe the line. For this reason, it was sometimes necessary to remind them of their place. One's hair was poorly styled, another was untidy; one's tone was distracted, another did not know how to choose appropriate friends. The verdicts passed judgment on the girls' way of being as much as on their work. Some were hauled over the coals in comments that seem quite surprising today: "Claudine is still frivolous. Her studies appear to hold little interest. Why continue?" "Superficial student. Lacking in maturity, does not really seem fit for intellectual work." Annie's comments were hardly brighter. She, too, was messy, sometimes unpleasant, lacking in zeal. Her report card did not mince words: "Annie must think about another profession: her inability to make the slightest effort is incompatible with the job of a primary school teacher."

Indeed, passing the competitive entrance exam did not guarantee success: the girls also had to work, to apply themselves. These words—effort, work, persistence, courage—reappear constantly in these files, as if to reaffirm central tenets of working-class morality. Four years of education were meant to produce perfect young women. They would teach but also know how to sew; they would speak clearly but not too loudly; they would have good posture but without arrogance; they would be discreet but not overly so; they would display confidence but not too much; they would be dynamic but not irritable. They would embrace work, they would have good morals, they would be organized. This was an imposing task for the school director and her colleagues: 400 young women between fifteen and twenty-one years old, mostly boarders in a building wedged between the École Normale des Garçons and military barracks. Even though discipline was strict and outings were limited, the girls could not be confined at all times. Most went home to their parents once a week, and they had free time—for two hours on Thursday afternoons. This is when love stories began, and problems as well.

Certain files contain letters. When the director wrote parents or the academic inspector, she kept drafts and replies. Shut away for nearly sixty years, these papers speak again. One can almost hear voices, with their intonation and their accents, in the way a capital letter is written. Take Claudette, whose report cards inform us that she was "childish," "chatty," and "exasperating." Though she pretended to return home to her family, in truth she spent an afternoon in town. A long series of exchanges followed, in which her parents—a primary school teacher and a middle school principal—attempted in vain to cover for their daughter. Anna's file is extremely thick, for she was summoned, with nine other students, to appear before the school's disciplinary committee. In 1962, Saint Nicholas Day (a widely celebrated holiday in the north of France) happened to fall on a Thursday, the day outings were permitted for students. Anna and her girlfriends met some boys at Chez Rémy, a café where she lost a bet and drank a mix of beer, soap, and ashes. Friends already signed her into the log of returned students (the girls were allowed to leave only between 2:00 p.m. and 3:30 p.m.). They were "falsely confirming her presence at the school," for, having fainted, Anna was brought back to her dorm in a car. This did not escape the monitor's attention. Anna and Martine were suspended for eight days and deprived of outings for several months, while seven other young women were denied outings for periods that varied according to their involvement.

The letters also report that certain girls were pregnant and as a result had to change institutions. The director defended students who worked hard and heaped criticism on those whose commitment was lagging. She protected Marianne, to the point of writing a dozen letters to make sure she would be allowed to marry and not be deemed a dropout. But she was uncompromising toward young women she deemed slothful. Due to lack of space in the dorms, those girls would have to repeat a year elsewhere.

Faces emerge from these lists of names and report cards. Silhouettes, fates. Louisa, whose Sicilian family had arrived in France in 1957 and whose father was a miner, married without requesting the director's authorization as she should have done because she turned twenty-one during her first year. The tearful mother of Georgette, who had made an unidentified mistake, requested leniency for her daughter: "I was abandoned by my mother at ten years old, and I've wanted my daughter to have everything I did not have: the love of a mom and dad. Madame, my letter is perhaps disjointed, but it is sincere and I am in such a poor state that I am writing to you from my bed, for this has so shaken me that I have not been able to eat anything since last night." And this poignant conclusion: "I beg of you, do not allow my husband to know anything. Punish Georgette, but let her have an opportunity." And Jocelyne, who had run away and tried to cut open her veins, Jocelyne whom the director defended by emphasizing her father's harshness: "This student's previous behavior did suggest that she might run away. However, her personality was withdrawn and gloomy; she suffered from her father's severity. We were not aware of any relationship she might have had outside the school; she did not receive letters. She worked decently, without much participation in class, but complained that she could not concentrate. [. . .] It would be unfair to deprive this young woman, who has not been the subject of a serious reprimand until now, of the possibility of taking her [baccalaureate] exam because she has found herself temporarily overwhelmed by family difficulties, because she lacked the energy to overcome these difficulties."

I thought that perhaps I could find these young women who had so moved me. They are now more than seventy years old. Most got married at a time when most women took their husband's name. I created an account on social networking sites that brought together former students. The accounts had to be created in the student's name, so I had to pretend to be my mother. I listed her birthdate and reconstructed her course of studies based on the documents I had recovered. I used the photo from her academic file at age fifteen. Very quickly, I received a message from Yvette, who asked for news. One person led to another: ultimately, I found close to twenty former students. My second move toward sociology occurred when I began conducting interviews. In retrospect, it strikes me that calling these meetings sociological interviews was not simply a question of terminology: It allowed me to justify a meeting even if the people involved told me they knew my mother very little or had few memories of her. I was able to introduce my work as research about my mother, the lives of women of her era, and, even more specifically, depending on the person to whom I was speaking, *écoles normales* or *co-opérants*. In addition, using a voice recorder allowed me to "pull back," make this exchange a "professional" moment, and emphasize my identity as a sociologist and university professor rather than merely "daughter of."

When Yvette opened the door, she was so moved that she started crying. And yet, she quickly told me that she had not known Christiane well. Yes, she remembered her, but what could she say with any precision? Christiane was kind, she was joyful, she was a simple, tall girl. I listened to these women, who were as old as she would have been, and I thought to myself: they knew her, they spoke to her, they shared four years with her. The same dorm cubicles with curtains made of Provençal fabric; the same cafeteria with the Lurçat tapestry, *Liberté*, hanging on the wall. The same park, filled with daisies in springtime and a statue of an urban and a rural teacher-in-training. Incidentally, the statue is still there, even though the park is now abandoned. With the exception of the food that some brought back on Sunday nights, all ate the same thing. The École Normale des Filles' archives contain the cafeteria's records—every meal served over four years, morning, noon, and night, and the fancier holiday meals as well. I was fascinated by these lists of dishes, with beer at every meal, lists that reminded me of Georges Perec's attempt, in his work on the "infraordinary," to record all he had eaten and drank during one year.[14] At long last, these menus reestablished the flesh and blood of my mother's body.

She probably complained about the meals, about the "dog food," the apparently inedible shepherd's pie. Did she also joke, like the other girls? "Where is the meat? Hidden under a pea!" Did she join the uproar when, one night, they really were not given enough food? She danced to rock music, she danced the twist in the common room with her girlfriends on Sunday nights: They were allowed to play trendy records until a new director, judging discipline to be too loose, reduced the length of Thursday outings and forbade Sunday night parties. Like the others, Christiane must have been surprised by the arrival of young women from the École Normale d'Alger. "I am ashamed of it now; we watched them while they settled in. We were curious," Annie told me. She, too, was stunned by the announcement of President John F. Kennedy's death on November 22, 1963. It was evening in France. They learned the news from the radio in the dorm, while listening to a show for teenagers, *Salut les copains.* Perhaps Christiane, too, passed notes to boys in the neighboring École Normale des Garçons, maybe through the girls who attended the coed choir and German classes, or in the cases that boys and girls exchanged when they shared film reels for their respective movie clubs, or through the windows of the bedrooms at the end of the hall, which had a view of a vegetable garden. She met Jean-Luc, my father, at the café, Chez Rémy.

I also found some of her elementary school girlfriends and saw how their bodies differed. Jeanne would have liked to continue her education, but her father raised her alone after her mother was institutionalized, and Jeanne found herself working in a candy factory by age fourteen. She made little Jesus candies, she told me, by stretching hot sugar with her bare hands. Her figure, like her way of holding herself and speaking, differs from those of girls who became schoolteachers. These girls had been taught to hold themselves straight, style their hair, clean up their accents, and avoid grammatical mistakes.

Women of the Sixties: Similar and Different

The last component of my inquiry revolved around these young women's socialization. I had already established that the life of Huguette, Karine's mother, did not simply shed light on Christiane's. Now I would pay attention to the differences between them and make these differences meaningful through a comparative approach. As the documents accumulated, I discovered that Christiane came from a working-class background. Her mother was a cleaning woman, her grandfather delivered coal, and her grandmother was a spinner; her father was a police officer, son of a mason and a dining hall employee. Huguette's family had greater means: her father was an engineer and son of two schoolteachers, and her mother, who worked for the post office, was the daughter of a shopkeeper and a court clerk. Though Christiane and Huguette both became primary school teachers, their paths into the profession differed. Paradoxically, they inversed social hierarchies: Christiane followed the best route to the École Normale de Filles, whereas Huguette, who had begun high school in sixth grade, became a teacher through substitute teaching. This was due to her pregnancy during her senior year and her refusal to listen to her parents, who wished their daughter to have an abortion to avoid an unsuitable marriage or a scandal.

But they shared common pathways of socialization. Both were young women, born in the 1940s, who grew up in the 1960s. They were twenty-seven and twenty-three in 1968. Because one lived in the Lozère (south-central France) and the other in Sfax, Tunisia, neither took part in the May 1968 social movement. But their paths speak to the erosion, beginning in the late 1950s, of "close domination" (*domination rapprochée*) in domestic spaces, a domination that took the form of asymmetrical relationships, relegation to the home space, physical proximity, and lack of mediation between individuals—in short, the impossibility of escaping bodily contact.[15] Close domination governed relationships between parents and children, husbands and wives, and, until the 1960s, homeowners and live-in servants. The 1960s undermined it through a series of silent transformations: young people and women "left" the home thanks to longer and more widespread education, a youth culture that distinguished itself from parents' popular culture, and paid work for women, even after marriage and childbirth. Young people and women requested a forum for expression, which they found in radio and television programs and magazines specifically intended for them, all of which allowed them to share experiences and provided the foundation for a political consciousness.[16] Huguette and Christiane grew up during this distinctive era, but they lived through different experiences—social demotion for one, social promotion for the other. Yet, both would protest, question, and resist in their own way. Christiane freed herself through her studies, and further broke away from her social world by becoming a *coopérante*, a teaching position in Tunisia that allowed her to travel far away and earn a lot of money. Her means of emancipation originated in an individual strategy and a will to control her own body: undergo a tubal ligation, ask for a divorce.

As was the case with the paths of primary school teachers, a comparison between Christiane and Huguette proved meaningful here. Huguette had cultural and social capital. She read, wrote, and brought to mind those "princesses of primary school education" discussed by sociologist Francine Muel-Dreyfus.[17] Though she taught in a run-down school, she asked for help by sending letters to writers: first to the novelist André Maurois, who helped her in a very material way, and then to Simone de Beauvoir. Their correspondence would have an emancipatory effect. Bolstered by de Beauvoir's example and encouragement, she would write and become a feminist activist.

Comparison opens concrete, empirical reflections on the concept of agency.[18] According to the documents I gathered, Christiane resisted and fought on an individual basis to make decisions about her life and fate. Through reading and writing, Huguette also aspired to shape herself as an individual, or subject. But she also became an activist. What social conditions made this commitment, this overcoming of the self possible? Beyond Christiane's and Huguette's specific paths, this was the question Janice Radway asked about readers of sentimental novels,[19] the question Eleni Varikas asked in relation to nineteenth-century Greek middle-class women,[20] the question Catherine Achin and Delphine Naudier posed regarding women of the 1970s:[21] What does it take for a situation to appear unjust? What does it take for an individual to revolt, for a personal tactic to become a collective strategy?

Returning to Literature

Each biographical component can thus be connected, woven into the life paths of all the men and women who spoke to me—about Christiane but also, and especially, about themselves. If my investigation sheds light on entire topics that history and sociology have left in the shadows (the Écoles Normales des Filles, *la coopération* at the end of the 1960s), if it allows people to speak, or to speak again, what does it ultimately have to say about the woman herself, nearly fifty years after her death?

For, at the end of this study (if such a study truly has an end[22]), I am left with an impressionistic portrait. Christiane was ambidextrous, walked rather slowly, and liked to wear ballerina flats. She did not close the collars of her blouses. She had a green dress and danced for joy (Annie, her primary school friend, would imitate her dance); she made a little gesture to tuck a strand of hair behind her ear. In the Sfax middle school teacher's room, she wore a light-colored dress but also a dress with pink, red, and orange, like the colors in the bouquet of roses that Aicha, one of her former students I found in Sfax, gave me. She was cheerful, but perhaps this cheerfulness was a little put-on since, at the end of the investigation, a mystery remains about a suicide attempt over a boy, in tenth grade.

What do I do with the frustration of what could have been known and what will never be known? What do I do with the regrets about what could have been known from the beginning if I had asked earlier. I cite Mendelsohn again:

> At night, I think about these things. I'm pleased with what I know, but now I think much more about everything I could have known, which was so much more than anything I can learn now and which now is gone forever. What I do know now is this: there's so much you don't really see, preoccupied as you are with the business of living; so much you never notice, until suddenly, for whatever reason—you happen to look like someone long dead; you decide, suddenly, that it's important to let your children know where they came from—you need the information that people you once knew always had to give you, if only you'd asked. But by the time you think to ask, it's too late.[23]

The impossibility of recovering everything is no doubt characteristic of investigations such as mine. This may be because secrets remain, because people are elusive and out of reach, because they never come back to life, no matter what we do. What images did Josiane, Francis, and Chantal have in mind when they said they could "see her again" as they talked to me? What image did Jacqueline have when she wrote me that she had dreamed of Christiane the previous night?

Most important, some memories cannot be captured in words. Sociologist Anne Muxel emphasizes the extent to which sensory memory—the core of memory, the key to lost time, as Proust describes it so well—remains inaccessible in testimonies and interviews:

> The memory of senses is located in the deepest center. It is the most buried, for it cannot be erased; it is the most dangerous, also, for it is subject to the capricious shifts of involuntary memory [. . .] It is the deepest, but also the most fleeting, for it does not lend itself to rationalization and cannot really be justified. Nor can it be handed down. It is experienced and felt. It is given once and for all.[24]

In *Camera Lucida*, Roland Barthes fails to translate feelings into words: "No anamnesis could ever make me glimpse this time starting from myself (this is the definition of anamnesis)—whereas, contemplating a photograph in which she is hugging me, a child, against her, I can waken in myself the rumpled softness of her crepe de chine and the perfume of her rice powder."[25] Herein lies my failure: When I look at the photos of my mother that I now have, no smell emerges from my memory. To feel and smell, I went to Tunisia by boat. I did so to experience the crossing, to hear the seagulls and the noise of the ferry. I slept in the housing development in which we used to live, I walked in the same streets, and I heard the *muezzin*, even if it is now a recording and Sfax does not much resemble the city my mother knew and that Perec describes in his 1965 novel *Things* (another coincidence).[26] I also listened to the songs that had been popular among teenagers in her time, telling myself that she had listened to them and maybe liked them. I sang these songs loudly. I do not know which one was her favorite, nor whether she preferred Sheila, Sylvie Vartan, or Françoise Hardy. But it delights me to join my voice with hers.

I still do not know my mother's voice. Voices, like smells, remain out of reach, unless one has a recording. While it is troubling to rediscover the lost on voicemails—in an incredible irony, my decision to make my late father speak at last about this secret means that I have his voice forever saved on my computer's hard drive—the investigation runs up against the irrevocable impossibility of making the dead speak. We can come close by listening to recordings from the 1960s, for voices are also dated, and diction, intonation, and even pitch indicate the period in which a recording was made, independently from the technological possibilities of the time. But I would like to end

FIGURE 2.1. With my mother and our pet dog Quiquine on the ferry *L'avenir* (*The Future*), which connected Marseille and Tunis. I made this same crossing years later with my twenty-year-old daughter.

this essay with an investigative delight (*un bonheur d'enquête*). I borrow the term from historian Arlette Farge, who has written about the archival coincidences that unearth a misplaced letter or a loose sheet of paper in a box.

Likewise, in the murmur of collected words, of analyzed correspondence, of all the speech generated by my inquiry, it was through a surprising detour that I was given, if not Christiane's voice, at least her way of speaking. In a wink that is not without irony for those who are interested in the silencing of voices, it was Aicha, one of my mother's former students at Souk El Zitoun Middle School in Sfax, who gave me the intonation of her voice by repeating something my mother had told her in class: a request that she speak to her in French. Returning to literature is also to give oneself permission: the permission to borrow from cinema, say Agnès Varda and Jacques Demy, because imagination and lightheartedness are ways of speaking about pain; the permission to replace my mother's laugh, which was apparently quite loud, by that of actress Françoise Dorléac, who laughed equally loud and was likewise

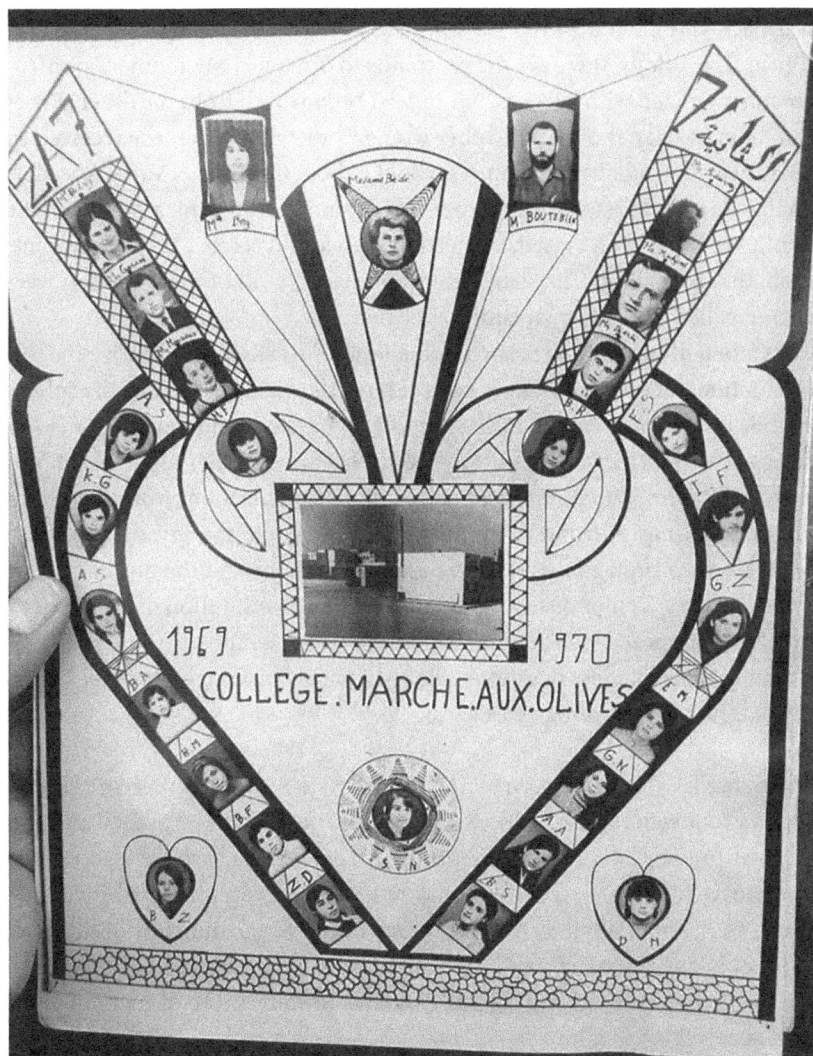

FIGURE 2.2. A photo of tenth-grade class A7m kept by Aicha. Aicha explained that the higher a photo is on the page, the more the teacher was liked by her students. My mother is all the way at the top, to the left. Aicha is the fourth student from the left, counting up from the bottom, under the initials "B.A."

killed in a car accident; the permission to write a text that does not darn the holes of the past, a text that resembles lace.

In the end, did I succeed at making my dead one speak? Maybe not, but the philosopher Vinciane Despret reminds us that reviving the dead matters less than re-viving them, than generating new stories. "The dead can certainly be recomposed, reconnected, but so can stories, histories that carry them, that start with them, and allow themselves to be sent elsewhere, toward other narrations that 're-vive' and that themselves ask to be 're-vived.'"[27] In this back and forth between the intimate and the collective, between literature and sociology, there are many strands to untangle. My mother's particular story, striated with silences, has indeed been woven from the other stories caught in my net: those of the other women I met, but also those received by email after the publication of my two books about Christiane. Various readers confided in me the story of a mother, a grandmother, an aunt, a woman of the family who had been erased, reduced to silence and secrets. It seemed to me, then, that by pulling Christiane from the shadows, all of these women were also "recalled" in their own family histories.

Among the countless research possibilities, we can also emphasize the role of emotions in social sciences. Long left on the sidelines by our disciplines as they sought to establish their scientific legitimacy, emotions have made a strong return in recent years, to the point that we can refer to an "emotional turn." The question concerns all stages of an investigation, from the scholar's positionality to her relationships with the people she investigates, from the ways each protagonist—the one asking questions and the one answering them—manages emotions to modes of writing and restitution of experiences. While it is impossible for inquiries into one's own family to ignore the emotional dimension, these questions belong in our scholarly templates regardless of the topic being investigated.[28]

Undoubtedly, we must return to Sophie Calle's question, and reverse it: not so much ask ourselves what we do with our dead, but instead what they do to us. Despret provides once again a response: "The dead turn those who remain into story makers. [. . .] 'Those who remain' thus carry out real investigations. [. . .] Above all, they make an effort to rise to the difficulty of the challenge of losing someone—and learning to find him or her again."[29]

So, after two books and a short film, has the adventure of reunion come to a close?[30] I think not.

This photo is one of my favorites: Christiane is fifteen, about to enter the École Normale. Her headscarf and raincoat indicate that she comes from a

FIGURE 2.3. The photograph of Christiane that never left her brother's pocket.

modest background. In all the photos I received during this inquiry (remember that I did not possess a single one of my mother at the outset), I encountered this strong, determined expression that now stays with me.

To me, this photo also visually represents the role of emotion in these distinctive investigations. It was sent to me by Raymond, my mother's older brother, who never recovered from the loss of the sister he adored. I shared my research progress with him, without ever receiving a response. One day, I asked him by email if he wanted me to stop talking to him about this work.

He replied by sending me this photo, with the following comment: "This photo never leaves the pocket close to my heart." In its damaged traces, in the folds and the rips, I seem to behold a brother's love and pain, and the tremendous difficulty of grieving when our familial inheritance consists of silence and loneliness.

Translated from the French by Hilary S. Handin

The Diary of a Twelve-Year-Old Hostage: Erasure and Survival in Family Memories, Stories, and Archives

MARTHA HODES

In 1970, my family was caught in a world-historical event. It was early September, and my sister and I were flying from Tel Aviv to New York. I was twelve years old, my sister was thirteen. We were flying unaccompanied because my mother had moved to Israel six years earlier to help start a modern dance company there. After my parents had divorced, my sister and I stayed in New York with our father and spent summers with our mother in Tel Aviv. That was the arrangement each of them wanted.

Not long after our stopover in Frankfurt, a man and a woman arose from their seats and ran up the aisle, shouting and brandishing weapons. They were members of the Popular Front for the Liberation of Palestine (PFLP), a Marxist-Leninist faction of the Palestine Liberation Organization (PLO), so radical that the PLO often disapproved of their tactics.[1] Obeying the hijackers, our captain reversed course and landed his US aircraft in the Jordan desert. A second hijacked plane, a Swiss airliner, landed later that night. The hijacking of an El Al plane had been foiled in midair earlier that day, and another US plane landed in Cairo where the hijackers blew it up within seconds of evacuation. Three days later, a British jet joined us in the desert. Our captors hoped to exchange passengers and crew from the three commandeered planes for Palestinian prisoners being held in Europe and Israel. While negotiations proceeded, my sister and I were among those held hostage, inside the plane, for a week. At the time, it was the biggest hijacking operation the world had yet seen—in the words of one reporter, "the most remarkable event in the history of aerial piracy." Journalists ventured out to the desert every so often, and when a member of our crew asked for news of the outside world, a reporter told him, "You *are* the news. You are the *only* news."[2]

FIGURE 3.1. Me at my mother's Tel Aviv apartment building the summer of the hijacking, 1970. Photo by Ehud Ben-David.

After we came home, we received no debriefing by authorities. No teacher sent us to a school guidance counselor, and no one took us to a therapist. Across the decades, then, my memories grew hazy and fragmented, punctuated by a few persistent images. Some were frightening: our copilot emerging from the cockpit with a gun at his neck, commandos wiring the plane with dynamite, a woman commando pointing her gun at me as I walked from the foul-smelling lavatory back to my seat. But there were cheerier images, too, and when I talked about the hijacking in the years afterward, which I did only rarely, I tended to focus on those: a strapping commando jumping rope with the children out on the desert floor, or the hostages laughing as we sang that summer's hit song by the folk trio Peter, Paul and Mary, changing the lyrics of "Leaving on a Jet Plane" to *living on a jet plane*.

Setting out to write a book about my experience nearly a half century after I came home, I queried old friends as to how I had recounted the hijacking to them. Their responses did not surprise me. "No harm done, no lasting effect," an elementary school friend told me. "I don't think I ever strongly associated your relating the experience with a sense of great trauma," a close friend from high school mused. "I thought you were not making a big deal of it," said my best friend from college, while a good friend from graduate school paraphrased my attitude as, "By the way, we were hijacked and it wasn't that bad." Others recalled my "very casual" tone and "air of detachment."

Among the most important questions historians can ask are *why* questions, and these are often the most difficult to solve, especially if they concern human motivation. When working with memories, historians must also ask: *Why did this person tell this story this way?* Attempting to understand my own experience of the hijacking, I set out to investigate why I had consistently narrated the event with a dismissiveness that startled my friends. I would find the answer in my father's experience of the hijacking and, more expansively, in my mother's departure from our family.

My presentation of the hijacking as almost entirely untraumatic relied for the most part on a single key memory: Soon after our plane lands in the desert, the copilot stands in the aisle to address the passengers. Tall and slim, his face kind and earnest, he tells us that he does not know how long we will be held, that we could be held indefinitely, but that our captors have promised "no bodily harm." I quickly memorize those words and hold onto them all week. In my memory, the copilot's words—spoken just as soon as we landed in a place with no airport—made me unafraid in the midst of everything swirling around me.

To piece together everything that happened around me that week, I pursued documents and records as any professional historian would do. I combed through airline archives, read press coverage, watched television broadcasts, and unearthed reporters' raw footage. I pored over moment-to-moment telegrams from the State Department and parsed debates over government responses. I contacted fellow hostages, scrutinized interviews with members of the Popular Front, and studied documents published by the Institute for Palestine Studies. I read reports from the International Red Cross about the hostages' health conditions, and I unearthed testimony from hostages who had brought lawsuits against the airlines.

On the evening of Sunday, September 6, 1970, Trans World Airlines Flight 741 made a precarious landing on a strip of earth, marshland hardened into a natural runway by the Jordan desert's remorseless summer sun. The British had named the makeshift runway Dawson's Field, after a Royal Air Force officer who used the toughened land for military exercises. The PFLP called it Revolution Airport. Known locally as Qā' Khannā, the spot was thirty miles northeast of the capital city of Amman. Given the falling darkness and hazardous conditions, our plane's landing was, improbably, a "greaser": smooth, with no damage to the aircraft. If fear filled the inside of the plane, outside a crowd cheered and fired weapons into the air. When someone propped a ladder from the back of a truck up to the aircraft's front exit, our hijackers descended, received as triumphant heroes. People dressed in military uniforms in turn ascended the ladder, carrying flashlights and rifles, lanterns and machine guns.[3]

A woman named Hallah Joseph, dressed in an army uniform, told us that we were "safe and welcome" in the country of Jordan, that the Popular Front members regretted the inconvenience they had caused. A man named Bassam Abu-Sharif said he was sorry, too, explaining his organization's motives and speaking about liberating his country from Israeli occupation. Armed men and women walked the aisles, guarded the exits, and confiscated our passports. The flight attendants, in their dual role as staff and fellow hostages, served dinner and distributed milk and water supplied by our captors, with particular attention to babies and young children. With an ambulance at the ready, a Palestinian doctor from the Red Crescent walked up and down inquiring whether anyone needed medical attention. The cabin crew set about making everyone as comfortable as possible for the night ahead.[4]

As the days passed, my sister and I found ourselves interested in the cause of our captors, which no one had ever told us anything about. Most of the commandos treated the children among the hostages with kindness. When a kid fashioned a game of "cat's cradle" from a piece of string, a commando communicated via sign language that his own children played the same game. When one of the commandos saw my sister wiping away tears, he said, in a way that felt fatherly, "Don't cry. We have children, too." But one of the women assigned to our plane frightened me. She always kept her weapon visible and rarely pointed toward the floor. Another hostage described her as "this one lady commando who constantly came in with a gun" and "looked like she was going to shoot everyone down." She was the one who pointed her gun at me when I was exiting the lavatory one day. Coldly she said, "Now *get* back to your seat," prompting me to compose my face to display no alarm as I walked slowly enough not to betray trepidation.[5]

There were plenty of other frightening aspects. Weapons filled the inside of the aircraft. Members of the Popular Front carried Kalashnikov AK-47 machine guns, and one time a man holding a hand grenade unsettled a flight attendant by feigning a tossing motion with a playful, "Here, catch." Some of the commandos, as one hostage described it, wore "bullets all around their waist," and some were very young; one hostage recalled that she did not "trust any child of fifteen or sixteen with a rifle." A stream of weapons-laden visitors also filed up and down the narrow aircraft aisle. During these visits, the hostages would quiet down and tense up, sensing that our captors wanted to make us afraid; some tried to project a dignified manner, others pretended to be asleep. Sometimes the visitors smiled among themselves, shook hands, or slapped one another on the back. Some pointed to the hostages and laughed, others acted like tourists taking in the sights. One hostage joked that we were "the main attraction at the Jordanian branch of the Bronx Zoo."[6]

Tanks and heavy artillery outside the plane accompanied the weapons inside. One reporter described "manned anti-aircraft and anti-tank guns in trenches dug round the three aircraft and a big detachment of guerrillas armed with submachine guns and hand grenades," at all times "on the alert." The three hijacked planes were surrounded in turn by the Jordanian army, signaling our position at the center of a war between the government of Jordan and Palestinian insurgents.[7]

Besides the guns and grenades and armaments, there was the dynamite. In his memoir, Bassam Abu-Sharif writes, "My PFLP colleagues went around wiring detonators to large lumps of plastic explosive placed under the seats." On the night we landed, our flight engineer watched a man carry a wired device to the back of the plane, then saw someone else place the same kind of device in the cockpit. Forcing himself to stay awake, the engineer reasoned that if the commandos suddenly left the aircraft, that would be his cue, so he kept himself from drifting into sleep by devising the speediest evacuation plan. One of the flight attendants remembered that, trying to lighten the mood, she would joke, "Don't come up here and trip over any wires!"[8]

In the course of my research, a document preserved in the National Security Council Files at the Richard Nixon Presidential Library in California gave me pause. It was a United Press International report, typed in all capital letters and dated September 7, our first day in the desert. The document quoted "guerrilla leaders" announcing that "demolition teams would 'destroy the planes along with their prisoners,'" should anyone approach the planes or should the demands of the Popular Front not be met "before expiration of the ultimatum"—meaning if Israel and the European countries did not release their Palestinian prisoners by a certain day and hour. *Along with their prisoners*: those were the words that gave me pause. The next sentence noted that a spokesman—that would have been Abu-Sharif—"hedged when asked if the passengers would be permitted to get off first but guerrilla sources said the plan was apparently to blow up the hostages also." Those words contradicted the commandos' promise to the copilot, and the copilot's promise to his passengers, on the night we landed: *no bodily harm.*[9]

Thinking back, I could call up an image of a commando wiring the plane with dynamite, but could recall no memory of a deadline and no memory of a threat to blow up the hostages along with the jetliners. My research, though, made clear that fellow hostages were aware of this possibility. One recalled "commando threats about what would happen if their deadline was not met." Another heard a commando say, "We cannot wait forever, and you will all go to a fiery death if this thing isn't settled soon." When I asked my sister, so many decades later, it turned out that she, too, remembered hearing the words "fiery death." She and I had never before talked about that, either in the desert or any time afterward.[10]

At twelve years old, I had already been keeping a diary for two years, and I loved to write on the crisp lined pages, recording incidents and thoughts I deemed worthy of preservation. That year I named my journal Claire, writing my entries in the form of letters. In that technique, I copied Anne Frank, who began her diary entries with "Dear Kitty." Anne Frank and I both wanted to be writers, and her birthday was the same day as mine.

In a carton in a closet, I found my 1970 journal, a bound volume of five-by-eight-inch pages with a red plastic cover. I had packed the volume in my carry-on bag, and during my desert sojourn I composed entries every day, setting down a little over a thousand words all together. Historians prize written records that date from the time and place under investigation, and when I set out to write about the hijacking, I envisioned the diary as my trusted scaffolding: an in-the-moment account of my thoughts and feelings up in the air, in the desert, at release, and upon return. With a combination of ingenuousness and self-consciousness, I could be an observant twelve-year-old, but I would soon find myself disappointed in the record I kept during that week in September 1970 in the volume I named Claire, meaning *clear*, as if to fool myself that I wrote my entries with any transparency. In the story I crafted in my diary, I deliberately constrained my powers of observation.

"Yes, I'm still sitting on the plane," I wrote the first morning I awoke in the Jordan desert. "It happened yesterday on the way from Frankfurt to N.Y." I described someone "running down the aisle shouting something I couldn't understand" and noted that "people's faces turned frightened." Surely afraid, I nonetheless did not record my own emotions during those first chaotic moments. Nor did I ever mention the gun I saw at the copilot's neck up in the air, or the commando I witnessed laying dynamite, or the woman who pointed her gun at me.

Indeed, reading and rereading my diary, I found that I had recorded only a handful of incidents that elicited fear, anxiety, or sadness. I noted when food became scarce and the pita bread grew stale, and when I wrote that we were subsisting on bread and water, I added a heartfelt "Oh dear!" I wrote that our captors took certain hostages off the plane to unknown destinations, and that a girl my age cried hard when she awoke one morning to find her older brother gone. When the commandos removed all remaining men from the plane on Friday night, capital letters and underlining became my deputies of dismay ("*all* the men PLUS the crew members that were men were to be OFF the plane"). That same night, I recorded my feelings for the old rabbi seated in the row ahead of us ("Poor man!"). My final acknowledgment of a troubled emotion came with the information that after evacuating all remaining hostages, the commandos blew up the three planes ("Gosh!"). At one point, I had recorded my sister's tears, then crossed out the words, revising the sentence "The hostesses comforted a crying Catherine and calmed everyone" to read "The hostesses comforted and calmed everyone." The inked-over words had clearly unnerved me since I counted on my big sister to protect me.

I found, too, that I had neglected to record the reassuring words imparted by the copilot to the passengers on the night we landed in the desert. This last omission in particular puzzled me. In my memory, those words had allayed my fears all during the week, so why had I not preserved them? I found an answer to this question in an interview my sister and I gave less than a week after our return, one of the only times we talked about the hijacking at length. Our interlocutor was an older cousin, an aspiring journalist who thought it would be cool to write about his two young relatives, just home from the most famous airplane hijacking in world history. A condensed version had been published in an alternative weekly out of Boston, but soon my cousin dug up the original tape, which contained a far longer conversation.

Listening in nearly fifty years later, I learned that my memory of the copilot's consoling announcement was incorrect in one critical way. That day in our living room in New York, I told my cousin that the copilot repeated to the passengers "what the guerrillas had said," that "the most they can do is keep us here as hostages, but there will be no bodily damage." I had recalled the key words pretty much correctly, but on the tape I said something else too. I said that the copilot's announcement came "around the fourth day." Given how close in time the interview was to the actual event, I had no doubt this timing was correct. I recalled the copilot's words as soothing, but in fact they must have alarmed me. There would be no bodily harm, but we were already on our fourth day in the desert, and the commandos had said—as I repeated to my cousin—that "the most they can do is keep us here as hostages." I must have wondered: Would I ever see my father again, or my mother? Would I ever see my best friend in New York, or my best friend in Tel Aviv? Would my parents ever see their daughters again?[11]

Now I understood that sometime after I got home, I shifted the copilot's words backward in time, in my memory, from near the end of my week in the desert to within hours of the landing of our hijacked plane, making them apply from the very beginning of the ordeal. By leaving the copilot's words undocumented, I was able to transform them into something I could invoke afterward, as a way to prove that there had never been any reason to be afraid. I was old enough to know that intense fear would be a normal reaction under the circumstances, yet I had erased my own feelings of dread from my personal record of the hijacking, which is why I did not dare write about the weapons and the dynamite either, and—if I knew about it—the deadline. I had crafted my diary entries to tell the kind of story I wanted to tell, if I ever got home, which would be a narrative that dismissed all manner of fear. Why had I done that? *Why did this person tell this story this way?*

I found the single slim folder in my father's self-storage unit on Eleventh Avenue. It was labeled "Hijack," and the handwriting on the tab was his, the folder wedged between files that sheltered family papers (letters from his mother and my mother) and professional papers (dance programs, performance reviews). What had my father been willing to preserve from the week his daughters were held captive in the desert?

Even though his own childhood was troubled, my father's outlook on life inclined toward joy.

"Did you have a happy childhood?" I once asked my uncle.

"No." My uncle stole a glance at his older brother. The three of us were having breakfast at a neighborhood diner.

"Did *he* have a happy childhood?" I flicked a thumb at my father.

"Evidently, he did," my uncle said, the two of us laughing at my father's invincible optimism and powers of denial.

"I did." My father beamed, missing the joke.

Stuart grew up in Brooklyn's Sheepshead Bay neighborhood, with a mostly absent father and a permissive and at times neglectful mother, who at one point dropped her young boys off at a violently abusive boarding school. My father left Brooklyn College after a semester, thrilled to be drafted into World War II and fly a B-17, eighteen years old and "heading into the unknown," as he said. After the war, at the age of twenty-one, he signed up for his first dance class at the Martha Graham School and a year later joined her company, which is where he met my mother.[12]

First in my father's curation of artifacts in the "Hijack" folder came a scrap of paper containing three telephone numbers, captured in his neat hand. These were the numbers he dialed several times each day, in search of information about his daughters. Since the people who answered the phone at the airline, the State Department, and the Red Cross would, in the end, give my father the good news that my sister and I had been released, this document became an acceptable memento.

The next item my father had preserved was a *New York Times* clipping from the day of our release, Sunday, September 13, bearing the headline "Released Hostages Tell of Their Ordeal in Desert." My father had marked the paragraph in which my sister was quoted: " 'Now I am going to thank God and have a bath,' said 13-year-old Catherine Hodes of Manhattan." Elsewhere in that issue, my sister's words were reprinted as the "Quotation of the Day," and my father had bought several copies, as if there could never be enough evidence of his daughters' safety. Notably, even though the *New York Times* ran multiple stories about the hijacking every day during the week we were held hostage, my father did not clip and save any of those articles, some of which speculated on our imminent death.[13]

Next in the folder came a note that my sister and I had written from the desert, which arrived several weeks after our return. The commandos had asked their captives to write messages to our governments, urging them to fulfill the Popular Front's demands, but my sister and I wrote to our father instead. "We are both okay and looking forward to being home," we told him. "Many people are watching out for us so please don't worry." While I have no memory of fearing for my life on the plane, I do remember worrying about my father. I worried about him because after my mother left our family his world revolved around his daughters. At twelve years old, I had long sensed my father's sadness over my mother's departure. How could he survive losing

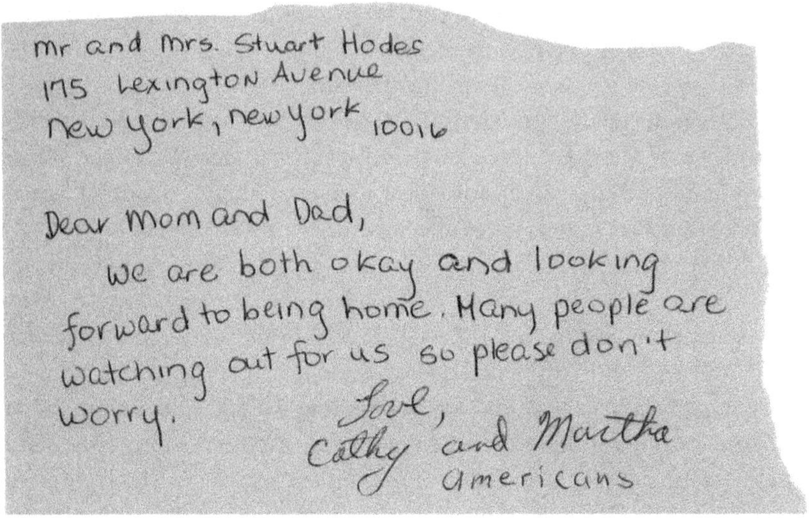

mr and mrs. Stuart Hodes
175 Lexington Avenue
new york, new york 10016

Dear Mom and Dad,
      we are both okay and looking
forward to being home. Many people are
watching out for us so please don't
worry.   love,
                    Cathy and Martha
                            americans

FIGURE 3.2. The note my sister and I wrote to our father and stepmother from the desert, which arrived weeks after we came home, 1970.

us too? It was important to reassure him that we were fine and that we would soon be home.

Next came a letter from the International Committee Against Air Piracy requesting participation in a lawsuit against the airlines, together with a copy of my father's decline. As he explained when I asked him so many years later, he believed that the airline had acted honorably. My father also did not want his daughters to be forced to dwell on the worst parts of the ordeal. Likewise, there was a letter from someone writing a dissertation, dated a year after our return, who hoped my sister and I would fill out a questionnaire. My father never showed us the questionnaire, not wanting us to dredge up thoughts of the hijacking after we all stopped talking about it for good.

The last item my father saved was a scholarly article by a sociologist, a fellow hostage who had interviewed my sister and me a few weeks after we got home—the second and last time my sister and I had spoken about the hijacking at any length. Entitled "Individual and Group Responses to Confinement in a Skyjacked Plane," it appeared in a 1973 issue of the *American Journal of Orthopsychiatry*. An accompanying note from the author was dated April 1974, indicating that my father had kept the folder at hand for at least several years after the hijacking, before packing it away and moving it into his storage unit.[14]

To this collection of documents I added one more item, this one preserved in the archives of the International Committee of the Red Cross in Geneva, Switzerland. There, sifting through four folders labeled "Détournements d'avions sur la Jordanie, aéroport de Zerka" ("Airplane hijackings over Jordan, Zerka Airport"), I came upon a cache of telegrams labeled "Messages pour les otages transmis par la Croix-Rouge américaine" (Messages for the hostages sent by the American Red Cross). Unfurling a sheet of paper more than five feet long, I made my way through the communications, until I came upon one composed by my father. My sister and I had never received this telegram, and when I asked my father about it during the course of my research, he recalled how carefully he had considered the wording. He wanted to write, "Keep your hearts and hopes up. We love you," but worried that even that hint of emotion might make us too sad. He considered joking—"Okay, enough of these side trips, it's time for you to come on home"—but someone at the Red Cross advised against that. In the end he wrapped his words in a breezy tone, speaking for himself and my stepmother. "Parents request children not be alarmed. Mom and Dad thinking of you. Rooms ready. Visited both schools. Great love from us and your friends." The parallel was striking. In the note my sister and I wrote to our father, we instructed him not to worry about us. In the telegram my father wrote, he instructed us not to worry about him.[15]

The contents of my father's folder and the wording of his telegram dovetailed with another kind of family archive. During my research, I posed a great many questions to my father, and the answers he provided almost invariably held a familiar ring. As I quickly understood, he was repeating the stock of stories about the hijacking he had honed across the decades.

One of these stories concerned what came to pass when my father first learned that his daughters' flight had been overtaken. Sunday, September 6, was going to be a full day for him. In 1970, as a former principal dancer with Martha Graham, he was running a small dance troupe, and that day his eleven dancers would open the matinee at the outdoor Delacorte Theater in Central Park. As soon as the dancers were offstage and the equipment packed up, he would drive to Kennedy Airport to pick up his girls. Coffee brewing, my father caught a news break on the radio: TWA flight 741 had been hijacked. Immediately he dialed the airline. Someone confirmed the announcement and gave my father a set of special telephone numbers, with operators available around the clock—these were the numbers (for the airline, the State Department, and the Red Cross) jotted on the slip of paper preserved in his "Hijack" folder. Soon after that, the telephone rang, my mother calling from the American embassy in Tel Aviv, frantic. My father wanted to travel to the Jordan desert, to come get my sister and me, but the man at the embassy said it was better not to draw attention to two unaccompanied children.[16]

My father decided to go on with the show. He owned two transistor radios, and New York had two all-news radio stations, so while packing up costumes and props he tuned one radio to each station and listened to both at the same time. Driving to Central Park in his Volkswagen bus, he decided to keep the news from his dancers. There was a performance to do, and, as he later put it, there was "no point upsetting them with my personal problem." The part of this particular story that my father liked best concerned what happened after the performance, when the dancers asked him to join them for something to eat. "I'd love to," he said, "but I have to go home to keep tabs on the hijacking. My daughters are on one of those planes." The dancers were "thunderstruck"—he often invoked that word as he imitated their incredulous reaction: "You did the show knowing your daughters were on one of those hijacked planes?" He would then recite his response: "I could see no good reason not to."[17]

I had heard this story many times across nearly fifty years when I located one of the dancers in my father's company. Clay Taliaferro, a sensitive six-foot-five Virginian who had grown up in the 1940s with only segregated theaters available to him, went on to a distinguished career as a principal dancer with the José Limón Dance Company, then as a professor of dance at Duke University. It was true that my father kept the news about his daughters from the dancers, Clay told me, but unknown to my father, the dancers could tell something was wrong. That day in Central Park, Clay saw something amiss: a forced smile, a too-intense focus, a hint of frenetic movement as my father set up the stage. Clay thought to himself, *This is not our Stuart.* At first some of the dancers wondered whether they had done something to make him angry, but among themselves they noted the morning's shocking news reports and recalled that Stuart's daughters had been in Israel for the summer, coming home to start school right about now. That afternoon, Clay saw my father "searching for some way to be with his daughters, somewhere far, far away." Disquieted, the dancers worked extra hard to get everything right in each piece. As Clay told me, "We all were Stuart that afternoon."[18]

Clay's version does not exactly belie my father's recollection of the dancers as *thunderstruck* since they surely expressed amazement when he confirmed their suspicions. But my father's story displays no hint of distress, a construction that fit with another of his favored stories about the hijacking. This one concerned the meeting he attended at my school. In the auditorium he waited patiently—parents prolonged the meeting because they were miffed about the color of the classroom walls—then sought out an administrator to explain that I would be late for the start of the academic year.

"Why is that?"

"She is being delayed by the hijacking"—his choice of words implied my certain return. The woman's eyes widened.

"And you had to listen to those parents complaining about the color of the walls!"

In both of these stories my father cast himself as stoic: placing the dancers ahead of his own agony or calmly listening to other parents fussing over trivial issues. In neither story did he express anguish, a fact contradicted by the memories of two people who saw my father every day that week. A neighbor on the fifth-floor hallway of our apartment building told me that it was impossible to interact with him, that he was utterly unreachable. As for my stepmother, she described my father as "a man on another planet," devastated and stricken. Just as I could talk about the commandos jumping rope with the children and how fun and funny it was when we all sang "living on a jet plane," my father could talk about the performance in the park and the conference at my school. These well-crafted narratives of our respective haunting days and nights were the stories each of us could live with.

Continuing my research, I asked my father a new question: Did he ever think we were going to die? His answer was immediate. "No," he said. "I always knew you were coming back." My research also revealed that after all the hostages returned unharmed, politicians and journalists debated whether our lives had been in danger. Commandos told a British reporter that they "never had any intention of killing or ill-treating any of the passengers"; a *Washington Post* reporter found that observers in Amman believed it "unlikely that they would carry out such a threat." Some people had worried less about deliberate murder than about other potential dangers: A commando, or even a hostage, might, as a British diplomat said, "break down under the strain," causing an "unpremeditated shot" to be fired, or the hostages could be "caught in the crossfire" between the Palestinian insurgents and the Jordanian army. Years later, Abu-Sharif maintained that one of the Popular Front's conditions, at least internally, was "not to hurt any civilian hostages, but to keep them only for exchange"—exactly what the copilot had conveyed in the words I had shifted in my memory, from the fourth day in the desert to our first hours there.[19]

During that week in September 1970, however, nothing was quite so clear. David Jenevizian, a Palestinian who worked for TWA in the Middle East, had occasion to listen to a phone call between a Popular Front commando and the Front's Beirut headquarters. When Jenevizian asked the commando point-blank if the Front was serious about blowing up the planes with the passengers inside, the man said—in light of the murder of Palestinians, with no sympathy from anyone—"Why not?" When a reporter asked the TWA flight engineer, upon his release, whether he had ever felt the lives of the hostages in the desert endangered, the engineer gave a sober, "Oh, many times. Many times."[20]

Beginning with the document that had given me pause at the Nixon Library ("demolition teams would 'destroy the planes along with their prisoners'"), I pieced together the information that was circulating about the lives of the hostages while my sister and I sat inside our stranded jetliner. According to a State Department telegram, "Time period for meeting all of the demands" was "72 hours starting from six a.m. local time," and "If demands are not met within this time, planes with all passengers will be blown up." According to a Red Cross representative, "We may face a tragedy. . . . There is perhaps one chance in two we will get everyone out." Daily communications between Amman and Washington, and between President Richard Nixon and national security adviser Henry Kissinger, contained similar speculations: if the Popular Front "destroys planes and kills hostages"; "if the hostages are murdered at Dawson airstrip"; "if . . . rescue . . . fails . . . and hostages killed." Diplomats ruminated on "the massacre of innocent travelers," and a New York senator said, "Today could be their last." On television news, my father would have heard the words, "The Arabs said the . . . planes would be blown up at ten o'clock tonight, eastern time, with the passengers aboard, if their demands were not met." *New York Times* articles—the ones my father had resolutely declined to clip and save—described the hostages "facing the possibility of being cold-bloodedly murdered," speculating on world reaction "if these helpless people were to die tonight."[21]

Here, then, was another narrative that my father had polished in the wake of his daughters' return, a narrative contradicted by the news circulating around him: that he always knew we were coming back. My stepmother, though, remembered something different. "Was he thinking of never getting you back?" she said to me. "Well, yes. Killed and never coming back, oh yes."

These are the tricks of memory that historians must account for. From the moment my father saw his daughters running toward him at Kennedy Airport, he would believe that he had never doubted we were coming home. As he told me decades later, a smile setting his face aglow, "You were home! Nothing else really mattered."

The contents of my father's "Hijack" folder stashed away in his storage unit. The carefully composed telegram saved in the archives of the International Red Cross. My father's honed and polished narratives about the hijacking—going on with the show, waiting patiently through the meeting at my school, his certainty that he'd always known his daughters were coming home. All of these shed a broad beam of light on the partial and limited nature of the entries I found in my 1970 diary.

"When left alone with memories, historians treat them as detectives treat their sources," writes Richard White; "they compare them, interrogate them, and match them one against the other." In *Remembering Ahanagran: A History of Stories*, White grapples with the tales his mother told about her Irish family. Comparing her narratives with his own research, White found that he could not "take even my own mother at her word." In the same way, I found that I could not take my twelve-year-old self at her word. My determination to craft a story about the hijacking that erased fear was impelled by the thought of my father awaiting—desperately hoping for—the return of his daughters. In my diary, I did not write about the guns or the dynamite or the deadline, or our possibly never-ending imprisonment, because I did not want to remember those things. I did not want to remember those things because I did not want them to be part of the story I would tell when I returned home. As a twelve-year-old hostage, the aspiring writer in me had constructed not a full record, but instead a tolerable story; not a truthful story, but instead a bearable one; not an honest story, but instead a story I could tell my father. Omitting fear and crossing out dangerous words in my diary was part of the process of formulating a story of the hijacking that my father could live with.[22]

"What do you do?," asks the historian Jonathan Scott Holloway, "when the memories of the actual participants in a specific event contradict official or archival records?" Holloway's research taught him to "embrace a faulty memory as a kind of reality, even in the face of a confirmable and objective truth." The value of my faulty memory of the timing of the copilot's assurance of "no bodily harm" was exactly that: a "kind of reality." Even after my sister and I were home safely, I did not want my father to believe that we had suffered because I did not know whether he could survive the knowledge of his children's fears: never coming home, maybe dying in the desert. As my sister, more honest and outspoken than I, told our cousin during his interview with us, "What wasn't okay was I felt my life in danger all the time." Here is where my mother's departure from the family helps to explain the story I crafted. Since she had already left, I could not risk losing my father too. I needed him to survive.[23]

Returning to the Jordan desert almost fifty years later, standing on a ridge overlooking the strip of sand where my sister and I had sat as hostages inside an airplane, it felt as if the hijacking had happened to someone else.

And maybe it had. Maybe the twelve-year-old girl who had worked so hard to forget was a different person from the grown-up searching to understand

FIGURE 3.3. My return to the Jordan desert nearly fifty years later, 2019.
Photo by Bruce Dorsey.

that experience. The diary that I, the historian, had approached as my prized then-and-there document proved instead to be a record and a relic of erasure. Just so, as a trace of my family's experiences of the hijacking—and of the kind of reality that my father and I were complicit in creating—my diary turned out to be the most illuminating document of all.

4

Peïra Cava, Hollow Stone:
Family Stories, Gendered Silence

STÉPHANE GERSON

The snapshot is small, easy to miss in the photo album. The photographer remains at a distance from a woman who almost vanishes within the mountainous landscape. This woman is hiking, with a dog by her side—a rare occurrence in the album. She is wearing a dark skirt and a white blouse. Her face is out of focus.

I do not recognize this woman, and neither does my mother, sitting next to me in her Brussels apartment. She recently found the photo albums that her mother, Zosia, compiled about her life in the 1930s and 1940s. They are yours, she told me when I came to visit.

Though Zosia is not the woman in the snapshot, she is present on most pages of the albums. Photographs show her childhood and teenage years in 1920s' Warsaw; her family life in Brussels, where they settled in 1933; outings in the Belgian countryside and further afield. They also depict Zosia's wedding to Jules Warchiwker, a diamond cutter from Antwerp. They married in the main synagogue in Brussels, rue de la Régence, in March 1942, shortly before the Nazis launched major roundups.

My mother, Francine, handed me these albums because I have become the custodian of our family archives and the story my grandmother fashioned about her war. Zosia told only one story, and it was this one: the story of a Jewish woman who, with her husband, survived persecution in Belgium and especially France. She framed it as an epic adventure, with near misses, sudden turns, and bold, ingenious moves by its heroine, Zosia herself. Francine, who was born in 1942, heard this story as a child, and so did I, in the 1970s and 1980s. My mother's memories and mine align. No one dies in this tale, and no one truly suffers either.

In 1994, I asked Zosia to tell her story once more, this time while I video-taped her. She was seventy-eight, still living in Brussels; I was twenty-seven, a doctoral student in history. In her living room, the two of us turned her oral story into a vernacular testimony and a memorial artifact. Family stories usu-ally vanish; they remain out of scholarly reach. Here, there is a singular trace. By virtue of my familial position, I have access to Zosia's voice, to the story's multiple iterations and afterlives, to their impact on relatives, and to family papers and photographs. This makes it possible to write a historical ethnog-raphy of her war story in its multiple dimensions: text, performance, self-fashioning, political intervention, and historical source into multiple lives, during the war and afterward.[1]

On the back of the snapshot, I find an inscription:

> Peïra Cava, lovely spot
> among the pine and fir trees
> which I miss deeply.
> June 1944
> Annie

Peïra Cava is a small village in Nice's back country, one of the earliest hiking and skiing destinations in the region. In local dialect, *peïra cava* means hollow stone. The words seem apt—I sometimes feel as if I am hollowing out Zosia's adventure story—but the more fitting metaphor is one of *accompaniment*. I accompany Zosia as a storyteller whose words and silences, whose inflections and verb tenses and staccato narrative rhythm shaped a war into an adventure. I seek to understand how, after the war, within various collective and familial contexts, an individual gave meaning to her experiences.[2] What could she see, what could she tell, what did we hear, what could we hear at home? Walking in her footsteps, I also accompany Zosia as a historical actor. I limn her quotid-ian experiences; I consider the forms of capital (money, languages, prior social experiences) a woman in her situation could tap to plot her next moves; I hope to learn something about her emotions. Out of temperament and necessity, Zosia walked fast. To keep up with her, I, too, must walk fast.

Sometimes my pace slackens, however. Sometimes I wander into side streets or linger in buildings Zosia left in haste. She framed an individual story, the story of a woman who made decisions, took risks of her own vo-lition, asked strangers for help, and ultimately saved herself. This story is meaningful: It represents a specific form of knowledge about the war, its af-termath, and the person who fashioned this particular narrative frame. This story carries its own emotional truths; there are reasons why Zosia needed a tale of adventure at a specific moment in her life.[3] Still, the scholar in me sees historical actors as social beings who rarely experience history or chart their course on their own. Walking at my own speed, walking alongside Zosia rather than in her footsteps, I encounter men and women who crossed her path during the war. Within her story, I uncover a web of Jewish and non-Jewish actors who, from their respective social and institutional positions, engaged with one another in relations "of mutual dependence and struggle."[4]

Zosia described some of these people in detail, others in a few words. There are yet others—the majority—whose existence she merely intimated, others who lived under the surface of my grandmother's words. To accompany Zosia is also to unearth the slivers of life and death, the ephemeral encounters, the shared experiences that are *contained*—both included and restricted to a narrow space—within her story. I accompany these men and women as well: relatives and neighbors, fellow refugees and detainees, the *passeurs* who promised to smuggle my grandparents into Switzerland, a landlord, a consul. Also: policemen, gendarmes, detention camp commissioners, all of them agents of the French collaborationist state in Vichy. These men and women are, in their absence and their presence, part of our family story.

Annie is part of our family story—even though Zosia rarely mentioned her at home. Sitting before my video camera in 1994, she did not once utter Annie's name. *Lui avec sa femme*, she said. *Him with his wife.*

Lui: Charles B., a Nice police inspector, provided my grandparents with advance information, false papers, the names of compliant doctors, and sometimes hiding places. *He became a great friend of ours*, Zosia told me. She said so twice. This great friend deserved gratitude and a place in our family origin story.

Sa femme: Zosia presented Annie as Charles's wife rather than a woman who made distinct though equally decisive contributions to this story of friendship and assistance. Zosia broke off contact with her soon after the war, turning Annie into a translucent filament in our familial memory. No wonder my mother and I did not recognize the woman in the snapshot. No wonder I asked my grandmother about Charles but not Annie when interviewing her. My questions were shaped by Zosia's narrative choices: the hierarchy of characters, the presence of some, the absence of others. War experiences are relayed not only through images and documents and injunctions, but also through gendered categories that, within families as elsewhere, organize reality and the past.

I started by researching Charles's career, his everyday life during wartime, his daily work at the police station, the help he gave to some refugees though not others. All of this is central to this microhistory. But focusing on the inspector alone, as Zosia's story and archival sources invite us to do, distorts the social dynamics at play. Months into the research, I began imagining a history that, inverting matters, began with Annie rather than her husband. Doing so would recalibrate assistance and rescue along gendered lines, broaden the social space within Zosia's story, and place the domestic realm on the same plane as the institutional one. It would also compensate for our familial silence. The scholarly, the political, and the personal are intertwined in this historical experiment.

I began with little about Annie—a few letters and photographs—and found but tidbits in public archives, which keep scant traces of women from working-class backgrounds. Scholars cannot "accept defeat," the historian Kate Brown writes regarding "people whose words and objects have not been considered important enough to record and catalog."[5] Still, Annie long remained a shadow within a history of postwar silencing. Then came the Peïra Cava snapshot. Two days later, I requested Charles's personnel file from his prewar employer, a French oil company, and learned that there were in fact two: his with his wife's. This opened lines of investigation. Not long afterward, I discovered that Annie had two siblings, and connected with descendants.

Annie remains a distant figure. There is much I do not know about her daily life and aspirations, the love she gave and received, and what she truly made of these Jewish refugees who suddenly entered her life in 1942 and vanished soon after the war. I am nonetheless able to sketch a family history that, without denying the necessity of Zosia's story or its silences, shifts the balance from absence toward an existence and a subjectivity, toward choices, commitments, and relationships that have been out of focus in our photo albums, our war stories, and—as I have discovered—Annie's war stories as well.

Zosia and Jules left Brussels in late July 1942 and arrived in Nice on August 4. They expected to be safer in the southern zone of France, administered by the Vichy regime, than in Nazi-occupied Belgium, where Jews were forced to wear the yellow star and receiving summonses to relocate in the east.

And yet. At dawn on August 26, three weeks after Zosia and Jules's arrival, French policemen barged into the five-story building in which they had rented a small furnished apartment, 13, avenue Maréchal Foch. Having agreed to hand over thousands of foreign Jews to the German occupying forces, Vichy had launched a vast operation of arrest and detention. In 1994, Zosia recalled the trucks awaiting outside their window, the screams of women, and the policeman who, when they did not open the door, promised to return with a locksmith but never did. She said that the police emptied the entire building except for them.

Unsure of what awaited, Zosia and Jules decided to obtain assistance. Zosia told me that she instructed Jules to approach the police inspector who had registered them when they arrived in Nice. Zosia trusted her instincts—*he was sympathique*—and made a tactical decision: better for a man to make this request than a woman. Still, she conceded that, for all she knew, this inspector might turn them in.

Charles B. did not turn them in. Instead, he accepted their dinner invitation and asked to bring his wife. *And so, he shows up with his wife, and we go to the Negresco for dinner.* This is when Zosia and Annie first met.

The two of them came from different social worlds. Zosia's father owned a successful textile business, first in Poland and then in Brussels, as well as an apartment building in Warsaw; her mother did not work in Poland, though she may have joined the family business in Belgium. They spoke French and Polish rather than Yiddish, evidence of their cultural integration and elevated status. In Brussels, they lived in a substantial three-story house, located between the Jewish immigrant neighborhood surrounding the train station and the city's smarter avenues; their store was on the ground floor. During the war, Zosia's father chaired the board of the Jewish orphanage of Brussels; her mother did the same for the Jewish retirement home. Annie, in contrast, spent the first years of her life a block away from Cannes's outdoor market, surrounded by artisans and small shopkeepers. Her mother worked in a bakery (a family business) whereas her father made a living as a band musician and salesman. These were people with very limited means, her great-nephew Stéphane told me during a video conversation. Around 1910, when Annie turned four, the family moved to Nice. They lived at 40, rue Dabray, in a four-story building with large gray bricks, green shutters, and a balcony that must have seemed enticing from their ground-floor apartment. Their neighbors were electricians, mechanics, and office employees. The regional train station, operated by the Chemins de fer de Provence, was just a block away. On weekends, the family sometimes hiked in the back country.[6]

Then came the First World War. Annie's father died in the Somme region in 1917, leaving his wife alone with three young children. Like other widows, she had them recognized after the war as wards of the nation, a symbolic adoption that provided scholarship money.[7] Education would ensure self-sufficiency and protect their modest social prospects. The boy was sent to military school; the youngest daughter became a saleswoman and then a department head at the Galeries Lafayette in Nice. As for Annie, the eldest, she obtained a Certificate of Primary Studies, a diploma that opened the doors of the *École pratique de commerce et d'industrie de jeunes filles de Nice*. This new professional school prepared girls from "Nice's working class" and "middling population" for careers as typists, secretaries, and accountants. Though the school was free, enrollment reflected parental commitment. "It is a great sacrifice for parents to deprive themselves for three full years of the fruits of their children's labor," the director explained.[8]

Annie's mother made the sacrifice because graduates were landing jobs in post offices, banks, insurance companies, department stores, hotels, and other venues in the booming service economy. Throughout the 1930s, Annie worked as a telephone operator (for the Havas News Agency), a "shorthand typist," and, by 1936, an "experienced shorthand typist." These were taxing, repetitive occupations, with few labor protections and slim opportunities for advancement. Still, shorthand typists—the "elite" of female office workers, according to historian Delphine Gardey—secured financial autonomy and a position above factory and domestic workers such as maids, waitresses, and housekeepers.[9] Annie's niece Monique, now in her nineties, remains impressed to this day: "She continued her studies, she was a typist. At the time, this was quite something."[10]

In 1930, Annie married Charles, the son of a lyrical singer of Belgian origin and a piano teacher who was born in Algeria and displayed manners that impressed Monique. Though Charles had more cultural capital than his wife (he earned a high school degree and spoke some English), he began his professional life as a hotel elevator operator. In 1932, a French oil company, Desmarais frères, hired him as a clerical employee. He was posted in the Saint-Roch depot, in a working-class neighborhood filled with mills, repair shops, garages, and warehouses. Charles and Annie moved into a small house nearby, 21, rue des Orangers; their neighbors were schoolteachers, drivers, and masons. In the neighboring Passage de la Tranquillité, workers celebrated weddings and baptisms. Still, tranquility was in short commodity in this dense, dusty part of eastern Nice. "Saint-Roch teemed," a local historian told me. *Cela grouillait.*[11]

This may explain why, between 1938 and 1940, Annie and Charles sought other horizons. Once Charles was promoted to assistant depot manager, they bought a 2,000-franc plot of land in the nearby village of Roquefort les Pins. All I have is the deed of sale, so we have to imagine the two of them gardening on weekends, hiking in nearby forests, or simply enjoying the quiet on their small property. Soon thereafter, they left Saint-Roch for Cimiez, a bucolic hilltop neighborhood of Nice that, in the late nineteenth century, had become a winter resort for aristocrats and rich bourgeois. Annie and Charles rented an apartment 13, rue Edith Cavell, in a stout two-story house that still stands, with tall windows, a narrow lawn up front, and washed-up yellow walls. This was Lower Cimiez, an in-between district in which retirees and businessmen

lived alongside nurses, secretaries, and the gardeners, cooks, and cleaning
ladies who staffed the posh villas and grand hotels of Upper Cimiez. Annie
and Charles now resided closer to Nice's elites, but not quite among them.
Their landlord ran a garage on the ground floor; their immediate neighbors
owned a bar-restaurant whose customers played *pétanque*. Down the street,
however, real estate developers called on potential buyers to build homes "in
good taste," without outdoor toilets, garish advertisements, or noisy and immoral businesses.[12]

In 1941, German requisitions forced the oil company to close the Saint-
Roch depot and lay off its employees. Having lost his job, Charles worked for a
wholesaler grocer and then, in February 1942, decided to join the Nice police.
At the very least, this was a stable, well-paid civil service job with benefits.
After passing the entrance exam, he was assigned to the immigration department, the *service des étrangers*. Every morning, Charles made his way from
Cimiez to the police station in central Nice where Germans, Poles, Austrians,
and others lined up to obtain the permits and stamps on which their futures
depended. I do not know what Annie did when her husband left for work. The
oil company had hired her to replace Charles after France declared war on Germany in September 1939, but let her go upon his return from active duty a year
later. Eager to restore traditional gender norms and rebuild France's virility

FIGURE 4.1. Avenue Edith Cavell, with plush villas and apartment buildings in the background. The
apartment in which Annie and Charles lived is in the foreground, where the photographer stood.
Postcard in author's collection.

following its disastrous defeat, the Vichy regime curtailed female employment. *"Definitive termination*, without severance," reads Annie's dossier for August 1940.[13] My research uncovered random facets of her daily life: walks with the dog she named Mazout (fuel oil), chats with the bar owner next door, get-togethers with English neighbors down the street.[14] And one evening in September, dinner on the posh Promenade des Anglais with Charles and two Belgian refugees he had met at the police station a few weeks earlier.

In our family story, as in others, survival begins with a request for assistance.[15] Zosia chose to make hers at the Negresco, a palace that presented itself as "the rendezvous of elite society," a hotel where, as a concierge put it in one of Patrick Modiano's novels, "everyone wears a dark suit."[16] Zosia was no doubt accustomed to such establishments, but I wonder about Charles, who began his career at the neighboring Hotel Ruhl, and Annie, whose *École pratique* sent interns to the Negresco.[17] Whether Zosia intended to impress or show respect, this dinner crystallized a complex social dynamic of distance and deference, attraction and exchange. Annie must have been intrigued by the elegant woman who sat across from her under crystal chandeliers, a woman who, though Jewish, seemed to belong to Upper Cimiez.

The story I have presented so far privileges class and mobility—the social categories that govern the public and professional records of Annie's life. Meaningful as it is, this story says nothing about her intimate life or the affinities between two women who, in 1942, both found themselves without parents, far from the worlds in which they had grown up. These possibilities must be left open.

And something else too. Annie was present that evening at the Negresco when, playing on registers of transparency and vulnerability, Zosia asked Charles for help. She was present when, according to Zosia, Charles hesitated, when he explained that falsifying registration records was *"very dangerous"* given the scrutiny of higher-ups. Annie was present when Charles ultimately said yes, when he agreed to disobey and break the oath he had sworn to Vichy, when he took risks that involved her as well.

Did Charles and Annie exchange glances during this conversation? Did he see resolution in his wife's eyes? I wrote these questions in my research journal in the hope of finding answers and to atone—again—for all I never asked Zosia. None of us at home registered the fact that Charles made this decision with Annie by his side. None of us imagined that he trusted his wife enough to include her within this decision process, even in a silent mode. To the extent that disobedience represents a specific form of politics, Annie's presence that evening also contains unrecognized political possibilities. These possibilities, too, must be left open.

Annie's great-nephew Stéphane told me that one of her grandfathers was a free mason—an affiliation that denotes attachment to the French Republic (Vichy outlawed all lodges in 1940). He also revealed that Annie's sister Jeanne had communist sympathies. Her husband had joined the resistance, and she may have resisted as well though no one in the family knows for certain. The French military archives contain a trace of her husband's activity, a 1952 request for certification as a resistant that, rejected though it was on procedural grounds, confirms at least part of the family story.[18]

These archives also contain a thick file on Annie's brother Étienne. He enlisted in the Free French Forces in London in July 1940, soon after General de Gaulle's BBC speech calling on France to continue the fight against Nazi Germany. Out of a French army of three million, just a few thousand rallied or remained in England at that time. Assigned to de Gaulle's staff, Étienne was soon dispatched to Western Africa, where he commanded a transmissions unit in Cameroon and then "helped establish the armies that would liberate metropolitan France."[19] His profile resembles that of other early *Français libres*: a career serviceman from a modest background; a veteran of the prewar colonial corps whose youth and taste for adventure made this commitment possible; a Frenchman for whom patriotism prevailed over ideology. While few of them had joined unions or political organizations before the war, a significant number had, like Étienne and Annie, lost fathers in combat during World War I. Stéphane told me that, without being "political," his family shared "a sense of duty," a "patriotic ethos." Étienne had "convictions."[20]

I do not know whether, like other gentiles who helped Jews, Annie had an independent streak, a history of good deeds, or prior involvement in humanitarian or religious organizations.[21] It is possible that the death of her father when she was eleven made her sensitive to the pain and the needs of others. All I know is that she inherited a patriotic ethos that led her brother toward de Gaulle and her sister toward Communism. As far as I can tell, Annie did not resist in this fashion. But when Jewish refugees asked for help, she remained present, she listened, she sat by her husband as he disobeyed on behalf of strangers.

These possibilities—the politics of assistance, rooted in inherited commitments, social dynamics, and interpersonal intimacies—are missing from our family story. Instead, we hear about *mon commissaire*, which is how Zosia referred to Charles. Her words bring to mind "Mon légionnaire," Edith Piaf's

1936 ode to the tattooed, blond-haired soldier who vanished after a torrid night of love making. But Charles did not vanish. Zosia described him as young and attractive; there may have been affection. Still, it is not romantic longing and abandonment I hear in her words but cultural affinities (both of their mothers played the piano) and especially regard for a bearer of male institutional authority who placed himself at her service.

The August 26 roundup forced every Jewish refugee in Nice to make a complex decision on the basis of little verifiable information: hunker down, hide elsewhere in France, flee the country?[22] Charles seems to have made the decision for Zosia and Jules. Soon after their dinner, he mentioned other imminent roundups and urged them to escape to Switzerland. Following his advice, my grandparents hired *passeurs* and, alongside countless other refugees, took a train to the Franco-Swiss border. Things did not go as planned. French gendarmes arrested them on the platform of the tiny station of Machilly, a mile or so from the border, and transferred them to the detention camp of Rivesaltes, near the Pyrenees. For many Jewish detainees in unoccupied France, Rivesaltes was a way station to the transit camp of Drancy and then Auschwitz. While their Belgian nationality and Zosia's pregnancy protected them from deportation at that time, neither factor ensured liberation.[23] Zosia says that, at her repeated urging, Charles intervened. Freed in November 1942, Zosia and Jules returned to Nice. They called Charles and Annie as soon as they arrived.

During the months that followed—until 1944—the four of them met for walks and meals, for theater and movie matinees (the Italian forces that now controlled the city did not make the arrest of Jews a priority).[24] An institutional relationship between a policeman and refugees morphed into a social and affective one—a friendship, Zosia said—between couples who fell on opposite sides of Vichy's dividing lines, couples whose social worlds would not have overlapped in peacetime. I do not know whether Annie and Charles had other Jewish friends, but am fairly certain that Zosia and Jules's circles were exclusively Jewish. On December 30, 1942, Zosia gave birth to Francine in a Nice clinic. She said that she and Jules found themselves alone with the baby, far from their relatives, but that Annie and Charles provided support. *They were extraordinary.* This is the only time Zosia praises Annie, although, again, she does so without naming her.

Some of their outings are documented in photographs that Zosia preserved along with wartime papers, in a file she stored on the highest shelf of a closet in the small spare bedroom at the end of her apartment. She seldom took these documents out, rarely showed them to us. Family papers have their own protocols of visibility, their own private or social lives.

FIGURE 4.2. Zosia, Annie, Jules, Charles (Nice, December 1942).
Zosia Warchiwker family papers.

The earliest photograph, taken just before Francine's birth, makes a formal impression: dark coats and dark shadows in the bright sun, full-body portraits, downward gazes, no physical contact. Zosia and Jules have just returned to Nice from the camp of Rivesaltes; the two couples are getting to know one another during afternoon strolls. They may have memorialized this moment because a street photographer crossed their path, though we cannot discount budding affinities.

Taken later, at less of a remove, the other photographs are warm, even tender. Cozied up on a bench, bodies touching, the four of them—five, if we include Francine—seem to enjoy these moments together. Posing for photographs creates mnemonic traces, but not only. It can also reflect and foster intimacy, trust, a shared compact, even affection. These photographs were taken outdoors rather than in domestic settings that may have felt less safe. Nearly every one is set in a public garden—a neutral space that is estranged from the History that hovers on the horizon. The images contain trees, bushes, and rocks, but no political markers, no refugees lining up at dawn, no signs forbidding Jews from entering. There is a long tradition, connected to Kodak advertisements and harking back to World War I at least, of snapshots hiding the horrors of war (and death, more generally) behind static, nostalgic scenes of leisure, camaraderie, and familial tranquility. "At the boundaries of the image, war and violence patiently await," writes historian Claire Mauss-Copeaux.[25] Indeed, wars have distinctive temporalities and social possibilities. People from different walks of life can, in the words of Stéphane Audoin-Rouzeau, "experience, feel, picture reality in comparable ways."[26] Some of them may equate this shared experience with friendship.

At the same time, middle-class codes seem to prevail in these photographs. Public gardens are more genteel spaces than mountain trails or beaches, where people pose in bathing suits. At the *École pratique*, Annie had learned how to hold herself, how to behave with "order, attention, and soft but firm discipline." She was also taught how to dress in a becoming fashion. The pearl earrings she wore on some outings denote a bourgeois style. She may have bought them from her sister at the Galeries Lafayette, the kind of store in which women from modest backgrounds could now purchase jewelry, stockings, or purses at affordable prices.[27] On a park bench or at the theater, Annie fashioned a middle-class persona within a world Zosia had long made hers. Her friendship with Zosia seemingly marked the culmination of her social acculturation; she appears at ease in the photographs. In fact, Annie marked this transition by adopting a different forename. On her birth certificate and other official papers, she is known as Anaïs. This was a family name, shared with two close cousins, and a regionalism, a Provençal version of Anne that

FIGURE 4.3. Charles, Francine, Zosia, Annie (Nice, May 1944).
Zosia Warchiwker family papers.

was uncommon outside the Midi region until the 1980s. With Zosia and Jules
and perhaps others, however, she did not use the name Anaïs. Instead, she
went by Annie, one of the ten most popular names in France between 1940
and 1945.[28] Her descendants and I were equally astonished when we discovered that for a time she had led parallel lives.

To my eyes, the photographs also depict the limits of Annie's acculturation. Her nails are short whereas Zosia's are long and adorned with varnish. In
addition to earrings, Zosia wears a ring, a watch, and a brooch (fig. 4.4). Her
jacket is more structured and traditionally elegant than Annie's wool sweater,
a *chandail* once worn by market women and now reclaimed by Coco Chanel
and other designers. Like her turban, this functional item denotes necessity
and fashion, two more distant horizons for women of Zosia's solid standing. Annie seems proud in these photos: proud to spend time with her new
friends, proud to pose in their company. She smiles in each one, her gaze directed at the camera that will enshrine these intimate moments and inscribe
her within this social world. Zosia, in contrast, does not always feel obliged
to either face the camera or smile. The (forced) smile had become a com-
monplace in snapshots during the 1930s, a "guarantee of modern, egalitar-
ian sociability."[29] Zosia's photo albums, however, are filled with prewar family

FIGURE 4.4. Annie, Francine, Zosia (Nice, March 1943).
Zosia Warchiwker family papers.

snapshots in which no one smiles, as if doing so reflected an inability to control one's emotions. Beyond the wartime circumstances, my grandmother's upbringing endowed her with a looser relationship to conventions that were becoming prescriptive for people from lower social stations. Yet again, Annie stands close to a higher social world, but not quite within it.

All of this makes me wonder whether the two of them fully breached the social distance that separated them. At one point in our interview, Zosia spoke about the town of Cros de Cagnes, near Nice: *It was tiny. Only tramway and railroad workers lived there.* There is something dismissive about her remark, a way of characterizing a town and a population for which she felt little affinity. Did Zosia use such language in the presence of Annie—or rather, as she must have sensed, in the presence of Anaïs?

In September 1943, Italy capitulated, and German troops replaced Italians in Nice. They closed off the city and immediately began arresting Jews. Thousands of refugees who had felt protected under Italian occupation searched frantically for escape routes and hiding places. *We hid.* Mon commissaire *rented an apartment for us.* Because it was difficult to hide with a crying baby, Charles and Annie offered to take in Francine for several months. At this point, Zosia's story of assistance and rescue takes on another dimension: building on its institutional and interpersonal foundations, it becomes— overnight—a domestic affair. Much about this turn of events echoes recent scholarship: the preexisting social ties between protagonists, the familial dimension of aid, the decisive action of women within the household. Also, the centrality of children.[30]

Charles continued to play an important role, but he spent his days at the police station. It was Annie who no doubt fed and bathed and cared for the baby, Annie who accepted to make their apartment a site of disobedience against French and German ordinances. Although she and Charles never had children together, Annie had, like other French girls, been taught about mothering as destiny and fulfillment. At the *École pratique*, she acquired "indispensable child care skills" and learned about "family life" and motherly "duties"—cooking, ironing, sewing.[31] Vichy embraced and magnified this idealized vision of women in its reactionary cult of France's supposed moral roots. By nurturing and mothering a Jewish baby, Annie both fulfilled the regime's gendered expectations and subverted its racial prohibitions.

The closest public garden to the avenue Edith Cavell, just fifteen minutes away, surrounds the baroque church of Notre-Dame de Cimiez and its abutting Franciscan monastery. I imagine Annie walking Francine to the gardens, Annie holding the baby along the stone parapet, Annie pointing toward the

FIGURE 4.5. Notre-Dame de Cimiez and the monastery, 1930s.
Courtesy Archives historiques du diocèse de Nice.

streets of Saint-Roch in the distance, the narrow alleyways of Old Nice further south, and, along the horizon, the blue depths of the Mediterranean.

Notre-Dame de Cimiez plays a crucial role in this story: It is there that, on
September 16, a week after the Nazis entered the city, Annie and Charles had
Francine baptized. Concerned about prying neighbors, they asked Zosia and
Jules for permission. There must have been traffic in the garage downstairs
and the bar next door. *They said it would be best for this child to be baptized,
so that we could prove . . .*

There is grounds to believe that Annie, rather than Charles, approached
one of the vicars at the monastery. Her family was traditionally Catholic, her
relatives tell me. All the children received their First Communion, and her
brother Étienne attended mass until the end of his life. Charles's descendants,
in contrast, say that religion mattered little to him; they do not recall familial
devotion.[32] Still, I struggle to compose this scene. There is no way of knowing
what Annie felt as she stepped into the church with a nine-month-old baby
bearing a Polish name, clearly Jewish. She may have heard—through Charles's
police work, perhaps—that the bishopric was hiding Jewish children, some
of them in the nearby convent of the Poor Clare nuns of Cimiez. She may
also have previously met this vicar, Jean-Marie Aventini, esteemed for his
devotion to "the sick, the elderly, and the most precarious." But would she

have known that, in March 1943, he had baptized a family of German Jews, Maurice and Irma Starer and their daughter Lucienne? Or that the bishop of Nice himself secretly baptized Jews, creating conditions in which ordinary priests could follow suit? Annie took a risk. That same week in September, Brother Aventini baptized Roger Dragoni and Michele Fighiera, two Catholic children whose parents had married in Notre-Dame de Cimiez. Brother Aventini also baptized Francine Warchiwker, whose entry in the parish registry contains a revealing blank when it comes to her parents, Zosia and Jules: "Married in the church of ____."[33]

Zosia and Jules did not attend the ceremony. Their absence that day mirrors the silence that has surrounded the baptism within our family. After the war, my grandparents never discussed an event that violated Jewish faith. Francine only found out, inadvertently, at the age of seventeen. In 1994, Zosia spoke briefly of her husband's pain that day—*you cannot imagine how much Jules wept*—but her own discomfort was palpable as well, and it went beyond the religious ritual. After all, other things are missing from this episode in her story: how the four of them organized Francine's stay in Cimiez (did Charles obtain false ration tickets in her name?); how long this stay lasted; what everyday life looked like in their home. More profoundly: What did it mean for Annie and Charles to suddenly live with a child? What did it mean for Zosia and Jules to live without their daughter? What did it mean for Francine to be separated from her parents and then, months later, from the couple who had cared for her?

In 1994, Zosia condensed all of this in six words:

Ils m'ont pris l'enfant.
They took the child from me.

Her tone was not resentful; Zosia felt gratitude. But her face tightened as she uttered these words, and she made a hand gesture, as if to dispel a painful memory.

They rather than *Annie and Charles.*
Took rather than *took in, took* rather than *welcomed.*
From me.

Then, for the first and only time that day, Zosia asked me to stop filming. She did so after declaring that she was *going to confess something*, a verb choice that jumps at me today. I have no memory of our conversation during this interval, but I must have persuaded her to say something about the baptism because she described it in a few words and then quickly moved on. Zosia said nothing about Francine's stay, or the separation, or the woman who both took care of her baby and took her away.

After a few months in hiding, Zosia and Jules reunited with Francine and left Nice, where they feared a denunciation. Under false identities, they rented an apartment in the neighboring town of Beausoleil and lived there until Liberation. The photographs in Zosia's possession show that they continued to meet Annie and Charles for occasional outings. My interview ends with their return to Brussels in October 1944. Jules resumed his life as a diamond trader in Antwerp. Charles left the police in March 1945, when the oil company rehired him as manager of the Saint-Roch depot, with oversight of thirty-four employees. Zosia did not work in the late 1940s, and I don't think Annie did so either.[34] "No need to tell you how happy we are," she wrote Zosia in June 1945, "especially Charles." In this letter, Annie discusses their health, her dog, food shortages, the oppressive summer heat. She also regrets Zosia's reserve. "Your postcard is awfully short and provides little information about your life in Belgium. Has Zosia forgotten how to write?"[35]

So many layers are embedded in this last sentence that I want it to sit on its own, a single line in the middle of the page.

Has Zosia forgotten how to write?

Zosia had not forgotten how to write nor in my view had she forgotten what Annie had done for her family. But, after the war, she could neither maintain this relationship nor acknowledge and later express in her story what drew her toward and at the same time away from this woman. Zosia saw Annie, with Francine, during a holiday stay in Nice in 1947. This was their last encounter, possibly their last exchange.

Long after the war, the historian and former resistant Jean-Pierre Vernant recalled the *philia* or loving friendship among individuals who during the war had come together, as equals, around a shared "dimension of existence."[36] This notion of friendship does not operate here. We must envision other stories about Zosia and Annie after the war.

The first is a story of refugees who sought distance from a couple who reminded them of their interrupted youth, a complicated past, and a truth that is not always easy to accept: how much we owe to others when our life veers out of control. While some Jews showed appreciation after the war to those who had helped them, others struggled with this position of dependency.[37] After all, the adventure story Zosia fashioned for herself was one of fortitude and self-sufficiency rather than suffering or trauma. It came into being in a specific memorial context, which preceded the advent of the victim as a public figure in Jewish memory, and an equally specific familial context.[38] On the eve of the war, Zosia's parents had forbidden her from studying pharmacy. Reluctantly, she sold buttons and ribbons in the family business, which her older brother inherited after her father's sudden death in 1946 and, within a few years, drove into bankruptcy. This loss of familial capital and status was compounded by Jules's professional struggles. The couple separated in 1956, leaving Zosia without resources. This story is less glorious, the story of a woman who was *exploited* in the family business until her departure for France, and later experienced rapid downward mobility. Author Emily Bernard has written about African American women who depict themselves in their life stories as "a source of power, not an object of humiliation."[39] I think that Zosia's own quest for dignity led her to experience or at least represent her war—the French years of 1942–44, outside the family circle—as a pivotal moment in her own becoming: a source of power. Charles and Annie had roles to play in her adventure, especially Charles, but as acolytes or *helpers* of Jews who were active in their own survival, not as *rescuers* of passive victims.[40]

The second story to be told about this postwar relationship is one of enduring social distance. It was not unusual for women from different backgrounds to experience a shared youthful friendship in different ways. What felt intimate and everlasting to the woman from modest origins could seem fleeting and less consequential to the other. Frédérique El Amrani Boisseau, a scholar of such dynamics, speaks of a "misunderstanding regarding the depth of the other's feelings."[41] Having returned to her bourgeois, Jewish world, Zosia may have felt with greater acuity all that now separated her from Charles and especially Annie. The two couples no longer shared a historical reality or a common escape from History. Nor did Zosia and Jules need the wartime social network and support structure to which she gave the name of friendship. I wonder what she made of the postwar letter in which Annie complained about food scarcity—a material necessity that did not afflict her in Belgium—and discussed the seven kittens she had to bottle-feed after the death of her rabbit. "Talk about hard work!," Annie wrote. I likewise wonder what, having returned to an elegant apartment in Brussels, Zosia thought of Annie and Charles's new lodgings. When Charles was rehired by the oil company, in 1945, they moved into an apartment inside the Saint-Roch depot, amid the fumes of crude, the boom of trucks on the busy road, and the stench of death drifting from the slaughterhouse just blocks away. From their street, one barely makes out Cimiez in the distance. The Negresco and its affluent guests lie far over the horizon.

And then Annie lost all of this. Around 1950, she and Charles divorced in circumstances that are unrelated to this story; Charles left Nice to take a position in one of the company's other depots, in eastern France; Annie moved in with her sister, in the building (and probably the very apartment) in which they had grown up rue Dabray. She also returned to work at the depot: The former manager's wife became an entry-level office employee. "What did the two of them have in common?" Francine asked me recently about Zosia and Annie. "Beyond the war, they might not have much to talk about."[42]

Still, Zosia stayed in touch with Charles after his divorce. Francine recalls that her mother sent him (and apparently him alone) birthday and Christmas gifts. *I did not forget him. It is thanks to him that I am here.*

This sentence escaped me in 1994, but today I hear what Zosia left unsaid: *It is thanks to him without his wife that I am here.* The final story to be told about Zosia and Annie after the war is hence one of gendered expectations and forebodings. In Zosia's eyes, Annie's contribution to their survival could not match Charles's. There is no room in her story for resistance as care, for a daily labor that melded assistance and affection. Standing at a distance, we might say that Zosia could not escape the hierarchies that, in postwar Europe, equated valor, courage, and true resistance with men and virility.[43] Standing a bit closer, we might add that her bourgeois lifestyle made it difficult for her to apprehend this care outside the domestic employment relationships to which she had long been accustomed. Upon returning to Brussels, Zosia placed classified advertisements for a live-in nanny.[44] Zosia never mentioned money exchanges with Annie and Charles, and yet this was the way of her world. Nannies remain invisible in such adventure stories.

Standing yet closer, I see a wartime separation between a mother and a daughter whose inclusion in Zosia's story could reactivate feelings of shame and guilt. Zosia is not the only Jewish woman whose testimony said little about wartime pregnancy, childbirth, or maternity—moments of intimacy, vulnerability, and, for some, trauma.[45] Nor is she the only Jewish survivor who, when recounting their wartime experiences, said little about their partings, either temporary or definitive, with relatives.[46] Zosia may also have felt unease, albeit unwitting, before a substitute mother who, in a country obsessed with babies and maternity, never had children of her own. Days after the baptism in 1943, a Nice newspaper urged its female readers to "devote everything to maternity, their flesh and their blood, the riches of their heart and the resources of their mind."[47] This language continued to resonate after the war, when France set out to rebuild its population. In her quest for maternal plenitude, might Annie not have laid emotional claim to the child she had welcomed into her home, the child to whom she had grown attached?

After all, Annie was not only Francine's caretaker and rescuer but also her godmother. "Give [Francine] a big kiss from godfather and godmother," Annie wrote Zosia in 1945. "Big hugs to our goddaughter," she wrote a year later.[48] While godparenting had long represented a spiritual mediation with the afterworld, by midcentury it constituted first and foremost "a spare kinship" that blended filial love, spiritual guidance, and obligations should misfortune befall the parents.[49] Blurring the divide between friends and kin, Annie's words in these letters were thus powerful. They asserted a visceral emotional and spiritual relationship; they made tangible a familial bond that would endure long after the end of the war; and they signaled—perhaps—a lasting Catholic presence within Francine's life. Zosia asked me to turn off the camera because she did not want posterity to know about the ceremony that, nominally speaking, made her daughter a Catholic, but her gesture erased something else: the affiliation that was consecrated at that moment, a connection that did not include her, a relationship she had ended decades earlier. Whether Zosia grasped it, all of this is part of her story. And not only hers: By effacing Annie, Zosia also effaced a facet of Francine's life.

They took the child from me, Zosia said: *the child*, nameless and disembodied, rather than *Francine*. A familial novel by Marie Richeux comes to mind: "First names were imparted in silence, without stories and hardly any images. What was passed on in this fashion?"[50] The letters that make up *Francine* encompass not only *France* and *Nice* but also *Annie*. What has this forename passed on in this fashion? And what has my mother's second name—Annie, as it turns out—passed on in its own fashion? Francine tells me that, as a child, she asked Zosia more than once why she did not do more for Annie and Charles, why she never invited them to Brussels. Francine remains stunned by this lack of reciprocity, a violation of protocols of hospitality. Still, I never heard her say that she missed Annie's presence. This changed once I began this research. One day, the two of us read Annie's letters to Zosia together; we did so out loud. Afterward, my mother told me in a measured tone that she had indeed lost something: "a person who would have shown me kindness, who would have played a part in my life."[51]

Annie felt this absence as well. "What's the latest regarding Francine?" she asked Zosia in 1945. "What's the latest regarding Francine?" she asked again in 1946. "I hope to see her soon and, before that, to receive a photograph one of these days."

FIGURE 4.6. Excerpt from Francine's baptism certificate.
Zosia Warchiwker family papers.

These letters voice what Zosia could not articulate in her story: the raw longing, the widening chasm, the separation on the horizon, the misunderstanding that was coming into view. Annie sometimes struggled to put this into words herself. Her relatives never heard her mention the help and hospitality she had provided during the war, the risks she had incurred, or the emotions she had felt with Francine and her parents. They learned about this through me. It was not only Zosia who silenced Annie, but also Annie who silenced herself.

"Many stories were never told at home," says her great-nephew. To maintain concord during a time of intense political infighting, the Gaullists and the communists in the family tacitly agreed to avoid discussing the war after Liberation.[52] One story resonated, however: the military exploits of Annie's brother Étienne. After fighting German troops across Africa, he landed in Normandy in July 1944 and, within days, was "seriously wounded while attacking with his driver isolated snipers who were shooting vehicles on the road between Sées and Montmerrei" (I am quoting his military citation). Following a long convalescence, Étienne rejoined General Leclerc's famed Second Armored Division in Alsace and fought all the way to Germany, until V.E. Day.[53] Promoted to captain, he earned the *Croix de guerre* and many other decorations that he displayed in his living room, public markers of a heroic, masculine adventure.

At a time in which few women obtained recognition for their wartime actions, Annie may have found her own story insignificant or even illegitimate in comparison to her brother's. She may also have deemed it too painful to share. If she did so, wouldn't relatives ask to see photographs of her Belgian goddaughter? Wouldn't they inquire about the bonds that had been sealed in Notre-Dame de Cimiez and then sundered? If Annie shared her story, wouldn't she have to explain why her wartime friends had forgotten how to write? Wouldn't she have to reckon with her own feelings of shame and sorrow?

If Annie shared her story, she might also voice another emotion: anger. Around the time Francine vanished from her life, Annie sent her supervisor at the oil company a letter that broke with the deference expected of female typists.[54] The context is opaque—her divorce, concerns about her workplace behavior—but her words ring loud. "How sad it is," Annie wrote in 1950, "that nowadays innocent people are hounded . . . whereas guilty and responsible parties alone get to keep their positions. This is so unfair." The politics of her rage bristle on the page. Annie was incensed about the ways she was treated by her superiors, although there is only so much I can know and say about this.[55] More revealingly, she expressed anger on behalf of other "innocent"

people from modest backgrounds, other women and men who found themselves close to elites but not quite among them, other women and men who
had to contend with the whims, the humiliations, the neglect of higher-ups.
It was perilous for female employees to complain about injustice in the workplace (in 1953, Annie lost her job in an apparent downsizing.) It may have
been equally perilous to voice such sentiments with family.

Peïra Cava drew me into the back country of our family story, and then into
a terrain that reaches beyond its boundaries, toward other ordinary men and
women. It is difficult to write a history that encompasses the experiences and
subjectivities of all protagonists in a relationship, in this case both Jewish
refugees and the people who helped them at their own peril. Scholars tell
us that "archives are generally silent on such matters," that "the chances of
reconstructing these relationships through historical sociology have probably
been lost," that each party's feelings and "profound motivations" are bound to
remain elusive.[56] A historical ethnography of Zosia's story delineates silences
and absences, with their political afterlives: the interactions and sentiments
my relatives and I could not imagine, the gestures we could not emulate, the
appreciation we could not express, the separations Francine endured on her
own because they were never named. It also enables us to approach one such
relationship within history and within multiple familial memories.
     Almost against itself, Zosia's tale of adventure opens Annie's social mobil-
ity and aspirations, her commitments and politics (Annie as nom de guerre?),
her longings and emotions. I ended with sorrow, shame, and anger, which is
appropriate but in retrospect insufficient. Despite all that transpired, Annie
may still—at certain moments, at least—have treasured her wartime adventure with Zosia and Jules. She may have felt gratitude for their shared experiences, she may have felt pride in what she accomplished.[57] Within the crevices
of Zosia's adventure story, all the possibilities of another woman's being come
into view.
     Annie died in 1970, of cancer. Her death certificate indicates that this
"secretary" had neither "visible assets" nor "known heirs."[58] When I first read
them, these words contributed to the deep sadness, tinged with intergenerational shame, that led me to seek her out with such desperation. Quickly, this
feeling gave way to discomfort before a document that obscures as much as
it reveals. Annie was a secretary, but not only. Though she lacked economic
assets, she left her mark in history. She had heirs too. In France, her biological kin do not know everything about her past, but they speak about her with
affection. In Brussels, Zosia could not utter her name in our presence, but she
did not abandon her, not completely.

After all, she kept the snapshot of Annie hiking with her dog.

This photograph is not only an image, but also an artifact, a gift from one woman to another. It is a memento, the trace of an extraordinary relationship that could not have left either one of them indifferent. Zosia accepted this gift—a shy smile on a country trail—and placed it in her album, alongside her parents and relatives, her kinfolk and close friends. She included Annie among her loved ones. Elsewhere in her apartment, she kept wartime photos, a baptism certificate, and Annie's letters from Nice. Her adventure story rested on specific procedures: selecting, sorting, ordering her wartime experiences into a narrative and a public performance. Her personal archive entailed more inclusive, more intimate gestures: collecting, accepting, bearing testament to fragments of human life. The family story and the family archive are distinct, yet entangled. Together, they reveal a rescue that all did not understand the same way. They flesh out an adventure that could not contain all the love and all the pain that, even at a distance, braided these lives together. They outline a friendship that was more fragile and more profound than any of us could have known in Belgium or in Nice.

Peïra Cava, hollow stone indeed.

FIGURE 4.7. Peïra Cava, June 1944.
Zosia Warchiwker family papers.

A Child of *Loving*

MARTHA S. JONES

I don't remember the day in June 1967 when the US Supreme Court decided the case of *Loving v. Virginia*, as monumental an occasion as it was. This, despite the dust-up that *Loving* generated all around me, as I came to understand. I was a child, less than two weeks from my ninth birthday; planning a sleepover party and then summer vacation mostly occupied my mind. Even as I now see, looking back, how New York's newspapers splashed the decision across their headlines, nothing of that interest registered with me. The nation's high court spoke directly to families like mine, but my only memory is of silence.

My parents took it all in. In those days, my father rode the Long Island Railroad forty or so minutes between our small town, Port Washington, and his office in Manhattan. Most nights he arrived home, carrying under his arm folded copies of the city's tabloids. "Interracial Marriage Ban Is Upset by Court . . . and the Decision Sets off a Hot Domestic Issue," New York's *Daily News* warned readers the day after the court's decision. Our local paper, *Newsday*, initially was mum on the subject, opting instead to herald the nomination of Thurgood Marshall to the US Supreme Court on its front page. Indisputably newsworthy! It took until two days after the *Loving* decision came down for that paper to mention the case. The editorial was so brief that it appeared like a whisper: "Marry Whom You Please."[1] If any of this news coverage generated discussion in our house, that happened only after we three children were in bed. I'm left to imagine my parents mulling over what it meant that the high court lent constitutional protection to marriages like theirs: Anti-miscegenation laws were unconstitutional.[2]

It's too easy perhaps to remember the *Loving* decision as nothing less than a welcome rebuke of laws that in eighteen states still banned interracial marriage. After all, never in its history had New York State imposed such a color bar. Still, as a child of the *Loving* years, I quickly learned that the court's ruling did not mean I should rest easy. My parents were within their rights to marry as they pleased, the court and public opinion affirmed. But I, as their child, remained among the monstrous, the mongrel, the fatally misplaced issue, a child who bore the regrettable mark of my parents' union. Even as today I recoil from such characterizations, ones promoted during the debates that led to *Loving*, I recognize how they spoke of me. Over and again, the defenders of anti-miscegenation laws touted the marital color line as a service and a concern for us, the children.

Before the Supreme Court, Virginia's assistant attorney general, R. D. McIlwaine III, leaned hard on this view. Yes, nothing about anti-miscegenation laws overstepped constitutional guarantees of equal protection of the laws. The same laws, McIlwaine urged, were also good public policy because interracial marriages were, by some accounts, less stable than those between persons said to be of the same race. This mattered, yes for the well-being of society overall, but it mattered urgently for the fate of children. The stigma that burdened children was such that they "are referred to not merely as the children of intermarried parents but as the victims of intermarried parents and as the martyrs of intermarried parents." He went on to explain that interracial marriage "causes a child to have almost insuperable difficulties in identification and that the problems which a child of an interracial marriage faces are those which no child can come through without damage to himself."[3]

In our home, no one endorsed such thinking. And still, my family didn't have an experience, a vocabulary, or an analysis that placed us in another light. Even those who loved us most strained to explain who we were in a world crudely divided between Black and white.[4] My parents knew well this binary regime, and earlier in their lives had conformed. In 1950, before they met, a US census taker found my mother living with her father, brother, and two maiden aunts in Buffalo, New York. In the box marked race, he recorded her with a "W" for white. An enumerator tracked down my father, a student at Boston University, living in a hotel-turned-dormitory for men returned from the Second World War. Of the nearly 900 students lodged together, only 22 were marked "Neg" for Negro. But that happened only after the enumerator curiously first marked the same 22 students, along with every other young man in that residence, as white.[5] Someone made an error, then corrected it by crossing out the "W" and penning in "Neg." My father's presence may have been unexpected to a bureaucrat who anticipated finding only white students in a BU dorm. But a quick correction restored order, one that imagined Americans as always divided by a color line.

There is, certainly, more than one way to be vexed by race in America. My parents had their own story, one about how they, as two people of different races, troubled law, culture, and the very idea of family. Still, the prospect of an empty box insisting that they indicate a race was straightforward. Race was, of course, always a social construct, a set of ideas arbitrarily associated with differences between human bodies. And their family pasts—of illicit immigration from Germany and of enslavement in the US South—meant that neither claimed to be all-American in an "Anglo-Saxon" sense. But there was a distance, even a real gulf, between their confrontations with the nation's racial regime and mine. This I learned one encounter at a time with forms, regulations, and people charged with keeping order. I had been called many things—including mutt, mulatto, and mixed—but no one quite had words for me once I became a child of *Loving*.

Family history, as in the history of my own family, is a tricky undertaking. Tricky in that I did not start out knowing precisely what I was looking for. My family archive includes memories, recollections, and snippets that, over time, have become my own. Curious stories passed down from folks like my parents, sometimes scrawled on all sides of fading stationary, mix with the ink and paper sureness of public records, certificates, and schedules. Family history asks who we are, how we came to be. Sometimes the answers are revealed in matters of flesh, of blood, of color, texture, and timber. They may be of girth and pace, grace and stillness. Still, they are also always stories.

It's a wonder my parents met at all given that they came from very different worlds. She was from the North—Buffalo, New York—a place of steel and prisons. A working-class, high school valedictorian for whom social mobility meant working in offices rather than factories. He was from North Carolina, the city of Greensboro, a place of tobacco and later civil rights sit-ins. A child of the cultural elite, his parents sent him to a New England prep school when the South's segregated system promised to fail him.[6] She, Sue, was a Catholic—one who only glimpsed Protestant kids from across an imaginary but very real line while growing up in East Buffalo.[7] He, Paul, was a Methodist, with a bishop for an uncle who refused to preside over their interfaith nuptials.

They joked that this difference—between Protestant and Catholic—was the great divide of their marriage. But it wasn't true. He was Black and she was white, and, at the start, nearly all else between them was subordinate to those facts. Only happenstance brought them together. In 1956, both roomed at the Lenox Hill Neighborhood House in Yorkville on Manhattan's east side. The place was founded in 1894, dedicated to supporting the European immigrant communities settling in surrounding tenements. Like Jane Addams's

Hull House in Chicago and Lower Manhattan's Henry Street Settlement, Lenox Hill by the 1950s expanded to support health care access, employment, and tenants' rights. Its headquarters were set up in a 1928 building that included a swimming pool, gymnasiums, a theater, a rooftop playground, a kitchen, offices, and—key for my parents—small, single-room residences for its affiliates.[8]

Their letters from those years went to 301 East 70th Street, where each found a community of sorts, not just a place to lay their heads. It was Paul's first independent home, and his missives to his mother included sketches that shared decorating schemes. It was her first time on her own, but Sue did not only rent a room at Lenox Hill. She took shorthand, typed, filed, and kept order as a secretary in the executive offices. Paul led an evening youth club—the Imperials—and, as my mother told it, played bridge with the older ladies and ironed his own shirts most Saturdays while opera blared from a transistor radio. They also found one another there while getting their adult bearings: he after troubled years brought on by service during World War II, and she after escaping the insular world of Buffalo's east side.

Nothing about Lenox Hill suggested that it would especially welcome them. The place was best known for its efforts to maintain an economically integrated community—many of those it served were working-class European immigrants and their descendants who lived in the neighborhood's old-law tenements. By the 1950s, gentrification—including expansion of the area's hospitals and the rise of large apartment buildings—threatened to push older residents out. Lenox Hill, in those years, had two faces. Up front were the neighborhood's needy, especially young people or, in the parlance of the day, juvenile delinquents. Behind the scenes were the city's elite who socialized at horse shows, the theater, and at the mayor's residence, Gracie Mansion, their donations filling Lenox Hill's coffers.[9]

Once my parents decided to marry, Paul's regular letters to his mother chronicled the strife that visited them, trouble that I heard them clash over years later. Sue's family opposed the wedding, he reported to his mother: "Sue's trip home was successful as I told you. i.e., She told them what she was going to do. However you can well emagine [sic] that none of this has set well."[10] My mother broke the news to her family in Buffalo, and not merely that she was planning upcoming nuptials to a man they had not met. She told them my father was Black, and this set off a campaign to stop the wedding. My father was her steadfast supporter: "She received a letter from an Aunt by marriage who outlined a long list of reasons for not getting married. The most [illegible] one was that she was cutting herself off from her family especially those whom she is closest to."[11]

Paul's mother followed their plans closely from her North Carolina home.[12] She not only kept up a regular exchange of letters but did what she could to ensure that things between them went well. When Paul advised his mother that their budget for the wedding looked tight, she sent rings—a small diamond engagement ring and a matching gold band from Tiffany's she wore as a young bride. Paul was the last of her children to marry, and the gesture—offered just months after losing her husband—suggests his mother put her concerns aside to support them. It mattered: "You knew I had wanted to get Sue a ring, but there are so many other things we'll need that she was willing to forgo it. But once [I] got it on her finger she was thrilled!! And really excited. So, thank you very much for your generosity."[13]

Their confidants in New York included a "young priest," whom my parents likely consulted at Sue's urging; she had relied on the counsel of a supportive priest when she left Buffalo for the city two years earlier. More than once, my father quoted the clergyman's perspective: "No matter what you do they (the Aunts) won't except [*sic*] it until it happens."[14] Attitudes were changing, even in the Catholic church, though not quickly enough. Nearly ten years before, in the 1948 case of *Perez v. Sharp*, attorney Daniel Marshall argued that anti-miscegenation laws barring the marriage of one Catholic to another interfered with the sacrament of marriage. Their priest did not bar Andrea Perez and Sylvester Davis from wedding one another, but the state of California refused their license because he was Black and she was Mexican. Marshall, an activist in the Los Angeles Catholic Interracial Council, regarded it as a victory for the religious liberty of Catholics when the state's high court struck down California's anti-miscegenation laws as unconstitutional.[15]

Lurking behind the exchanges between Paul and his mother was the law, not of California, but of his home state, North Carolina. Likely no one seriously considered that my parents marry there. Since 1715, over nearly 250 years, lawmakers in North Carolina consistently barred marriages between white and so-called non-white people. Paul may have been frustrated by Sue's family: "As for myself I have somewhat a feeling of frustration in that I'm unable to help her, really. I'm taking one from my Daddy's book and standing by willing, wanting to do what I can to help."[16] But he could afford to be patient, knowing that New York law would allow them to take a license whenever the time was right.

Most striking about the months leading up to their wedding is how resolute my parents were. I knew them only later in life when the circumstances of their marriage, including strained finances and a string of infidelities, weighed heavily on them. After some acrimonious years, they separated for the last time in the early 1970s. But in the months leading up to the ceremony, as they confronted her family's entrenched racism, my parents became increasingly sure. They talked about giving up, but, my father explained, Sue "has ruled this out." An aunt suggested that Sue return home to Buffalo and take time to think things through. But they decided otherwise: "I have suggested this [delaying matters] would be good if she wanted to, but we both thought it would not certainly help especially with her mind made up. We feel that it would only serve to aggravate the situation."[17]

They wed on a Saturday, June 29, before a Catholic priest who first made my father submit to church rules. Everyone assumed that children would come along, and Sue's clergy member made sure that Paul committed—in writing—to having us baptized and raised in the Catholic faith, even as he remained a Methodist.[18] It wasn't until 1970 that the pope's apostolic letter "Matrimonia Mixta" loosened this requirement.[19] In 1957, a promise was enough to reassure everyone that the crooked lines of faith would get straightened out. And when the time came, we were dutifully baptized Catholics. Still, nothing in church doctrine prescribed who we, their children, would be when it came to America's notions about race. My parents set up housekeeping in a West 107th Street walk-up. Then, just one week shy of their first anniversary, I was born.

It took no time at all for me to meet up with the color line. It happened within moments of my birth when a doctor filled in a blank. For my generation, race was a fact not unlike sex, weight, and length. Birth certificates, along with the regulations that set their terms, ensured that infants were scrutinized, surveilled, and otherwise held up against that measure of human difference that was race.[20] I was born amid turmoil over this long-standing practice. Civil rights organizations—the NAACP and the National Urban League included—urged that recording race on birth (and death) certificates served no legitimate purpose. New York State officials pushed back, making the case that the health data derived from birth certificates justified the practice. In December 1961, New York City Health Commissioner Leona Baumgartner announced a compromise. Birth certificates would continue to record a child's race, but that data would be kept for statistical purposes only. No longer would birth certificates publish what a physician saw.[21]

But my earliest encounter with officialdom predated that change, and the designated agent of my race making was an obstetrician who completed a box that could determine where I was allowed to live and attend school or who I might marry. Were physicians suitable agents of racial determination?[22] American courts certainly thought so and deemed them qualified to assign us a race. In one of many examples, historian Peggy Pascoe explains how, during the 1939 trial in *Estate of Monks*, a court heard from a range of possible experts: a hairdresser, a physical anthropologist, a cultural biologist, a biologist, and a surgeon. At stake was the race of Marie Antoinette Monks who, if found to be Black, would have her marriage invalidated and any claim to her late husband's estate extinguished. Discrediting other testimony, the trial judge relied on the insight of a physician who practiced medicine in the US South and served as a missionary in Africa. Mrs. Monks was one-eighth Black, the court concluded, Black enough to run afoul of a state anti-miscegenation law that forbade her marriage to a white man.[23] The doctor "seemed to hold a very unique and peculiar position as an expert on the question involved from his work in life," the California Court of Appeals reasoned.[24]

So it was in New York City hospitals. In the dark anteroom of a ward, a doctor filled in a blank and gave me a race. All this out of my parents' sight.[25] Manuals such as the *Physicians' Handbook on Birth and Death Registration*, published by the Census Bureau in 1939, aided doctors in fulfilling their duties. But they did not offer much guidance when it came to parents of differing races: "Color or race of father and mother. When either parent belongs to the white (Caucasian) race, write *white*. Otherwise, racial origin should be described by stating to what people or race each parent belongs, as *Indian, Negro, Chinese*, etc. Avoid the use of terms such as 'American' or 'Canadian,' which express citizenship rather than a race or people." No guidance there about how to note children like me.[26]

Only years later, as a nineteen-year-old preparing for a semester's study abroad, did I have a good look at my birth certificate. I was more concerned with rail passes, backpacks, and the right gift for my host family than formal paperwork. But to secure my first passport, I had to present the document that lived in my parents' strong box at the back of a bedroom closet, folded into well-worn thirds. It was a reverse sort of copy, black background and white print on shiny heavy paper, with a raised health department seal. There were my parents: names, ages, places of birth. I recognized them. My father, the Atlanta-born southerner, eight years my mother's senior; she, born and raised in Buffalo. Amid all this data, one word stopped me cold. That word was "white."

I knew my mother to be a white person. In twenty-first-century parlance, we say that she was someone believed to be white, but, in the 1970s, her whiteness figured more like a fact than a social construction.[27] On the other hand, upon finding my father—and by implication me, his daughter—designated white, I frantically scanned the paper. Was this *my* birth certificate? If so, it included a terrible mistake. My father was not white at all. He was Black, and so was I.[28]

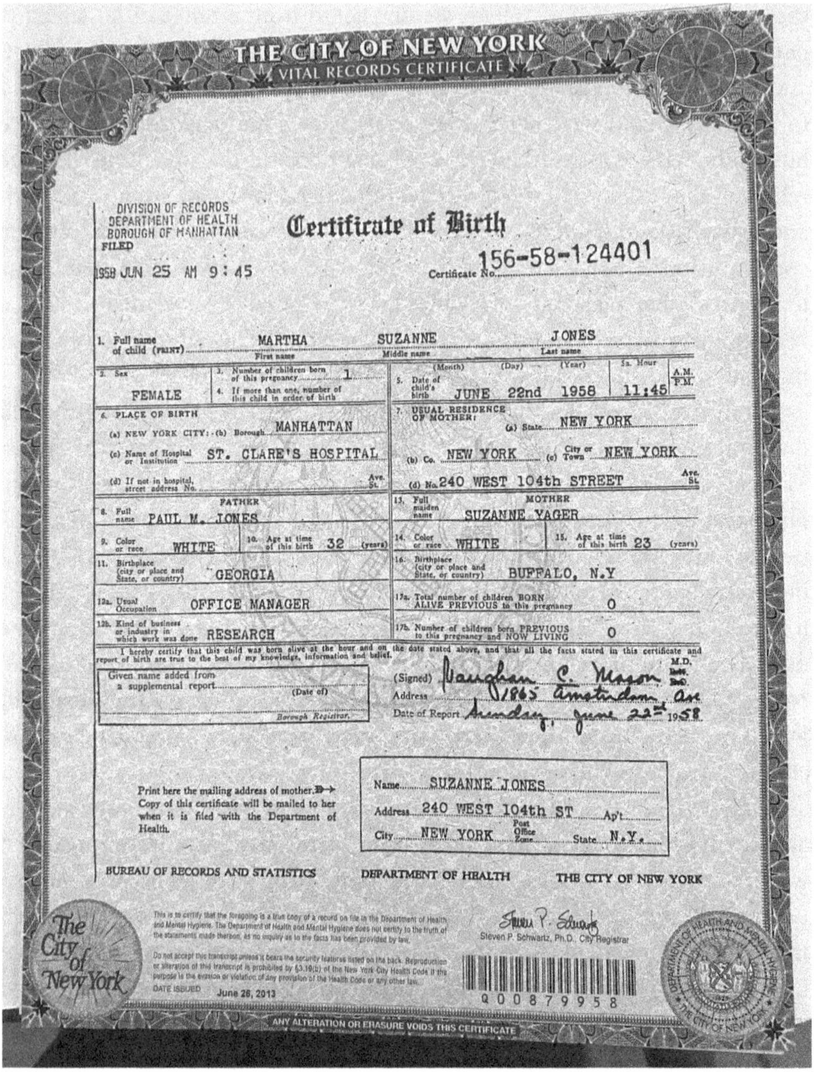

THE CITY OF NEW YORK
VITAL RECORDS CERTIFICATE

DIVISION OF RECORDS
DEPARTMENT OF HEALTH
BOROUGH OF MANHATTAN
FILED
1958 JUN 25 AM 9:45

Certificate of Birth

Certificate No. 156-58-124401

1. Full name of child (PRINT): MARTHA (First name) SUZANNE (Middle name) JONES (Last name)

2. Sex: FEMALE
3. Number of children born of this pregnancy: 1
4. If more than one, number of this child in order of birth:
5. Date of child's birth: (Month) JUNE (Day) 22nd (Year) 1958
5a. Hour: 11:45 A.M. P.M.

6. PLACE OF BIRTH
(a) NEW YORK CITY: (b) Borough: MANHATTAN
(c) Name of Hospital or Institution: ST. CLARE'S HOSPITAL
(d) If not in hospital, street address No. Ave. St.

7. USUAL RESIDENCE OF MOTHER:
(a) State: NEW YORK
(b) Co.: NEW YORK (c) City or Town: NEW YORK
(d) No. 240 WEST 104th STREET Ave. St.

FATHER
8. Full name: PAUL M. JONES
9. Color or race: WHITE
10. Age at time of this birth: 32 (years)
11. Birthplace (city or place and State, or country): GEORGIA
12a. Usual Occupation: OFFICE MANAGER
12b. Kind of business or industry in which work was done: RESEARCH

MOTHER
13. Full maiden name: SUZANNE YAGER
14. Color or race: WHITE
15. Age at time of this birth: 23 (years)
16. Birthplace (city or place and State, or country): BUFFALO, N.Y
17a. Total number of children BORN ALIVE PREVIOUS to this pregnancy: 0
17b. Number of children born PREVIOUS to this pregnancy and NOW LIVING: 0

I hereby certify that this child was born alive at the hour and on the date stated above, and that all the facts stated in this certificate and report of birth are true to the best of my knowledge, information and belief.

Given name added from a supplemental report (Date of)
Borough Registrar.

(Signed) Vaughan C. Mason M.D.
Address 1865 Amsterdam Ave
Date of Report Sunday, June 22nd 1958

Print here the mailing address of mother. Copy of this certificate will be mailed to her when it is filed with the Department of Health.

Name: SUZANNE JONES
Address: 240 WEST 104th ST Ap't
City: NEW YORK Post Office Zone State: N.Y.

BUREAU OF RECORDS AND STATISTICS DEPARTMENT OF HEALTH THE CITY OF NEW YORK

The City of New York

This is to certify that the foregoing is a true copy of a record on file in the Department of Health and Mental Hygiene. The Department of Health and Mental Hygiene does not certify to the truth of the statements made thereon, as no inquiry as to the facts has been provided by law.

Do not accept this transcript unless it bears the security features listed on the back. Reproduction or alteration of this transcript is prohibited by §3.19(b) of the New York City Health Code if the purpose is the evasion or violation of any provision of the Health Code or any other law.

DATE ISSUED June 26, 2013

Steven P. Schwartz
Steven P. Schwartz, Ph.D., City Registrar

Q00879958

ANY ALTERATION OR ERASURE VOIDS THIS CERTIFICATE

FIGURE 5.1. My birth certificate.
Courtesy of the author.

Worried that my passport application might be in jeopardy, I went to my mother. I might be denied that all-important document, or, worse, subject to a penalty for perpetuating a racial falsehood. She couldn't reassure me about the fine points of law but did have a story: My father had not been present for my birth. From the perspective of the 1970s, when fathers coached and caught babies and cut umbilical cords, I needed reminding that, in the 1950s, they more likely sat in waiting rooms, paced linoleum corridors, or smoked ciga-rettes outside on the curb.

That's what my father was doing out in front of West 51st Street's St. Clare's Hospital, with his buddy Bobby, while I was being born, my mother recalled.[29] And I can imagine him sitting there. Harder to imagine is that upstairs on the ward, my mother's obstetrician did not know who, or what, my father was. I've turned the story over and again many times and suppose it makes sense. The doctor who completed my birth certificate didn't see my father. He wasn't greeted by my father's colloquial drawl, didn't observe the flare of his nose, did not shake his strong, wide, brown hand. The obstetrician who delivered me, my mother thought, looked at her, looked at me, and recorded all of us as white.

A few years later, a case brought by Susie Guillory Phipps reinforced my sense that birth certificates were high stakes. Phipps made the news after appearing before her county records office, like me, on her way to securing a passport. The clerk emerged from the records room, document in hand, and called Phipps to the side in hushed tones. Phipps, the clerk advised, had African-descended forebears, and many years before a physician marked her as colored. In a slim moment, Phipps went from being a white person to one without a vocabulary, without a scheme, without a construct that captured her family history or her identity.[30] Phipps wasn't content to quietly get her passport and tuck away the certificate. She sued the state of Louisiana, claim-ing her right to be a white person. She possessed a property interest in her white identity, she argued, and Louisiana could not summarily take it away. The entirety of her life rested on that fact. Judges disappointed her. Louisiana not only upheld, in 1985, the state law that provided for racial distinctions among and between citizens, it also allowed that anyone with at least one Black great-great-grandparent was Black and not white. Phipps was said to be 3/32s Black, enough to justify the terms of her birth certificate.[31]

Phipps was adamant, but her husband, undisputedly a white man, took the revelation in stride: "It didn't bother me." His wife, it seemed, was an exceptional Black woman, if she was in fact a Black woman at all: "But she's white, and if she's not black, why not right it?" Still, in no way was he indiffer-ent to the color line: "It doesn't mean I'd jump up and marry a black woman or want my kids to marry a black woman." His objection lay not in a concern about his own whiteness, but in the grandchildren he imagined would result should his own sons marry Black women: "It ain't them that suffers, but the kids in the future."[32]

My mother and I might have talked about amending my birth certificate to mark me and my father as Black. It was the sort of scheme she might have entertained, but I didn't have the nerve to follow through. I knew I could not emphatically claim either designation, white or Black, before a judge. And I had no alternative. Terms such as mulatto and octoroon, once part of official American racial parlance, were now pejorative throwbacks.[33] I got my passport, headed to Europe, and hid the birth certificate, like a secret, an artifact I regarded with confusion and even shame.

In 1962, my parents looked to move their small family from Central Harlem to a New York City suburb. There, we confronted a world shaped by redlining, restrictive covenants, and other discordant echoes of Jim Crow. In Port Washington, where we finally settled, it was mostly recalcitrant neighbors who plagued our search for a new home.[34] This was a lonely time for my parents, who had not fully known what to expect. My mother turned to poetry, a slim but moving record of how, once the movers had left them to sit quietly amid the boxes and furniture still to be arranged, an unfamiliar silence enveloped them. It was not that they had left the bustling sound of Harlem's streets for the quiet of a suburban cul-de-sac. My parents were entering what was for so many Americans the uncharted territory of living side by side.

I spent that vexed summer with my grandmother in North Carolina, while my parents tended my toddler brother and readied for my sister's July due date. I've heard more than one version of how they finally landed 64 Wakefield Avenue: a postwar cookie-cutter cape, battleship gray, a postage-stamp-sized front yard, three bedrooms, one bath, and a back garden that spilled into a country club golf course that would never accept us as members.[35] My mother explained that the purchase was possible only because the owners were not Americans—sometimes they were French, other times South African. In either case, the point was that the sellers signed a contract with my parents because they were not invested in enforcing the logics of Jim Crow. Or they were even a bit vengeful, delivering a final insult to the neighbors who opposed any incursion of Black people into their all-white enclave. Returning to homes far away, they'd never be accountable for breaching the social compact. I grew up believing that the only people who might welcome my family were non-Americans.

There are other stories. I've heard it said that locals organized, hoping to buy the house out from underneath my parents, but they were not well-heeled enough to pull it off. More recently, I heard another story from a childhood babysitter. He explained that his mother, a white artist who lived around the corner, banded together with others to support my parents' quest at home-ownership. Getting there required some subterfuge. This loose team of local activists posed as prospective buyers, secured a contract, and then transferred it to my parents, all the while keeping the sellers and other neighbors in the dark. I suspect the story may be apocryphal. But however they got there, my parents managed to parlay a small inheritance and a GI Bill mortgage into a home.

The first months were filled with snubs and slights and even included bomb threats. On the winding, tree-lined streets of our neighborhood, I avoided the stalwarts who maintained that we did not belong. There were kids whose yards I was never allowed to enter. Still, the worst of it eventually let up, leaving us to find some peace. My more vivid memories are of a house filled with artists, priests, teachers, social workers, and activists. Many were members of the town's Community Relations Council. Radical by its own lights, critics viewed the group as conservative in its approach to civil rights, with one remarking that CRC had spent a long year "educating the community before showing any homes in white areas to Negroes."[36]

"Had that been us, those Negroes?" I wondered when reading the news coverage more than a half century later. Perhaps. Our lives became enmeshed in the era's movements for change: antipoverty, antiwar, and civil rights. At home, I was in the company of grownups committed to transformation. My father chaired the local Community Action Council, and my mother ran its office. Dinner talk was of protecting civil rights, running low-cost public transportation, standing up a credit union, stocking a food co-op, staffing a health clinic, and clearing the way for a new, moderate-income housing development. Watching my parents work taught me how to fight the good fight.

One of my father's biggest battles hit close to home: He challenged the de facto segregation of our local high school. My high school. Where we lived, on this part of Long Island's North Shore, no law kept Black and white students in separate classrooms or school buildings. Still, a color line was evident in the town's only high school. It was not that Black and white students were kept apart. The discrimination was evidenced in outcomes: graduation rates for Black students fell far below that of their white counterparts. In the same classrooms, Black students did not get the same teaching, mentoring, and opportunities that were extended to white students. Segregation, in this sense, was a shorthand for how students in our high school were educated differently, even as they shared the same school building.

My father saw in these outcomes a version of the trouble that *Brown v. Board of Education* aimed to remedy in 1954. Both he and my mother experienced their own versions of school segregation. She attended a Catholic girls' school on Buffalo's east side where the students were local kids, second- and third-generation Irish and German. They were white, like their school. In 1940, after the Black population of Buffalo boomed to nearly 18,000, there still were fewer than 100 Black residents in the neighborhoods that surrounded her family's Grey Street home.[37] His father sat on Greensboro's school board in 1954, its sole Black member, when that city announced that it would not delay complying with *Brown*'s desegregation demand. Compliance was at best halting, but by 1957 Black students began to attend what were previously North Carolina's whites-only schools.[38]

By the 1970s, Port Washington did not much look like the places my parents had come from. Still, racism was felt there. My father encouraged local Black parents to file a class-action suit against the school district on behalf of all the town's Black students. The plans were fraught—many doubted that a court would entertain a discrimination claim that did not involve the physical separation of students—and I recall my father's sharp disagreements with the local NAACP head over the wisdom of a direct challenge. Years before, in 1964, activists in the neighboring town, Manhasset, won concessions from the local district board after charging that schools there were de facto segregated: that is, segregated in practice and by custom rather than pursuant to law.[39]

Eventually, my father's suit went forward,[40] and it became time to choose named plaintiffs—children who, by name, would represent the entirety of the Black students. My name was not among them. Perhaps my father aimed to keep me out of the headlines. But more likely, he knew that choosing me to stand in for all Black students might complicate an already difficult case. I knew who Linda Brown was—so too did many Americans who recognized her as the lead complainant in *Brown v. Board*. My father—the Black activist—took the lead. I remained in the shadows. His critics were right, and, in short order, his suit failed. No fault of mine.

"We just don't label them too much," explained my grandmother. It was 1977, twenty years after my parents' marriage—and well after we, their three children, were born—when she was asked to explain who we were. It was a friendly enough encounter. The interviewer, historian Dr. Merze Tate, and my grandmother were already acquainted for decades. They first met in the 1930s, when Dr. Tate was a faculty member at Bennett College, where my grandfather was president. Four decades later, my grandmother and Dr. Tate sat together in a familiar place, my grandmother's home. They spent two days with a tape recorder running as my grandmother recounted the details of her life. She was just past her eighty-sixth birthday, and Dr. Tate gently prodded her through those many years. Dr. Tate was on assignment from Harvard's Schlesinger Library, where today the interview is on deposit as part of the Black Women's Oral History Project.[41]

Toward the end of their interview, the two women sat at my grandmother's dining table with family photographs spread about. Dr. Tate used them to elicit details about my grandmother's children and in turn theirs. My grandmother had nine grandchildren in total. "Now these three I've kept together because they are in color and they belong in the same family," Dr. Tate prompted. It was us, I recognized. My grandmother was sharing with Dr. Tate our public school portraits; we sat for them every year in the 1960s and 1970s. Dr. Tate knew where her questions were headed and was warming up for a tougher query. I wonder whether my grandmother felt it coming.

"Yes, these are Paul's children." My grandmother dutifully introduced us as the children of Paul, her middle son. I was just starting my sophomore year in college, she explained, and there were my siblings. "Oh yes. They're very interesting," Dr. Tate replied, an observation filled with subtext. We'd been called things worse than "interesting," especially in the school yard. Was there any polite way to ask about the race of my parents' children? Dr. Tate tried, first by simple observation, referring to my sister: "She has almost blondish hair and light brown-bluish eyes." I should be clear that this does not describe my sister at all. But the point was made. We were descendants of my grandparents, but that was not all. Looking at us, Dr. Tate thought she saw some mark of my parents' illicit union. It was blond with light eyes.

Dr. Tate never asked *what* we were, at least not directly. Instead, she turned to questions about our mother: "What is her mother, do you have a picture of her mother?" My grandmother kept a photo of my mother nearby in her sitting room, she explained. Listening to her interview with Dr. Tate, I can feel her discomfort. This was not a topic she deemed appropriate. As a general matter, she was not one to speak of people in terms of types, including gradations of color, at least not on the record. But in this case, the interview veered close to a subject about which she had too little experience, too little to draw on. I expect that she didn't quite know what to say.

"Their mother is white American," my grandmother went on, cautioning Dr. Tate: "But there too, you remember, situations have so much to deal with these kinds of things and so we just don't label them too much." The recorder was still running. Looking back, I am sure that Dr. Tate knew who—or *what*—my mother was. Likely at some moment they had met socially. Surely, through the networks that knit Dr. Tate and my grandmother, the subdued scandal that my parents' marriage generated had reached Dr. Tate's ears. But on that day, her purpose was to get my grandmother on the record, about many things. And among those things was what we were. That we had a mother who was white might have said enough, but Tate pressed my

FIGURE 5.2–5.4. Photos my grandmother shared with Dr. Tate.
Courtesy of the author.

grandmother with firm gentleness to explain what made us so "very inter-esting." No one placed a label on us that day. Though they were searching for one.[42]

Nearly half a century ago, my mother told a story about my birth, hoping to explain (away) my troublesome birth certificate. It was the story she knew, I suppose. It was also a story I needed; it released me to board that flight for the University of Copenhagen. I held onto the story for more than what it said about my birth. I also loved the image of my father and his best friend Bobby perched on a Manhattan curb anticipating my arrival. I can nearly see them, young, handsome, strong, and charmingly playful. Whatever they talked about, it was laced with the sort of bravado that perfectly attends a momentous but also unnerving occasion such as the birth of a first child. At thirty-two, my father would finally be just that: a father. And if the doctor who delivered me had only seen him—a man brown, baritone, and full of just the right bluster—perhaps then he would have also seen me.

My mother's version, it turns out, is but half the story. Only at the age of twenty did I take in how my birth certificate reported my race. It then took another four decades for me to look carefully at the doctor's name. He'd completed the boxes and then signed: Vaughn C. Mason. The name had not registered at all in the 1970s, but as I tried to better understand what had happened on the day I was born, I soon discovered something else my mother hadn't shared. Scouring my databases, I easily found him: Dr. Mason, with privileges at St. Clare's where he delivered me. Then on the staff at Sydenham Hospital, in Harlem, where later he birthed my brother and sister. There was Dr. Mason, with an office on Amsterdam Avenue at 152nd Street, in Harlem's fabled Sugar Hill.[43] The same Dr. Mason who, in 1961, became head of the National Medical Association, the alternative to the American Medical Association. Dr. Mason, the Black physician who marked my father and me as white on that birth certificate.

Dr. Mason had known better. I was certain that he had known us. I went to a cousin whose mother was also a New York physician in the same years; my aunt was a peer to Dr. Mason. And while my cousin didn't recall him, I was able to connect the two through their professional networks, especially their service for the Black-led National Medical Association. While I can't be certain, it seems very likely that my aunt, sister-in-law to my father, advised my parents about who to secure as an obstetrician. My parents always valued her medical advice.

My cousin then told me something else; it was about the direction her mother had given her about filling out forms. It went something like, "When

asked to indicate your race, simply leave the space blank." Her mother suspected that such data might be used against us, "to round us up," my cousin
explained. Here my mind went directly to legal scholar Derrick Bell's fantasti-
cal story about "space traders" who appeared in the United States looking to
take all Black Americans back with them into the universe. In that story, birth
certificates did indeed matter for they distinguished who was required to go
to a fate unknown from those who were permitted to remain on earth.[44] But
my aunt was thinking not like a legal scholar with a penchant for fantasy. She
was thinking like a physician.

Historian Susan Pearson has closely studied the birth certificate and explains how Black physicians increasingly objected to marking newborns by
race after World War II. My aunt was not alone in thinking that there was
something sinister about boxing infants in, especially when ideas about racial difference were used to justify unequal treatment in health care settings.
Black doctors knew that race was a social construction that drove law and
policy. It was not a fact. And there was even a small cadre of Black doctors
who, when completing birth certificates became part of their regular duties,
substituted the word "human" for terms that public health officials looked to
elicit: "Negro," for instance.[45]

Had she been an obstetrician and not an oncologist, my aunt might have
been among those who left that box on birth certificates blank. Perhaps
Dr. Mason had been purposeful rather than careless or presumptuous when he
completed my birth certificate. Perhaps it was his way of protesting the requirement altogether. Or maybe he thought he was giving me an advantage.
With a birth certificate that marked us all as white, Dr. Mason may have been
shielding us from the roundup that my aunt feared and Bell anticipated. As
a family, we never looked to that certificate to tell us what or who we were.
Shortly after I was born, we moved to Central Harlem where the assumption
was that we were Black, whatever our paperwork may have said. Still, Dr. Mason gave us an out if we chose to take it. In 1958, that was an infinitely more
practical gesture than any effort to report me as somehow Black. White. Both.

The time has long passed for correcting the certificate. You don't care
much about what it says, and neither do I. We have lived whole lives now,
filled with stories that make plain that when Dr. Mason was wrong, he was
also right. In that first, very first moment of misapprehension, mislabeling,
misunderstanding, he told the whole story of my life as a child of *Loving v.
Virginia*. I was there—the certificate proves that. And still I was unseen—an
incomprehensible, illegible, troubling child. Dr. Mason is long deceased. So
are my mother, my father, and his pal, Bobby. Now, the story is simply mine.

6

Who Gave You Permission?
Race, Colonialism, and Family Photography

TAO LEIGH GOFFE

"Who gave *you* permission to write about your family?"

A loaded question, heavy with assumptions. I was asked because I am Black, and some of the family members I am writing about are Chinese. I am a color, and they are a country. Blackness is a political and racial identity formed out of a rich history of competing modernities and multiple African experiences. Black is a diaspora born from the theft of a continent. China is not a race, but a diaspora, too, a nation defined as much by overseas intimacies and commercial ports of exchange as by the mainland seat of governance. At the transoceanic crosscurrents of the Black Pacific and the Chinese Atlantic, my family came into being. For centuries the branches of family trees have connected people descended from Africa to people from Asia. Black and Asian racial formations in the Americas are distinct and divergent but not mutually exclusive. For me, writing about kin places Black people and Asian people within the broader currents of global history fulfilling my filial duty. My Qingming, or tomb sweeping, which is a Chinese holiday of honoring the dead, is addressing the past and the future through writing. While in some way all societies venerate ancestors, there is a particular resonance in how African and Asian diasporic cultures overlap in performing spoken and unspoken rituals that, as a duty, invoke dead family members. Incense is lit by descendants as ancestors are presented with offerings of food and libations. Researching the dynamics of colonialism is my humble offering and responsibility. Everyone does not need to, nor should they as a given, embark into family research or writing about kin.

In part, my permission to write about my family comes from being an academic whose research takes place deep within the archives of British and Dutch colonialism. My doctoral training explored what colonial history cannot tell us about cultural formations between Black and Asian people in the United States, Caribbean, and Latin America. In the British Library, several times I have been surprised to unexpectedly encounter the faces of ancestors in colonial-era documents. Though European bureaucrats did not design colonial records as genealogical finding aids for people of color, they inevitably are so, especially for descendants of racial slavery. How, we might ask, does this work differ from genealogy?

Genealogists and historians differ in motive and method. Both pore over the meticulous note taking and recordkeeping of empire. They cross paths in archives, but their questions are not the same. Due to the comprehensive documenting of the Church of Jesus Christ of Latter-Day Saints, many colonial records are digitized and freely available, forming a genealogical guide. Countless marriage, birth, and death certificates from colonial countries provide valuable clues about the lives of ancestors who were legible to the government. For Mormons, genealogy is a responsibility too. It is a way to save souls, baptizing ancestors by proxy, increasing the "eternal family unit."

Genealogy is an enjoyable pastime for those who wish to regale relatives with family crests and coats of arms at family reunions. For genealogists of color, heraldry is always invested with a different politics than for white genealogists. It is common to find Moor's heads as insignias, or trophies of conquest, in European family crests: the terrain of family history is thorny. Sometimes genealogists write community histories, which can be vital to understanding quotidian life in ways that historians would not necessarily render it. As a scholar, I try to help these genealogists through my access to institutional resources and archives. I admire their dogged attempts, through historical records, to fill out branches of family trees. It is noble work, but I am acutely aware of the branches that will always be missing if we depend solely on colonial archives.

The noble work of saving ancestors from oblivion, to restore them to nobility, does not interest me. I center instead structures of extended kin that have always existed beyond the nuclear family. While there is talk in my family of the *Mayflower*, business magnates, and the regicide of King Charles I, I would rather learn about the texture of life of the seamstresses, washerwomen, and domestic workers who form my pedigree. Class determines whose records are deemed worth preserving in official archives. Neither the fabric of family life nor the events of global history are as certain as the archive suggests. Histories that do not conform to heteropatriarchy are conveniently and consistently absent. It is a perverse irony that many who do not conform to gendered notions of family and biological relation are left to preserve the family record. More and more I have noticed a rescripting of family history by such guardians of the family Bible, who include spinsters and men who never married.

Legal documents are a form of evidence created by the colonial state. However, birth certificates are putative. Behind each one is a potential shadow genealogy. There are putative histories, based on assumptions and uncertainties. Treaties written by the colonized who never agreed to the terms of surrender represent one reality among many. Once one fully reckons with what is putative, assumed, and alleged, multiple histories become possible. It has been suggested that the future is fixed while the past is multiple. I am writing against the presumed linear temporality of colonial historiography as a hagiography of the state.[1] Hagiographies, the biographies of saints, serve the purpose of creating myth and demanding reverence. The nation-state is a relatively recent fiction whose power functions as if it had always been, and so it requires such sanctioned myth making. That people could be chattel was another fiction that sustained the state and its capitalist economy. To deny the logic of chattel, one must challenge the logic of inheritance as a given. Property is both a gendered and racialized matter in Western society, and tracing surnames show us the cruel fact of what was taken.

"Who gave *you* permission to write about your family?"

The answer to the provocative question lies in its reciprocal grammar. The possessive grammar of pronouns takes ownership of property that cuts differently because racialization is an uneven process that creates social difference. Race continues to operate after death through a taxonomy of rites and rituals of remembrance, including tomb sweeping. Sexual consent is often a fraught intergenerational matter for diasporas with family trees branching across seas. Families like mine, with blood relatives of different races, have existed for centuries. Do I belong to them, or do they belong to me? Often, family members who do not identify as Black ask me questions that I cannot answer, as if I were their Black ancestor. While we share ancestry long ago descended from Africa, my cousins do not inhabit the experience of what it means to be read as Black. This does not mean they are not Black or they are. Some members of my extended family are read as Asian who are also of African ancestry. Some relatives are read as white and identify this way because race is a construct and a formation. These distant cousins live in New Zealand and London, Kingston and Rotterdam. Whenever we get together, one will inevitably ask me to recite the family tree as if it is not theirs to memorize as well. "How are we related again?" They repeatedly ask me about Black Lives

Matter, President Obama, and *The Wire*. I grow tired of the role of the Angry
Black Woman and Black Studies professor, so I refuse to rehearse the litany of
colonial crimes and generations removed.

Historically, everyone has not been invested with the right to own property. Some people were owned as if humans could be property. Others were
forced into contracted periods of temporary bondage. In the context of these
labor histories, I situate myself as part of a different act of genealogy, Afro-
Asian and feminist, formed across continents, the plantation economy, and
imperial circuits of trade, through multiple surrogate births. After the aboli-
tion of the transatlantic slave trade in the British Empire in 1807, Asian men
were brought to plantations en masse as a surrogate labor force—some by
force, others by choice—that would replace the enslaved Africans who for
centuries had tilled the soil of sugarcane production. Though not equivalent
to slavery, it was a brutal institution—racial indenture—and, in the twentieth century, waves of merchant Chinese shopkeepers followed the racialized
channels of migration to the Caribbean and Latin America.

Black and Asian women who would never meet because they were separated by oceans raised each other's kin. While they did not choose to do so,
many raised children who were not biologically their own. Children of African and Asian heritage were born to Chinese men in the nineteenth- and
early twentieth-century Caribbean. A choreography of second and sometimes third families, ghost marriages, common law unions, marriages by the
glove, and split-family households between the Caribbean and China has
shaped Afro-Asian families for two half centuries.[2]

"Who gave *you* permission to write about your family?"

Is this the full answer I was supposed to give? Though it was not intended
to be accusatory, the question took me aback, as if I had answered it a million different ways, all at once. I calmly said, "They are mine; I am theirs."
The question could easily have been mistaken as a confrontation. I am often
the only Black person at Asian and Asian American studies conferences and
university alumni soirees. There is an inevitable moment when an Asian or
Asian American person asks for proof of my connection to Asia, as if for
identification papers. Why am I in attendance? Legitimate curiosity can lead
to inappropriate questions. White people are not interrogated in the same
fashion at these events. Orientalism is a European tradition. White scholars
are expected to be present; they are welcomed because they created fields
that, like Asian studies, bolstered colonial projects of dominance.

But the question was asked several years ago in a more intimate space, an
event on family history in New York's Manhattan Chinatown, which is why I

was taken aback. I wanted to hear the vulnerability in the query. The scholar who asked me about permission was, like me, of African and Asian ancestry. I wanted to know why permission was not required or sought after to write about our Black relatives. It was our first meeting, both of us invited to a panel in a quaint shop turned community hub to mull and meditate on the work of family history and oral history, both of us invited to speak about our experiences navigating the territory of family research. The two other speakers were Chinese and, to my knowledge, not descended of other racial heritages. At a time of increasing friction between Black and Asian communities in the United States, we all understood the inclusive optics of our panel's casting.

The encounter conjured the awkward opening passages of Nella Larsen's 1929 novel *Passing*, a reflection in a mirror. Two Black women of mixed heritage notice each other, exchanging knowing glances. Though the other panelist did not look like me, she was searching for her point of access to a family history that her relatives had likely denied her. The territory was not unfamiliar; it is my job to be a guide. I am, after all, a professor of Black Studies who teaches a course called Afro-Asia: Food, Futurism, Feminisms. I am lucky to spend most of my days considering the gendered, historical politics of coalition, encouraging the next generation to build Afro-Asian political futures beyond the dictates of colonialism. Students often ask me for permission or the license to write freely and authoritatively about their family histories. While I should not have to do so, I am happy to grant this license inside the classroom so that it may spur further exploration. Eventually they must find permission within themselves and from their communities.

Writing about family has been a reflex for me since graduate school. I have written about my great-aunt Hyacinth, a woman of Afro-Chinese heritage who migrated from Jamaica to the United Kingdom in the 1950s.[3] I have published speculative recipes that connect the kitchen of Guangdong, one of my ancestral provinces, to the pantries of Kingston, the city where my mother was born.[4] I imagine the muscle memory of both of my grandmothers' hands. I seek the choreography of their kitchens in rural Jamaica. By learning to cook chop suey as it is made in Curaçao, I have charted Afro-Asian women's genealogies. This Chinese dish proved popular across the Americas because it is tasty and cheap. It was widely consumed across the United States during the Depression era, nourishing the nation. All mixed up, chop suey has become something of a cultural stand-in for celebrating multiculturalism.[5] Chop suey taught me there are many ways to trace a genealogy. Which recipes did our ancestors not pass down to us?

As I considered the shifting barriers of race within families across the Americas, I felt as though I understood where the question originated. Disinheritance, denial, disavowal: These terms define Afro-Asian relations for many people of African and Asian descent. Though it would be easy to presume Black and Asian solidarity exists across the Americas, the axis of Afro-Asian relations has for centuries been a hard-fought terrain of tensions and intimacies, even for women and men of color oppressed by colonial overlords. For people like this scholar and me, Afro-Asian solidarity is a matter of charting alternative pedigrees of coalition beyond blood, a matter of intellectual genealogies. For centuries, Black people and Asian people have been racialized against one another because they have historically been granted different modes of access to capital.

Papa's Maybe

Putative paternity as a form of legal familial relation is the norm in the Caribbean. Like the legal category of the common law, "the putative" is an assumed category. The porous boundaries of race buckle as they attempt to shore up and uphold a pigmentocracy built by fictions of shade invented by white supremacy. Eurocentric values derive from the valuation of humans as a regime out of the political economy of the plantation that existed for centuries across the Americas. Family would seem to a fixed category, but it is porous. If it were not, laws would not be needed to police and enforce these boundaries of relation. Such laws were used to order the familial dynamic of the plantation, determining who was allowed to own.

In the colonial Caribbean, fathers had the right to acknowledge their children or not, determining in many ways whether the child would be treated as a social pariah or not. Because they were born out of wedlock, many were excluded from opportunities that could have provided social mobility. To be enrolled in certain schools, one's paternity needed to be verified. In the 1970s, Jamaican Prime Minister Michael Manley passed the Status of Children Act, a transformative legislation that "removed the legal disabilities of children born out of wedlock." The post-independence society began to shift as it did away with illegitimacy as a legal category of scorn. Discrimination, of course, still takes place against many Jamaican children born without birth certificates or with their father's name absent from the form. The colonial regulation of birthing and marriage was a form of social control that is difficult to distance from its oppressive origins.

The denial of blood relation or paternity is common. The term "jacket" is used in Jamaica when women knowingly misidentify the father of their child to ensure parental financial support. Hortense Spillers famously played with the grammar of the African diaspora family in her 1987 essay "Mama's Baby and Papa's Maybe."[6] Gesturing to the shadow dynamic of plantation familial structures, she asks about the status of the bastard who is born a girl child. We have heard of William Faulkner's Joe Christmas and Emily Brontë's Heathcliff. Spillers asks about girls and what they stand to inherit. One's fate is as determined by the circumstances of birth as by ethnicity, gender, and complexion. Spillers writes of gendered categories thrown in crisis, of motherhood by theft of the body. Enslaved fathers were described as progenitors, mothers as breeders. After the end of the plantation regime, they were both demonized as deviant and irresponsible reproducers who were incapable of determining their own reproductive futures.

A European Christian ordering of society and family is but one way of structuring inheritance. Amerindian culture in the Antilles teaches me this. In the Kalinago territory of Dominica in the eastern Caribbean, inheritance is matrifocal: The youngest daughter inherits. While Chinese society is patriarchal, adding Asian norms to the familial dynamic of the Caribbean upends and complicates Christian formulas that dictate paternal obligation in colonial societies. It was common for Asian men to take ownership of their children in and out of wedlock in the early and mid-twentieth-century Caribbean because they had the financial means to do so. While this was not so much a magnanimous act, having multiple wives and families in and out of wedlock was not aberrant. In some cases, it gave Chinese men a foothold in society to have children of African descent who could negotiate the culture for them, especially as Chinese women did not migrate by and large.

To be part of overlapping African and Asian diasporas is to understand race as a verb that shifts across continents. Racialization starts within the structure of the family and can divide the lives of siblings, who might look different. Race is not a fact, but skin is a passport. The lives of sisters and brothers can diverge according to color, with differing access to socioeconomic power and transnational mobility. The prejudices that have ordered and shaped colonial plantation society persist. Class cuts with race, color, and pedigree to dissect families into haves and have nots, mirroring its structure. Paternity was a fraught matter because of inheritance, but the disinherited fashioned creative kin strategies to subvert colonial laws. I imagine what was done to circumvent discriminatory mandates that denied the right to inherit.

"Who gave *you* permission to write about your family?"

"They are mine; I am theirs."

Nothing is uncertain about this. I answered thinking of Toni Morrison's character, the infant ghost Beloved. "I am BELOVED and she is mine."[7] Morrison gave us the poetry of the Middle Passage, a fever dream of intergenerational trauma and nonlinear temporal possibility. Babies were born at sea. Consent was stolen. I belong to them, my kin. I have always pictured the feminist genealogies of women of color in this expansive way. My grandparents were saltwater children born of port city intimacies on an island in the Caribbean Sea. The four of them crossed multiple oceans, as had their parents. This is not a romance of wanderlust. My grandparents' transoceanic itineraries were those of colonial subjects, embedded within competing modernities, braided threads of West African, British, Dutch, and Chinese empires.

I have found extended family members who generously welcomed me in Eindhoven, Shenzhen, Newcastle, and Paramaribo. Ann Stoler notes that "racial thinking secures racial designations in a language of biology and fixity and in the quest for a visual set of physical difference to index that which is not 'self-evident' or visible—neither easy to agree on nor easy to see."[8] When difference is not easily or visually distinguishable, colonial management invents categories of division to separate and segregate life. This happens precisely because difference is not always legible. Where the West meets the East Indies, British and Dutch greed for spices converge. Searching for the British colonial presence in Chinese port cities necessarily leads us from the Caribbean to Southeast Asia. The records of the Dutch East India Company (V.O.C.) tell a tale of competition with the British East India Company. The commercial history of both entities is interwoven with the histories of family members who are not racialized in the same way. Some are the inheritors of these port city intimacies, some are the disinherited. Some are pictured in the family album, some—usually the darker-skinned individuals—are absent because of colorism.

For Papa's Maybe, these children born in the shadow of colonial economies, inheritance is uncertain. We are all to some extent Papa's Maybe. But the putative is not just a category of deniability: It is also one of possibility. Fathers have historically claimed these putative rights to secure representation. For those who have never stood to inherit, inheritance is as heavy a question as that of history. Parental rights were not a given under racial slavery. They were maintained under racial indenture—a critical difference. For Black people, the status of slavery was heritable; for Asians, the condition of being indentured was not. When one chooses to write about family, the weight of permission is both ethical and racialized. Those of us who have been inherited as chattel by European aristocracy and the white planter classes of the Americas understand the juridical nature of race as a relation.

Some Black families have existed as the invisible branches of white family trees, a history hidden in plain sight across the Americas. Black families like mine contain invisible Chinese branches and roots that sprout in saltwater harbors like Hong Kong's. For this reason, I have always understood Kingston and Paramaribo as Overseas Chinese port cities deeply connected by commercial and familial ties. Because I know my way to the Chinatowns that no longer exist in Jamaica and Suriname, I can order from the secret menus of diaspora. Though I do not speak Hakka or Putonghua, I recognize the shrines of our tutelary deities in hidden corners of Chinese shops and restaurants across the world.

"Who gave you the permission to write?"

The question is never asked of those who have historically denied subjecthood to others. Those who attempted and failed to disinherit our ancestors by rendering them as chattel have also wielded the pen as if it is the last word of history. Who gave them the permission to do so? In the hands of the disinherited, though, the pen is an act of power. In Suriname, some Black people use a curious strategy, owning and disowning Europe by inverting their surnames. Olsen becomes Nelso. Mok becomes reversed as Kom. They rewrite their genealogy each time they put pen to paper and sign their names.

The category of the putative shows us what is possible. The putative father is alleged or claims to be the biological father of a child born to a mother who is not his wife. Presumed fathers, they can claim paternal rights. When kin is extended as a horizontal category of relation beyond biology, new forms of inheritance become possible beyond wedlock. In African diaspora genealogies, speculation is a necessary tool. I learned of Afro-Surinamese putative strategies of rescripting kin when I presented my work at a conference at Suriname's Anton de Kom University, named for the resistance fighter and revolutionary Black figure. From Afro-Surinamese people there and in the Bijlmer neighborhood of Amsterdam, I learned how such Black diasporic strategies flourish. We have never needed permission to embrace one another in the diaspora. Nor have we asked for it.

As a legal term, "putative" shows us how uncertain parentage is viewed as a threat to the social order. With no choice but to disobey, irreverence toward the violence of the European colonial archive has been my only orientation from birth. Though I was born in London, my mother was born a colonial subject. Jamaica had not yet achieved independence from Britain. The colonial present extends the colorist regimes of the past. To deny the logic of human chattel requires challenging the assumed logic of inheritance, which is not universal.

Writing is one of many disobedient strategies of the Black diaspora. We take license and liberties with the grammars of European languages that are intimately ours, languages that disinherited us of our mother tongues. Our true family trees are written in dialects unknown to European linguists. Hakka, Hokkien, and Cantonese inflected with remnants of Twi and Yoruba make vernacular unwritten forms beyond the transliteration of Pin Yin. This blended accent of Black and Chinese patwa does not hide the fact that, in many Chinese families with Black descendants, Blackness is disavowed with shame. It is all too common. Anti-Blackness and colorism, global currencies of exclusion both, are learned quickly—beyond European or US colonialism.

Jiapus, Femme, and Nonbinary Genealogies

Black feminisms do not position kin as a given because so much has been taken without consent. It is not only consent that has been taken, but kin. To choose kin is to choose a politics of inclusive possibility. Choice from choice-lessness. In *Sula*, Toni Morrison, again, gives us this language for defining what she calls New World Blackness and womanness.[9] In a speculative mode, family history can be a source of power. It is choice. It is an act of taking the permission to imagine the intimacies that official archives cannot contain. For Chinese people in the Americas too, fictive kinship was formed out of paper daughters and sons. While the bureaucracy sought to limit Chinese futures by denying visas and US citizenship, the new familial intimacies that grew for those not biologically related stretched beyond the bounds of Chinese Exclusion in the United States (1882–1943).

In a course I teach on Afro-Asia, I braid this feminist tradition via the fictional worlds of Maxine Hong Kingston. While Morrison provides an entangled temporal genealogy and a baby girl ghost in *Beloved*, Kingston gives us a girlhood of ghosts and talk stories. Forgotten aunts and other phantasms form a putative genealogy. Kingston's aunt, the No Name Woman, jumped into a well after bringing shame to the family by giving birth out of wedlock. Kingston's mother says, "You must not tell anyone what I am about to tell you."[10] And yet, in *Woman Warrior*, the reader is pushed to rely on unreliable narrators telling secrets to tear at the seams of putative histories.

Colonial histories are haunted by armies of No Name Women. As an Afro-Asian woman, I have inherited an army of shadows that perform the labor of haunting the colonial archive through storytelling. A women of color feminist approach to history from the 1970s and 1980s gives me not only an alternative method but also the grounding for a political orientation toward family history. Only in this way can we ward off the seductive power of nostalgia in exploring the lives of our ancestors. I understand that I cannot be objective because I am an inheritor of this gendered history. I also understand that I will likely be subsumed in multiple future family trees, as a No Name Woman.

I know this because there are beautiful generational poems that record family histories in Chinese tradition. In these poems, only the names of male heirs are included. Male lineage determines inheritance. Jiapus (家谱), Chinese genealogical clan records, date back thousands of years in some cases. The generational poems preserve genealogy, written to connect the generations. Stanzas form over millennia as evidence of those who came before. Each verse begins with a character, a hao, denoting the ancestor's name. The name is extended in poetic form to create a record for future memory. The honorific follows the name of the ancestor who founded the clan.

While primogeniture is a European notion, Chinese women and nonbinary people are also forgotten and disinherited by poetic design. Genealogy is a gendered practice of exclusion in East Asia too. One cannot say women have been erased since their names were never recorded. Though they are most often the ones preserving familial traditions across the generations and performing filial duties, they are subsumed.

What of the femme and nonbinary Hakka and Cantonese genealogies? I have come to ask this question in my art making and teaching. My course syllabus provides an answer of queer, radical, and feminist genealogies. Patricia Powell's *The Pagoda* and Kerry Young's *Pao* give us palpable Afro-Asian literary worlds in which Black, Chinese, Indian women, and nonbinary characters are central to archiving history.[11] Far from ancillary to history, Powell's and Young's characters present wounded familial intimacies and stories of disinheritance in the shadow of the Jamaican plantation. My syllabus is an alternate jiapu of feminist and nonbinary possibility. My students and I write our own generational poems of putative intimacy by reading and writing together.

The woman who posed the question in Chinatown was looking for a permission slip of her own. Though I hope she found one, I could not grant it to her. I do not know where my jiapus 家谱 (or zupus 族谱) are, or hers. I felt at home, though, in the cramped Chinatown shop. You break, you buy. These are the rules of the shop and the rules for navigating family history. People are afraid to approach fragile histories for which they may have to take ownership and responsibility. But we, Black people, are often token curios displayed on pedestals in Chinese spaces such as these. For this reason, it was the perfect stage for the panel on the oral histories of Black and Asian people. Negotiated over the counter, this history has been a transactional one of tender and tense intimacies. The merchant is always the stranger, it is said. Across continents and oceans, our ancestors formed gray economies that evolved after transatlantic slavery. Shops, marketplaces, and dancehalls became spaces of sociality for Black and Asian people who, in the Caribbean, made something out of ruins.

Black and Asian people across the region saved and invested in their own community microfinance structures. While they did not always invest in one another across racial lines, they provided one another with loans, on rotating systems of trust within communities.[12] The colonial denial of mortgages did not stop invention, joy, or pleasure from flourishing. Aware that they have long underwritten European colonial markets as human collateral, they devised their own financial instruments. My African and Asian ancestors never requested the permission to exist from the British government. I approach the aftermath of these post-abolition Afro-Asian transactions to make sense of the racial formations and political economy of the Caribbean plantation.

I heard in the scholar's question an understandable longing for acceptance by the Chinese, common among those of African and Chinese descent. But who are *the Chinese*? Why is it that seeking acceptance from the Black community is less common? One can be the descendant of a continent, but not of that race or experience. While race is not a biological fact, it is real because it shapes our historical realities. What does it mean to be of a different race than people from whom you are descended? This is a common question for Black people in an era marked by racial slavery and its aftermath. Why is the onus left on us?

Family Photographs as Portals

A sepia-tinted passport photograph of my grandfather, dated 1934, opened a door. A permission slip, the photo compelled me to begin writing about my family. How do you tell a story that you are uncertain is yours to tell? Silence communicates for generations of the dispossessed, torn by the psychic injuries of war and occupation. Anne-Marie Lee-Loy has recorded the oral histories of countless Afro-Chinese children who made transpacific journeys from Jamaica to Hong Kong.[13] There are harrowing stories of perseverance. Through them I extrapolate what my grandfather could not tell me about his Pacific passages. Who were the Black people that navigated the Pacific? These routes form an abject and unwritten circuitry of the Black Pacific.

In archival images of Hong Kong, I have wondered where to locate Black people such as my grandfather. In back issues of *National Geographic* of Hong Kong, I find similar images, technicolor glimpses of Kowloon's vibrant

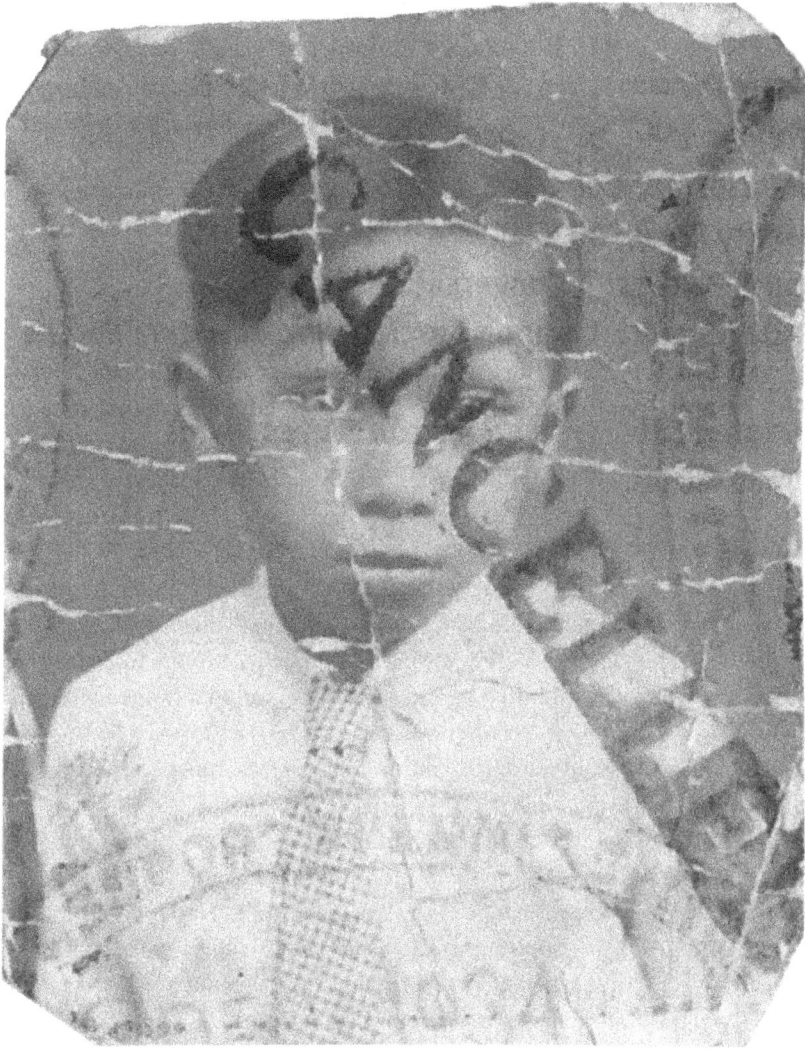

FIGURE 6.1. Passport photo of the author's grandfather, Kingston, Jamaica, 1934. Courtesy of the author.

night markets. I flip through the pages documenting US colonial desire with excitement—this is a photographic portal—but also apprehension. Persons of color never know whether they will encounter the face of an ancestor in these pages. The US colonial appetite was as voracious as Britain's. In *Hawaiian Islands, Edge of China, Manila*, a book written by an American tourist, Burton Holmes, in 1901, I found photographs of the Hong Kong my great-grandfathers inhabited. They departed in the early twentieth century for business opportunities in Jamaica. "The Chinese, of course, object to being photographed, and for that reason try to dodge the camera not knowing that the motion-picture camera is a photographic Gatling, certain to hit its victim no matter how fast he may be able to run."[14] This sentence made me think of the missing photographs of this era. The gun/camera analogy reveals an American tourist's violent desire for capture. "How does one revisit the scene of subjection without replicating the grammar or violence?" asks Saidiya Hartman.[15] She crafts elegant research-driven methodologies and strategies, such as critical fabulation, to write about the past. Who gave Hartman permission?

Permission is granted in an inheritance that is an arc, the shape of the Caribbean archipelago. A chain of islands and landmasses hugging a basin of water. Four islands tell my story. Britain, Jamaica, Hong Kong, New York. The accretion of debris and biomatter in these four archipelagoes are layers of colonialism and ongoing struggles for sovereignty. Hong Kong continues to protest its layered occupation twenty-five years after the British left. Released from the clutches of imperial rule in 1997, maybe there are lessons for the United Kingdom from Hong Kong. Brexit has shown that, even if no man is an island, every island does not want to be part of the main. Born of different wombs, my grandfather and his siblings found a home together in Hong Kong. Raised by their father's Chinese wife, his first wife. Two brothers, Edwin and Ashley, and a sister, Sookeaw, of the same Chinese father and different Black mothers on the island of Jamaica in the 1920s.

In this story, that which was brought forth did *not* follow the womb. *Partus sequitur ventrum.* Black mothers and Chinese mothers raised each other's children across five continents: Asia, Africa, Europe, North America, and South America. Two tropical islands, Hong Kong and Jamaica. A silence, what they could not articulate. In Jamaica, Chinese paper sons wed picture brides. My great-aunt Sookeaw was a Black picture bride. Dressed in a qipao, her passport photo was her ticket across the globe. The same purple ink, the same stamp run across her image and her brother's passport photo. The bureaucracy of the state legitimizes what might be putative. Through a proxy marriage by power of attorney in absentia called *trouwen met de handschoen* in Dutch (marriage with the glove), this young girl was married off to an older man she met for the first time in Suriname.

Most would describe my grandfather and his siblings as half: half in relation to each other, and half Black and half Chinese. But I challenge this rhetoric of racial hybrids. Familial and racial mathematics do psychic damage while dividing and segregating enmeshed colonial histories. Arithmetic is applied to the body, and racial fractions are rooted in the logic of blood quantum.

FIGURE 6.2. Passport photo of the author's great-aunt, Hong Kong, ca. 1940s.
Photographer unknown. Courtesy of the author.

Half is an epistemic violence that splits in two, as if people could be chimeras. My grandfather and his siblings became a class of exceptions, permitted to travel freely between the two islands because of their dual parentage.

My grand-aunt Sookeaw was born in 1925, two years before her brother Edwin. After his birth, their father took her on a ship named Kingston to Hong Kong, where she would be raised by their stepmother. I was lucky to meet Sookeaw in Toronto in 2009. Although she was eighty-four, memories of the 1930s were still lucid. My mother had never met her aunt Sookeaw, but she discovered her phone number in her father's address book when he died. A long-lost sister, she lived just across the border with her daughter Mary and grandchildren.

We learned that Sookeaw became a picture bride after a traditional match-making process. The arranged marriage was a long-distance one. Following *trouwen met de handschoen,* she would not meet her husband until she had traveled across the world to what was then Dutch Guiana (Suriname). Marrying by proxy of attorney took place when the parties could not be in the same location. Sookeaw told us that her passport did not provide her true age. The date of birth was falsified so that she would appear old enough to travel alone from Hong Kong to South America, by train and then boat. Her arrival was an initiation into Dutch culture from the British cultural mores of Hong Kong. She arrived at the port wearing a yellow raincoat. Sookeaw stood out among the other Chinese brides. There was a thriving and growing Chinese community in Suriname of Chinatown shopkeepers. Though Sookeaw was of childbearing age, the couple waited several years to have children, when she was older. Life and business flourished. Their multiple children connect the histories of Jamaica, China, Suriname, Curaçao, Aruba, Indonesia, the United States, the Netherlands, and Canada through the strands of British and Dutch colonialism.

Through Sookeaw's remembrances—translated from Srnan Tongo by her daughter Mary—I learned about my grandfather. Sookeaw said that, as a child in Hong Kong, he was often found asleep, an open book on his chest, when he was supposed to complete his homework. Sookeaw shared a later anecdote. When Edwin visited her in Canada in the 1980s, she found it hilarious that, at a dim sum meal, he hid unfinished plates under his chair. A frugal man and trickster, he did not expect to pay for what he had not eaten at the buffet if he could get away with it. These little details, the way she remembered her brother meant everything to my mother and to me.

I asked Sookeaw about the racism, discrimination, and prejudice she faced as a child. To my surprise, she said she did not experience racism because there were so many children of African-Chinese heritage in her village. An incredible statement if true, it led me to imagine the possibility of a generation of Afro-Chinese saltwater children born out of oceanic intimacies because Hong Kong is a port city. There are similar familial histories between Cuba and China, between Mexico and China, and elsewhere.[16] Merchant fathers spent time docking between two continents with at least two families and businesses.

Sookeaw recalled bombs exploding in Hong Kong and seeking shelter from the Japanese invasion during World War II. I have followed the routes of her family to Suriname and to Amsterdam. In Holland, I met a woman introduced to me as Tante Anne. Cousins of mine from Suriname, who were visiting Amsterdam, graciously took me to see her, knowing that she was one of the last of this generation of Surinamese Chinese elders. Tante Anne told me of growing up with Sookeaw. She had been a picture bride, too, traveling from Mainland

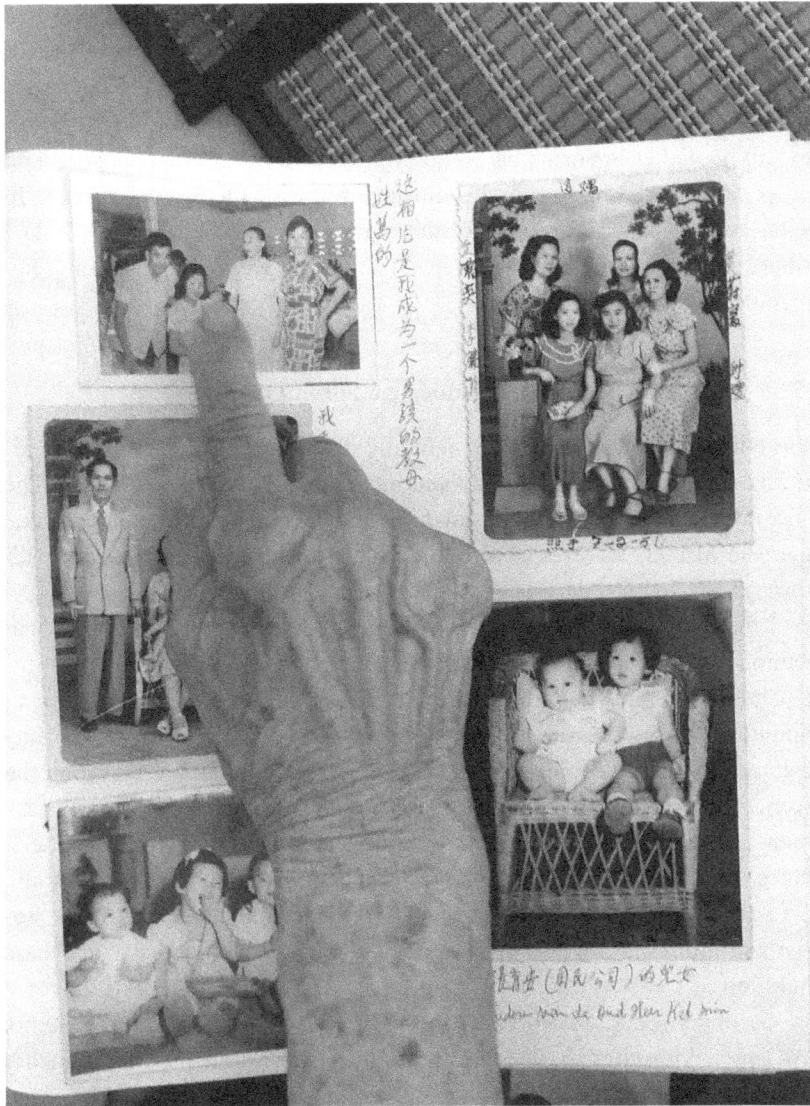

FIGURE 6.3. Tante Anne's family photo album (Amsterdam, 2019).
Courtesy of the author.

China to Tahiti to Hawai'i to San Francisco to New York to Trinidad to Suriname. While Sookeaw made her journey by train and then boat, Tante Anne's family could afford plane fare. Itineraries crisscross the globe.

Tante Anne cried for two years when she arrived in Trinidad as a teenager. From the moment she landed at Piarco Airport till her departure from the island, she could not be consoled. Her father, whom she barely knew, had arranged for her to marry a wealthy Chinese man in Port of Spain. Perhaps he was thirty years her senior, I am not sure, but eventually the groom grew tired of his marriage to a forlorn teenage bride. He booked a ticket for her to join her father in Suriname, where Anne met my great-aunt Sookeaw and other women who had made the journey from China to South America. To Sookeaw, I asked what I could not ask my grandfather. To Tante Anne, I asked what I wished I could have asked my great-aunt. I weave fragments and figments into a braid of possibility.

Being Led: Producing a Filmic Offering

The ethical terrain of writing about family, of seeking a path, requires humility. An acceptance of uncertainty and intergenerational trust is crucial. The ancestors whose names are unknown to me were *once known* to many at one point in history. My eyes closed; I allowed the unnamed to guide my path through the archival densities and scarcities.

I found a deep sense of kin with someone related to me by Afro-Asian feminist genealogies rather than blood. I learned more about rituals of intergenerational healing from Carmen LoBue, an Afro-Pilipinx American film director who identifies as queer and nonbinary, than I could have in any colonial archive. We took Hartman's question seriously about revisiting the scene of subjection without replicating the violence of the grammar. Carmen and I were both searching, and so together we considered our inheritance of African and Asian ancestry. We did so in "Ask a Chinese question, get a Black answer," an episode of Hulu's program *Initiative 29* on Black stories and futures. It is a part of my creative and research practice to ask these questions.

Carmen's roots are African American, Native American, and Filipino. We laughed together about colonial island chains and the invisible branches of family trees. Carmen and I both knew that ancestral veneration has been central to African and Asian diasporas; we wanted to explore this ritual together, making it our own. Libations are poured as an offering in many Black cultures. Carmen chose oranges as symbolic of Asian rituals of presenting food offerings to the dead. Family photographs became portals and part of the altar too. We filmed the episode over two days on a beachside property in Long Island.

The TV episode we shot includes many gestures toward historical waves of migration. Photographs of Black men of the Windrush generation in the

1940s; new migrants to the United Kingdom dressed in smart overcoats and hats are featured in the beginning. Carmen chose to include photographs of my Chinese relatives who were shopkeepers in Jamaica in the 1920s. Their film was a visual poem imbued with the ethos of tomb sweeping and ancestor worship. Inspired by work that I have done with sound, they chose to include African and Chinese prayers and chants. While the sounds on the audio track are barely audible to the uninitiated, this was an encoded auditory incantation.

There was also a deliberate though unspoken choice to omit European ancestors. When Carmen held a casting call, they asked actors of color to play my ancestors. Everyone selected was Asian or Black; some happened to be Jamaican Chinese. Others were Jamaican Thai, Afro-Guyanese, and Filipino. In her novel *Kindred*, Octavia Butler shows us that consent is an intergenerational matter of permission.[17] Her main character Dana, an African American woman, is violently pulled into the plantation past where she meets her Black and her white ancestors. While traveling through time, she even loses a limb. This is dangerous yet necessary work, Butler warns.[18] Some of us may

FIGURE 6.4. Photographic shrine from the film set of the Hulu series *Initiative 29*, episode "Ask a Chinese Question, Get a Black Answer," directed by Carmen LoBue, 2021.
Courtesy of the author.

FIGURE 6.5. Photograph from the film set of the Hulu series *Initiative 29*, episode "Ask a Chinese Question, Get a Black Answer," directed by Carmen LoBue, 2021.
Courtesy of Romil Chouhan.

be biologically connected to slave traders and holders, but we would not call those people kin. Disowning with Carmen was a political gesture; it was claiming an inheritance.

Qingming became a ritual and a filial act of the page and the screen. Carmen and I embarked on this journey without knowing where it would lead us. We began with the discontinuities in our family trees, gaps that we did not need to fill. We made composite Afro-Asian kinships with the film as a ceremony for the dead. In China, there are dilapidated ancestral halls containing thousands of years of neglected genealogical records. Incense is no longer lit. These halls have been abandoned by modern China. Two Black people who are also of Asian ancestry, Carmen and I decided to pay a diasporic tribute through art. Connecting the Philippines and China, we spoke about the ritual of games such as mancala and mahjong. Holmes's 1901 treatise lumps "the edge of China" with Manila under the colonial eye of occupation. By connecting Chinese and Filipino genealogies framed by a Black diasporic aesthetic, Carmen commanded the camera otherwise. Our camera is not the Gatling gun Holmes describes. The art of motion pictures is full of possibility—for refusing as well as reclamation.

Together, we found the permission to imagine Afro-Asian histories. Carmen honored the nonbinary ancestors of the diaspora family tree with the actors they casted. They also gave me the gift of DJ'ing a séance, a dance party on the beach for my ancestors. A young actress named Yuri, an Afro-Japanese girl, depicted me as a child. She was the charismatic maestro of the filming. Yuri orchestrated the future for us with her playful spirit, taking turns DJ'ing with me for our unnamed African and Asian ancestors. There were so many happy coincidences on set including an encounter with a former NYU student from my global Chinatowns class who happened to be working as a production assistant. She was able to see the global intimacies I had taught come to life on the set.

The ethics of writing about family are inscribed in the reciprocal clauses of the social contract of kin. Family is not scripted by blood: Rather, it is expanded by the uncertainty of what is putative. Beyond wedlock, the name of the father is traditionally given and cannot legally be taken without permission. Embracing the putative grants us permission and compels us to sit with difficult questions, such as anti-Blackness within Asian families. What does it mean to seek embrace from a biological family that rejects you? What does it mean to embrace that which defines itself by rejecting you? This abject, ambiguous space is a quicksand. Many become mired in the quest for identity.

Somehow, Carmen and I found one another in a different space, embracing the power of indeterminate origins with the permission granted by being part of the Black diaspora. Somehow, Tante Anne and I found each other in circuits of the overseas Chinese in Amsterdam, with family photographs as portals to the Dutch colonial past. We all reclaimed our kin together. We are theirs, and they are ours.

Who gave us permission?

Mine: Kinship in Deep Time along the Pennsylvania Salient

AMY MORAN-THOMAS

It's all in our family albums.
W. G. SEBALD

I am an ethnographer interested in how history lives in the present. Most of the time, I don't use history the way historians do. I relate more to W. G. Sebald's relationship to the past. He couldn't bear the archives for long; everything was an archive to him. He recalled how he would gather whatever photos or fragments he'd chanced upon in the few hours he spent in a given state archive and then flee the building with a sense of urgency and nausea and no plans to return. But he saw memories of loss and histories of violence archived everywhere: missing buildings, ordinary objects, the altered shape of tree lines, removed stones.

The book I most wanted to read by Sebald is the one he never got to finish, his own family history. He died while working on it. His famous earlier works blurred the lines between fiction and personal history. But in his last book, he reached for nonfiction. He remembered seeing pictures of his father during military leaves, happily standing in uniform with his mother and son in front of their garden. This, too, was a picture of the war, Sebald began to realize: a family on a Sunday at a remove, the presence of kin and care at the same time as an unfathomable human atrocity was happening.

I've been thinking about this lately when looking at my own family albums. In some of the photos, I'm the child; in others, myself a parent. The albums index some of the most precious and joyful moments I have lived, reminders of the family who raised me with tenderness and love. But they bear much more uneasy traces too: traces of what else was happening during the times we were alive, what else had already happened in the places we call home. The processes of planetary destruction that now promise to shape much larger futures were transformed in part in one of the places I grew up and regarded as foundational to my own ancestral origin: my father's

FIGURE 7.1. *Burning for Three Days,* Pennsylvania oil country.
Photo by William H. Rau. Library Company of Philadelphia.

hometown in western Pennsylvania. It is part of the region in which oil is
said to have been first commercially drilled, on land that was once home to
generations of Erie and Seneca Haudenosaunee people. I was an adult by the
time I learned that the earliest name for the petroleum extracted there, before
it became Standard Oil, was "Seneca Oil."

The traces behind that name—and the larger patterns for which it became
a global template—seemed to surface associations between fossil infrastructures and Indigenous land dispossessions that tap into much deeper legacies
of buried harm. When climate scientists measure the planetary disruptions
to designate dates of the Anthropocene, one of the key turning points they
report is the plummeting carbon level in the atmospheric record, linked to
the period of mass death when catastrophic epidemics and colonial violence
brought by Europeans caused the Indigenous populations of the Americas
to plunge from at least sixty-one million to around six million.[1] There are
many degrees of remove across such spans of time, but so much gravity to
acknowledge for a white American family living on that same land today. As
I tried to understand how to hold and face these responsibilities, my parents
were willing to travel with me and glimpse collective history together in its
knowns and unknowns.

My daughter is still a toddler, sleeping next to me as I write this in a room
filled with cute toy animals. My heart sinks to realize that one day soon she'll
learn that many of the animal species her toys resemble are pressed near extinction, and that these toys' synthetic bodies are made of the very petrochemicals iconic of the ways our planet and so many of its residents are being

so unevenly harmed. Still, we play with the stuffed animals; they are gifts, tokens of connection from our kin, and my daughter cuddles the soft toys to practice caring for others. Whenever I take a picture of her doing so, I know that printing it would mean giving shape to my love by reflecting her image in oil-derived petrochemicals. This materiality almost seems like a coincidence. But with closer study, it instead appears as a reality made possible by thousands of moments and repetitions. I don't know what it means, or if one day I'll be able to find a more honest way to tell her about origins and what took place on this land over time. But if there are any historians of the future, they will not understand what is happening right now if they stick to the endless pictures of melting glaciers and billowing smokestacks in the headlines. Those are the repeating images of climate disasters and not the story of how we got used to them. The policy events of technocratic negotiations that usually miss a subtler intimacy: how historical and ongoing catastrophic harms come to be lived with as ordinary, part of the social fabric available for us to know or express kinship and care. I'm starting to think that Sebald's words also apply to settler colonialism and planetary destruction. "It's all in our family albums."[2]

In the town square, daytime Christmas lights in front of us outlined a leaking derrick. "BIRTHPLACE OF THE OIL INDUSTRY," read a sign: "THE VALLEY THAT CHANGED THE WORLD." In 1859, a train conductor used coal-powered steam engines to drill the world's first oil well in Titusville, Pennsylvania, along the edges of the county where my father was later born. On the drive there that day, my dad showed me where he and his father—transformed into tall tale bedtime stories for us as "Swamp Rat Joe"—used to run their traplines. They sold these so-called swamp furs to an old man on Thurston Road who paid eighty-five cents for a muskrat if you peeled the skin off yourself. I asked my dad once if eighty-five cents was a lot of money then. "Not really," he said. What he valued was the time with his father.

Now all the muskrats, grouse, and rabbits are gone. They say the young forest is overrun with coyotes. Nearly all of them are crossed with dogs, some with extinct kinds of wolves. My uncles try to hunt them, too, but say they are so smart that it takes a whole team of men with radios to pin them down. Who has the time? Some other relatives point to the rusty pump-jacks that line the road. They might appear to be ruins, but they are not. They are just waiting for their chance. When the price of oil goes back up, the weighted levers will creak back into motion. Among the ruins is McClintock #1, with a sign calling it the longest-producing oil well in the world. It still extracts residues of petroleum every day, accumulating just enough money to fund

FIGURE 7.2. Remains of rusting oil infrastructures, western Pennsylvania, as visited with my parents. Photo by author.

the state park dedicated to oil history, the train lines we keep returning to for reasons I can't always explain. Maybe it's the place where, as a child, I felt closest to origin myths.

By 2019, the velvet seats of the Wabash Cannonball passenger car were growing mildew, so my parents and I chose the open flat car instead, holding onto the bars and watching the forest creak by. The folk songs that we grew up with told about a once-fictional train called Wabash Cannonball as the first engine to burn petroleum instead of coal. Older hobo versions of the song said that, after death, souls could ride a Wabash train straight into the afterworld. Decades later, companies seized onto the folklore as a market opening and built an actual Wabash Cannonball line that sliced through various dispossessed ancestral territories, including those of the Wabash Confederacy.[3] I never managed to find out how this particular passenger car labeled Wabash Cannonball made its way east from the now-defunct line to Pennsylvania. Song lyrics boasted the train was so fast it could arrive at its destination an hour before leaving the station, but along the Oil Creek Railroad it chugged slowly with the rest. Riding on it felt like being an uneasy passenger in settler mythology, a glimpse into how fantasies turn material. Or like a mundane form of time travel into a forest filled with questions I don't know how to ask.

My parents had brought us to ride the Oil Creek train as kids, sparking my early sense that our family origins were bound up with the origins of oil. The train station and its attached souvenir shop have changed only slightly. The classic Johnny Cash song about Pennsylvania oil still crackled over its speakers, telling the well-worn story one more time: Edwin Drake's seeming folly, attempting to drill an oil well, finally paid off one Sunday morning in 1859. People grabbed laundry tubs because they had no structures to contain the gushing oil. Today, old framed photographs of terrible ecological destruction line the walls of the train station and its makeshift museum, pictures of extraordinary disasters grown familiar in the century and a half since: tanks of chemicals consumed by roiling fires, oil-spilled rivers, forests razed for barrels, burned-out frames of houses.[4]

As kids, we each received an artifact from this place: a roughly used railroad spike painted gold, the metallic spray paint holding together its irregular shape over the rust. "Oil Creek Railroad" was handwritten in black letters over the chipped varnish. My dad had selected these three spikes from among the museum shop's bric-a-brac, shelves full of tiny souvenir bottles of petroleum from the late 1800s and boom-era sheet music for songs like "Oil on the Brain." The rusty golden spikes stayed in our rooms for years, mine near my bedside alarm clock. My brother and sister and I each curated our own artifact with a sense of responsibility. Maybe because nothing else had been passed down to us from our ancestors, no keepsakes or inheritances. Yet some of our kin once lived in the place where these relics originated, zone of the world's first oil boom. This small piece of it was ours to keep; it was the closest I felt connected to previous generations across time, a tie to something larger our ancestors had made.

Nowadays, that remnant carries other meanings for me. I suppose that whoever spray-painted our relics gold was thinking of the iconic "golden spike" that once completed cross-country railroad lines. As an adult, I think of that term as linked to violent land dispossessions from Native peoples; and I wonder and worry how ideas of ancestry through infrastructure connect me to those histories too.[5] "Golden spike" is also a term some scientists use to reference the Orbis spike, the mass-death events across the Americas during the seventeenth century when the terrible loss of life left haunting traces in the geological record of air trapped in ice cores.[6]

"Family history is colonial history," Tao Leigh Goffe writes. "How, then, to understand the vernacular photographic record and what is missing?"[7]

I used to spend a lot of time on ancestry websites, wondering in what ways my ancestors were connected to such violence stretching back in time. So far, we never found any particular record of complicity among all the marriage licenses and death certificates, or other traces that added up to an easily graspable story; just uneasy fragments of proximity. At the same time, such records are so incomplete that nothing could be ruled out. At what point do these genealogical particulars come to matter less or somehow position us all? Some white Americans today attempt to address such questions by sending their DNA to companies or uncovering stashes of papers that, in an attic box or basement trove, yield secrets and clues.[8] My own searches didn't reveal any specific implication. Instead, our complicity was more diffuse and common: Living on land that had once been taken violently from others, we now watched it being mined for carbon so harshly that before long no one will be able to live here.

As my parents and I stared out of the train's windows along Oil Creek Railroad, history seemed written everywhere around us, in the composition of each breath we drew from the carbon-warmed atmosphere, in each spike that held the tracks to the ground. Traces of something like an ancestral responsibility felt palpable everywhere, and I wanted to think that paying attention to these traces might offer clues about what those complicities meant. Park signs sponsored by petroleum companies proclaimed all nearby wildlife as "Oil Heritage" plants and animals. They brought to mind our last visit, one early January. Flowers were blooming out of season because it was so hot, and suddenly the surreal park signs seemed matter of fact: These climate change blossoms, about to die out of season, *were* Oil Heritage flowers.

I used to imagine that there was an era of coal, followed by an era of oil, and then one of gas. Even famous histories like *Carbon Democracy* tell the story of Pennsylvania fossil fuels in this way.[9] But the scenes from Oil Creek Railroad tell a much messier story, one in which oil started early and coal never ended and gas dates back to the 1800s too. None of those eras can be easily separated from each other or from the people and kin who made them possible.

When new gas well drilling cuts into the hollows of an old coal mine or a forgotten oil bore, innumerable toxic chemicals and radioactive materials can infuse local water supplies. This recently happened in Greene County, a few counties south in Pennsylvania where some of my ancestors moved for work in a mine. The companies simply said that the new wells were "communicating" with historical wells below the ground. In addition to water interactions, there are implications for air. It is estimated that Pennsylvania has more abandoned coal mines and oil and gas wells than any other state.[10] Many of the old structures were undocumented, according to the Orphaned Well and Cleanup Act, which presents drillers and their drillings as parents

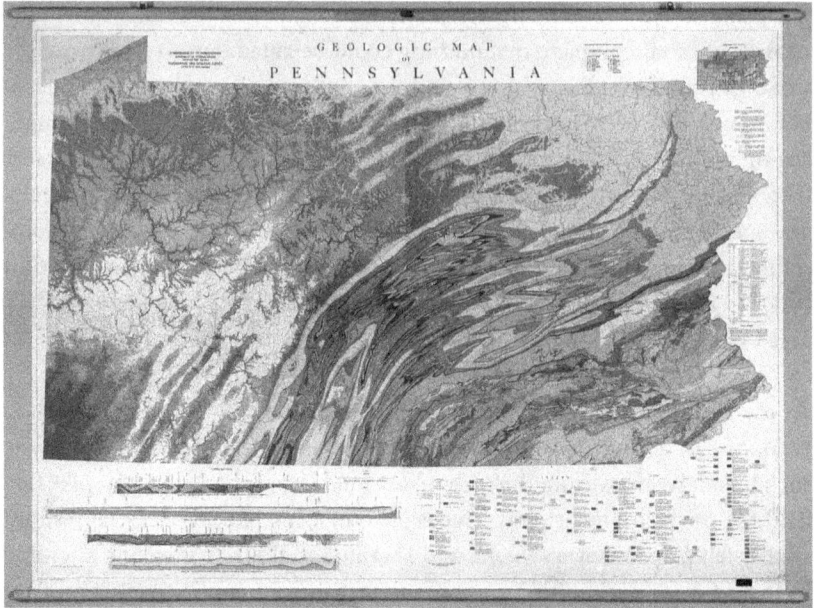

F I G U R E 7.3. Geological map of Pennsylvania, 1960.
Commonwealth of Pennsylvania.

and abandoned children. The act was intended to remediate the methane and
other toxic gasses such structures emit long after their last use. It was a con-
tinuous reminder that, whether or not anyone remembered it, the unmapped
past would continue to unleash material forces into the present.[11]

The geological contortion called Pennsylvania Salient reportedly traces to a
collision of the North American and African continental plates during the
times of Pangaea. This event intensified the climate change that killed nearly
two-thirds of species at the time; for this reason, geologists called the Appala-
chians "the mountains that froze the world."[12] Several hundred million years
later, the carbon sequestered underground by these ancient processes constitutes the region's prime commodity. Families like mine have lived for generations along this ancient collision zone, inhabiting economies that are fueled
and defined by extracting carbon deposits—coal, oil, and natural gas—even
though scientists warn that burning the traces of this earlier catastrophic extinction will be certain to trigger another.

No one in our family talked about it like that when I was a child, and
we drove our overstuffed van between the constellation of towns where our

relatives lived. On the way across Pennsylvania every summer, my father brought us into leaky coal tunnels dripping with bright orange water and told us how his grandfather had been among the itinerant Slovene miners who dug coal in a scraped-out drift mine without working for any company, just dynamite and a mule. He died of black lung. The only words of his passed down to us were *follow the seam*. His daughter, my grandmother, worked in the mills that made steel from coking coal extracted from those seams. She sometimes used to dress me up as she dressed herself, like Rosie the Riveter. She was the one who held me on my first ride along Oil Creek Railroad, I know from photos that date back longer than I can remember.

FIGURE 7.4. The author and her grandmother.
Photo by author's father.

When miners first encountered oil and gas while digging for coal, they did not know what to do. But industrialists were already making chemicals from nearby salt. It didn't take long until oil stills were devised in Pittsburgh to refine crude oil into kerosene for lamp lighting. Soon, hydrocarbons replaced the functions previously offered by whale tissues: Even before plastics supplanted bones and baleen, lamps came to be fueled by petro-kerosene instead of blubber oil. "Oil's well that ends well," read the banner spread over a black-tie party of humpback and right whales celebrating the Pennsylvania oil boom in one popular 1860s' magazine cartoon published days after the start of the US Civil War.[13] Before long, engineers were learning to rearrange molecules and make chemicals from the ethylene and benzene byproducts of coking coal, opening doors to the creation of the Standard Chemical Company. Decades before the boom in uranium milling brought Marie Curie to western Pennsylvania in 1921, Chinese investors and Russian engineers—including Dimtri Medeleev, creator of the Periodic Table of Elements—passed through the boomtowns. By that time, a floating darkroom had been established on Oil Creek so that prospectors could have their portraits rendered in photographs that also involved various experiments in fossil fuel chemistry.

When Seneca Oil became the world's first petroleum company in 1859, beckoning cartoons of Indian figures decorated the bills of sale printed by Edwin Drake's funders.[14] And long after John D. Rockefeller purchased the company and renamed it Standard Oil, petroleum companies continued to commission Seneca men to pose with Jesuit priests and reenact what they called Petroleum Sunday.[15] The US Navy gave Iroquois names like Soubarissen—the name of a Haudenosaunee chief they claimed first offered the US petroleum—to their oil tankers.

Yet from the train ride along Oil Creek Railroad, it was hard not to notice that these floating appropriations were missing from the very place they're supposedly sourced. Early chroniclers of Crawford County noted that the complex infrastructure—some two thousand surface oil collection troughs—was too old to have been built by Jesuits. "They had been used for gathering what we now call 'Seneca Oil' (petroleum). . . . Those pits were not made by the Indians. Their regularity, their number, [and] the averseness of the Indian to labor all forbid the idea that he could have been their creator."[16]

Eager to claim the technology and place but forced to reach for explanations beyond *terra nullis*, local historians attached the oil infrastructures to a popular theory about a great lost white race they called Moundbuilders. Variously said to be descended from Danish explorers, Welsh metallurgists, or

FIGURE 7.5. Petroleum Sunday reenactment, 1948.
St. Bonaventure University Archives.

wayward Vikings, these purported Moundbuilders were said to have arrived in the Americas first, building all of its impressive architecture before being murdered in a massive genocide by Native Americans. The theory gained wide traction nationwide as American mining and archaeology grew up together. By the late 1800s, Congress awarded a research grant and insisted that its new Ethnology Bureau make Moundbuilders studies a top funding priority.[17]

FIGURE 7.6. Erie Lackawanna trains under the family Christmas tree.
Photo by author's father.

In Titusville state park, the earliest oil infrastructures appeared on maps only
as "THE MYSTERY PITS." One winter years ago, my mom and I went on foot.
We had found the pits on the furthest edge of the park, past a pavilion of
picnic tables, up against the train tracks. There were patterned hollows in the
ground as far as I could see into the woods. In some pools, you could watch
traces of oil bleed up into the snow.

I first learned about coal and oil from playing with our train set under the
Christmas tree. It was not a toy, my parents always said. All the engines and
coal cars were Erie and Erie Lackawanna, the lines my grandfather had worked
for as a switchman. My dad was sixteen when he found his father dead of a
heart attack. He started a short-lived job for the railroad as a gandydancer,
maintaining the ties and tracks. In the set he inherited from his dad, we moved
the coal and oil around in loops. The tracks got nailed to plywood draped in
white sheets. We made the rivers out of nonstick tinfoil and mirrors. There
was no underground for fossil mines, but as we grew older, my mom created a
cemetery with tiny handmade clay tombstones for each of our dead.

It might be a myth that railroad tracks inspired the invention of the zipper.
But that is the story they tell in Meadville, home of the Talon Zipper factory

where coal miners's wives like my Granny Tressa sewed zippers onto military gear. Pulling something together; toward what? *Plessy v. Ferguson* began on a train, too, enshrining "separate but equal" segregation into law that would take *Brown v. Board* to overturn. In 1886, *Santa Clara County v. Southern Pacific Railroad Company* was one of the key cases that established American corporations as legal people, a landmark that would transform oil and gas along with most industries in the world.

Long before my grandfather worked for the Erie Lackawanna line, the anthropologist Lewis Henry Morgan had been involved in the railroad's court case. He was already dubbed the father of American anthropology by then, working with the young Tonawanda Seneca tribal diplomat and engineering student Ely Parker to write *League of the Iroquois*. But Morgan's models often theorized societal evolution as stages in a unilineal "progress." These ideas reinscribed the very racial typologies Morgan said he hoped to counter, and they had real-world effects. He was a vocal proponent of the reeducation model that, from Carlisle, Pennsylvania, became a template for all other Indian boarding schools, infamous for the philosophy "kill the Indian, save the man." The school's archives contain pictures of students shoveling coal into giant power generators made in Oil City, thirteen miles from Titusville, amid bins of black fossil rock.

Back at the station, I stared at the vertiginous space between the steps and train tracks as we disembarked. It had been below the tracks of another towering trestle that my parents first told us about deeper histories. Built as passage for the state's earliest coal and oil train tracks, the Kinzua Viaduct was famous for looking like it stretched into forever. Once, all of us stood at the top while my dad told us what happened to the last piece of Seneca land in Pennsylvania when he was our age: the active breaking of what was then the oldest treaty in the United States, backed by George Washington.[18] But when a corporation wanted to build an electric dam at Kinzua a century and a half later, the US Army Corp of Engineers sided with the company, one of many such cases of the time. From the top of the high bridge, we could see past treetops into the distance. It was there that, authorized by the Supreme Court, the government burned down 145 Seneca houses, four churches, several general stores, a longhouse, and the reservation schools and cornfields before flooding 10,000 acres to build Seneca Power, an energy company whose executives included no tribal members. In the museum built in Salamanca after Seneca families from Pennsylvania had been pushed to New York, there is a simulation of each destroyed residence and details of its history. Today, the lake at Kinzua is full of motor boats.

I didn't know back then that the destruction surrounding Kinzua Dam was not an isolated incident during the hydroelectric boom. Or how many other broken treaties I never heard about at all. Still, standing on the bridge stuck as a memory of the first time I heard an adult plainly state that our country had knowingly done something so wrong. Following my family down the path below the Kinzua Viaduct tracks, I remember feeling afraid. It was so much bigger than us.

The word "pipeline" was coined in 1859, the same year oil was first commercially drilled. The world's first oil pipeline was buried in western Pennsylvania in 1865, near Oil Creek. It ran the five miles from Miller's farm to Pithole, circumventing the teamsters who delivered barrels of oil by stagecoach wherever the train tracks didn't go. The oil companies armed private security forces to police the lines. This pipeline was the ancestor of all the others that followed, the template for an architecture that soon spread from western Pennsylvania across the world.[19]

On the morning we buried my grandmother in the same county where that pipeline had run, I could see into our small plot of the underground. My little sister and I stood at the edge of the place we thought we'd likely be

FIGURE 7.7. Erie train over Kinzua bridge, ca. 1888. From Oil Country of Pennsylvania. Library Company of Philadelphia.

FIGURE 7.8. Unfinished Dakota Access oil pipeline during the protests at Standing Rock, view from Sioux Falls.
Sinisa Kukic, Getty Images.

buried too. But we would confuse any archaeologists of the future. Nowadays living things incorporate so much carbon from the atmosphere into our bones and tissues that carbon decay ratio curves fall apart. Like all Americans of our generation, we contain amounts of carbon in our bodies that would make us appear to have been born decades before our great-grandparents.[20]

The night after my grandmother's funeral, the local bar was filled with fracking guys from out of town. They called their work "shale play," proudly showing off broken fingers and twisted knuckles from laying pipe below a winter stream. One man drew on a napkin the common tattoo he was planning to get across his shoulders, a skull with gas pipes instead of crossbones. It looked like the poison symbol on a bottle of chemicals, but whatever the lines carry or leak will not be labeled. After the workers move on, the pipelines left behind will run liquid to distant refineries or leave waste water to be injected into ground wells, most frequently in communities of color. "What does the skull mean?" I asked when he handed me the sketch. He just laughed because obviously the answer was danger. But I didn't know to ask *for whom*?

There are rumors that wastewater from Pennsylvania fracking is later injected into the ground as far away as Louisiana. But not everything can be displaced. "Look at how it's part of the homestead!" my mom kept repeating every time

FIGURE 7.9. Early pipeline being buried in the ground near the Pennsylvania-Ohio border, ca. 1860s. Pennsylvania Historical and Museum Commission. Courtesy of Marathon Oil.

we passed a capped well in my dad's hometown. She stopped for me to take more pictures. It's funny to see them as visual images now because the sensory experience of taking them was all smell, less like chemicals and more like trying to breathe in another atmosphere. Still dizzy hours afterward, I kept wondering if it was what the Ordovician smelled like. That is the layer being shattered for vapors during the fracking of the Utica shale, a mile deeper than Marcellus, from the era following the great Cambrian extinction. The world then was dominated by volcanoes, and life could not survive on land. The oceans were filled with mollusks and cephalopods.[21]

When fossil fuel use exploded during the Industrial Revolution, explaining the otherworldly atmospheric haze became a whole genre of storytelling.[22] In some fireside stories, a genie would come out of the coal's smoke to narrate, but in other stories the burning rocks just started talking. A piece of coal would tell the children sitting around a fire: *x million years ago, I was . . .* and narrate where it came from, conjuring scenes of tropical swamps with towering ferns and ancient forests of pillar-like blackened trees frozen in carbon. Some say that these stories told by coal were the origin of ideas about time travel and the "dying world" tales they shaped.[23]

But in the western Pennsylvania forests we traveled to each August, everything felt alive. My great-uncle George used to clear out his wagon every summer and have us pile in for a tractor ride past the cornfields and cows and electric fence, out past the elderberry patch, the place our families brought their kids and told them to listen. Once the earth there was exhausted of arrowheads uncovered when the first pipelines were dug, farmers like him planted homemade tomahawks and cattle skulls for us to find as evidence for their horror stories. As the oldest, I was the first to wonder why the artifacts contained duct tape.

Kids with ears pressed to the ground, we didn't know we were listening to the hiss of oil or gas rasping through an old pipeline. He told us that it was the restless spirits of dead Indians, that the chiefs who had been murdered there were watching everything we did. The adults would ask us: "Can you hear them breathing?"

My dad used to take us swimming at the beach on Lake Erie. Back then, I was not aware that it was a Superfund site. He said that whenever they used to drive up there for fun in the 1960s, everyone knew to expect twenty or thirty feet of dead fish choking the coastline, bobbing layers along the shore as far as the eye could see. I remember giggling at the terror of this mental image as a child. At the time, I used to think that what frightened me were the ominous fish. Now it is the depths of collective denial that must already be in effect for families like mine to cheerfully, knowingly travel hours to such a portending landscape with plans for a picnic.

And now here we are, and I don't know what to do either. In the summer of 2021, I stood on a mountain that used to hold thick seams of coal, looking out

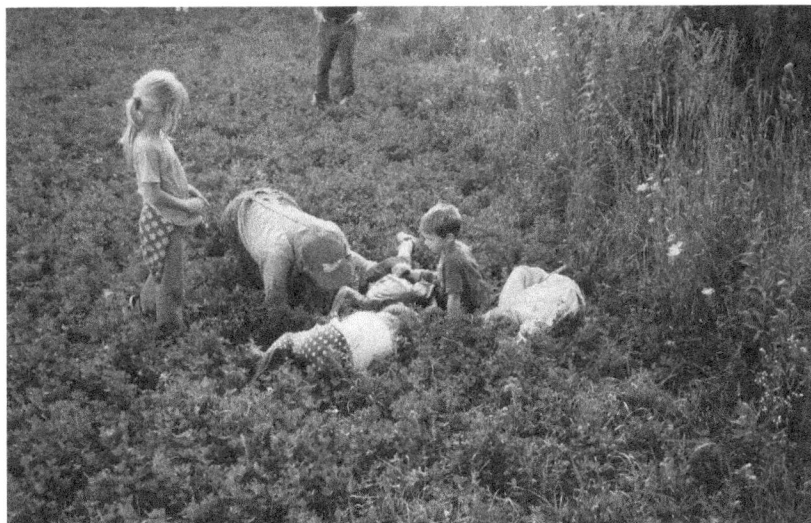

FIGURE 7.10. Children listening to the ground, western Pennsylvania. Photo by author's father.

FIGURE 7.11. "Indian Steps" at Coal Hill, Pittsburgh.
Pittsburgh City Photographer Collection, 1901–2002, Archives & Special Collections, University of
Pittsburgh Library System.

at the city below and wondering what it will mean for you to be born into this. This place already looks different to me since I first saw you, even though you were smaller than a blueberry then. We had thought you were no longer alive, and I was bracing myself to hear the technician say it. But then I saw your heart beating on the fuzzy pixels of a blue screen. She said that according to what they knew about that stage of pregnancy, you were forming around 100 brain cells each minute. I left the clinic that day with a surprised smile under my mask and an inscrutable picture in my hand, along with instructions to take vitamins and supplements. Later, I read that the calcium in such pills is usually sourced from sedimentary rock strata around oil and gas mining. The pulverized rock layers in each tablet were likely accreted from extinct coral reefs or evaporated rain, back when the Pennsylvania mountain ranges we traveled that summer formed under an ocean. It was one of the many ways I realized that, if we could manage to bring you safely into the world, you would not be new even then.

Unearthed skeletons from ancient epochs contributed to the rise of kinship studies in the 1800s. In Dream Cave and other places of incidental excavation, British miners found the fossils of ancient woolly mammoths and other giant creatures while extracting rock and lead. The invention of kinship was bound up with such findings, scholars later argued. "First had come the expansion of earth time, of geology, then that of life time, of the extinct forms of living species documented in the fossil record. Human time was the third and last to expand out of the short chronology of the creation narrative of the Bible, and the explosion of human time was the precipitating cause of the formation of anthropology. . . . At the center of that new configuration was kinship."[24]

While most studies of family ties followed old European conventions and drew genealogical trees, Lewis Henry Morgan produced diagrams that resemble electrical circuits. At the time, anthropologists wanted to imagine "culture" outside historical time, and treated a society's systems for naming kin relations as a language fossil for the study of cultural evolution. These ways of drawing family had corollaries in property laws of the underground.

Studying Morgan's archive, I had hoped to unpack old stories about what historians call his "invention of kinship." Instead, I found a surprise among his papers: He had written about fossil fuels and *their* kin as well. In his 1841 "Essay on Geology," Morgan disagreed with some contemporaries about the origins of oil.[25] Contemporary debates—was oil organic or volcanic?—were in part a fight about whether supplies were finite or endless. These disagreements had started even before commercial drilling began to escalate. . By that time, scientists had already reported that burning coal was causing worrying carbon release into the atmosphere. Nearly 150 years after those public debates started, I watched processions of coal trains that could include 175 cars, stretching more than two miles long—meaning that just one train can carry thousands of tons of coal toward the plants to be burned.

Up close to the coal generators, there is something you feel deep in your bones. From a distance, it's impossible to sense their true scale. But driving up to the towers in Pennsylvania's Conemaugh Valley that January, alongside the slow coal trains, I realized this generator has been here since before we were born; and despite the ongoing climate battles, smoke may well continue to rise here long after we are gone. From the generator's base, I could no longer fully see the toxic steam because we were too close and it was just so high. Behind the wire fences, even in the middle of the day, there was no one in sight, only endless machines: conveyor belts and rock piles, train cars converging from all directions, motion day and night. The massive gray concrete smoke stack was larger than the biggest building I'd ever seen. Imagine if the great pyramid of Giza suddenly became smoothly rounded and grew about three times higher into the sky; or if two city blocks melted upward into a single concrete tube with no windows, tall as the Empire State Building, higher than four Statues of Liberty. The coal tower rising before us in Homer, Pennsylvania, was the tallest chimney in the United States and the third largest chimney in the world.

People don't often think of energy infrastructures like these as part of our society's monumental architecture. Most debates about contested monuments focus on statues of men. But they are entwined materials and stories. For half a century, this place has sent electricity to millions of homes across hundreds of miles, lighting up grids all the way between here and New York City—a fact discussed daily by most people in western Pennsylvania and hardly anyone in Manhattan. Being up close to the imposing generators that power so many grids made me think of the moment in a science fiction movie when the characters finally see how a society obtains its energy, and this reveals something about the deepest heart of that civilization. These are the places to which all the other tracks crisscrossing the country eventually connect.

The night after our latest ride on Oil Creek Railroad, we slept in a motel whose rooms were repurposed train cars, stopped long ago in their tracks. After saying goodnight to my parents, after leaving them at their Erie car door, I walked to my car and collapsed on the cheap floral bedspread in a daze, overwhelmed by the weight of history. It had been a long day. I paged through old geology maps that charted the ground below us, the only books I'd brought on the trip. The more I studied the names given to layers marked for extraction, the harder it became to imagine Seneca Oil as an idiosyncratic coincidence of local history. The geology charts of nearby counties were also full of racial slurs. "Most of the oil in this field comes from the Big Inj*n sand" below the Pittsburgh coal seam, read one 1907 report.[26] "Practically all the gas produced in this township comes from the Big Inj*n sand." The geologists added: "An unproductive sand, usually less than 50 feet thick, is infrequently reported at distances . . . below the base of the Big Inj*n. Wherever found it is known as the Sq**w sand."[27]

Names like those go back further than oil. Where my mom's family mined, the coal seam was called Kittening, named for a legendary Lenape and Shawnee village in the area that had been destroyed with particular violence. Growing up, I had never met a Lenape or Shawnee person to my knowledge. Yet much of the coal burned around us to electrify offices and homes was named for their village and its inhabitants, who were once burned alive. The soldiers who carried out the massacre, whose victims included women and children as young as two years old, received the first medals of honor forged in what would later become the United States. Centuries later, the energy plant built nearby to make electricity from the carbon from Kittening seam was named for General John Armstrong, who led the attack. How is it that every day Armstrong continues to burn Kittening?

I had bad dreams that night and woke up before dawn to the smell of burning. Probably just the nearby plastic factories, I realized. Plastics derived from petrochemistry have a long history in this state, too. One prominent factory was built on an old petroleum venture purchased by Standard Oil. An early harbinger of what later became a rising petro-plastic empire, by the 1940s it specialized in plastic tubing. The place was recently destroyed in a fire. I lay on the cheap mattress on the train car, trying to ignore the smell and go back to sleep.

I thought of those smells recently when I saw a museum exhibit about fracking. The depictions looked like a familiar living room but with a pipeline running through it, a rocking chair, a cabinet of poisonous fracking chemicals on the wall, the sound of hissing in the air—audio recordings from Pennsylvania pipelines, I learned later. The scene conveyed bodily tensions between intimacies of domestic care and industrial harm, a play of absences and presences, as the artist intended.[28] But toxic infrastructures reaching into a homestead marked by love also recalled an uneasy feeling older than fracking: the tension between knowing and not knowing the grounds of an American family history, the way attempts to assemble its pieces constantly span a realization of the need to acknowledge, and a deep human fear of learning something poisonous.

In shale maps, the fractured strata looked like the latest in centuries of cracked Rorschachs, acted out on the region's ground, all transgressions and regressions. "It makes you schizophrenic," John McPhee's interviewees always said about trying to move between human and geological time.[29] My family's small coal parcel was taken over by the county a few years ago, decades after anyone stopped digging. When my great-aunt unearthed the old mine map for us, it made our trip feel like a quest. But I squirmed when the GPS led us toward one of the most notorious names in Pennsylvania's "Black Valley." Seen from another angle, the highway we drove along had been built over crumbling coke ovens—paved today with asphalt, which means petroleum residue and bituminous tar. The road east leads to Three Mile Island. But we headed west, past confederate flags and trailers with alpacas in the yard. I knew we were getting close when the road joins up again with the old train tracks. *Follow the seam.*

We located it within minutes of climbing out of the car, tracking the creek's bright orange acids until the water ran clear. That was how we found a seam of coal, cut out of the bank long ago, chiseled as far as you could take the face without collapsing everything above. The creek's water flows out to the Monongahela River that everybody just calls "the Mon," the remaining syllable of a Lenape word for erosion.

My dad repeated the same stories I've been hearing for more than thirty years about the seasons they lived in tents and how everyone imagines coal miners standing, but his grandfather dug crawling with an axe held sideways,

FIGURE 7.12. Glass heart found near the family coal mine, 2017.
Photo by author.

and everything except his eyes was covered in rock grime when he returned from inside the mountain. "He let the Black man who worked for him build a shack somewhere over there," my dad said suddenly. I was taken aback. "I thought it was just dynamite and a mule," I said. In the countless times I've heard about this place, the man had never been mentioned.

Two cathode television sets had been dumped between the creek and the mine, screens pressed in the dirt. Later, I had a nightmare that we plugged them into the motel's coal-powered electric sockets and watched the scenes they've been absorbing from the ground.

My mom and I stood staring at the place where the water mixed against an ancient seam and tumbled its toxicity forward. I thought of Claude Lévi-Strauss's comment in *Tristes Tropiques*—inspired, he said, by Marx, Freud, and geology—that most human meaning is structured by buried forms sunken somewhere deep out of sight.[30] I could tell that my mom did not want our trip to end like this. She searched around the debris for something to cheer me up, uncovering in one pile of dead leaves a casserole dish shaped like a transparent heart.

We walked for a while past old beer cans and used needles, loosely circling the mountain. I began to doubt that either of us actually wanted to see what was further inside.

The Genre of Inheritance:
Dancing with Grandma

CLARE HEMMINGS

I. Dancing with Grandma

My mum always told grandma's story to me and my older brother Julian in exactly the same way. She would start by reminding us what a fabulous dancer Grandma had been. All the men in the small South Wales village she grew up in were in love with her because of her flashing midnight blue eyes and impossibly long legs, mum insisted. She could stay up all night, a different partner for each dance till dawn, and still wake up fresh the next day. Flo was a wild one, a real beauty, who didn't give two hoots what people said about her. . . . She met grandpa—Reg the policeman from the neighbouring village—when she was arrested along with the other girls trying to snatch some fun at the social club. Drinking was illegal in Wales on Sundays, mum told us, and so grandma must have been caught with a tipple. Grandpa bailed grandma out, vouched for her otherwise good character to the court, and they were married within the month. They moved from South Wales to the South of England, and the rest is history, mum would say with satisfaction.[1]

So begins my unpublished short story "Grandma Was a Dancer," which follows the many incarnations of my maternal grandma Flo through the stories other people tell about her. It is a story of generation, class, and gender, a way of telling multiple and sometimes competing stories that resist straightforward memoir, let alone History writ large. My mum tells the story of grandma's grand romance to my brother and me, both of us rapt in the breakfast room of our 1930s' stucco house on the outskirts of Brighton (that queer haven only ninety minutes' drive from London). It is the 1970s, and in keeping with this supposed era of sexual freedom, my brother and I long for the story's glamour while being delighted with its familiar, reassuring contours and nostalgia. My story continues:

I loved this tale of grandma and grandpa, and I begged mum to repeat it on a regular basis. I appreciated what I now know was the perfect narrative arc, as we moved from restrictive Welsh hills to the sophisticated South of England. Grandma's arrest and release recast my frail grandpa as leading man, and old photos on the mantelshelf at grandma and grandpa's house confirmed the centrality of her beauty to the story's momentum. The story made sense too: grandma certainly caught the eye and held it. There was still something of the leading lady in the way she styled her bright-white hair so carefully every morning, applied discreet make-up and never wore the same clothes two days straight (despite having only three full sets of daytime clothes that could be mixed and matched for any occasion). And in the cupboard on the upstairs landing, there was a row of dresses robed in tissue that she never wore. She had made all of them herself, she said proudly, except this one, gently pulling out an exquisite light coral coloured silk dress, cut on the bias, with an ornate darker coral beaded fringe. That one was a gift, she added with a wink.

It is a story of Grandma that allows her to be simultaneously young and old, and casts her as the heroine in a historical romance that moves across space as well as time. Grandma is so glamorous and so adventurous, and though she must have told this story a hundred times, the pride in my mum's voice is undimmed. She loves telling this story of geographical and romantic transition; it helps all of us make sense of how we got to where we are now, the familial within and as the historical. While mum tells the story, I wait for the denouement, holding my mum's hand hard as we follow Flo's unfolding fortunes. Grandma moves from Wales to England, from laboring class to respectable class, from single to married life, from her home to ours. My mum's tale of Grandma captures my youthful imagination; it allows me to enter a realm of fantasy outside of my own experience, safely within the space of the familiar made temporarily strange.

When my brother and I stayed with grandma and grandpa, I took every opportunity to sneak into the landing cupboard and sit on the floor in the middle of the row of grandma's dresses, touching one with careful fingers, rubbing a cheek against the fabric of another. Long or short, beaded or plain, heavy or gossamer light, the dresses felt and smelled of a different time and place, and I wanted to be there. I made up stories about the occasions grandma would have worn them, imagining myself her beau. Do be careful of the step, Flo, I'd say, helping her out of a Hackney Carriage. Or I'd remove my silk-lined cape with a flourish, floating it over a puddle so that grandma wouldn't have to get her feet wet, and even more importantly to protect the pearl satin slippers she was wearing to go with that coral dress. This time grandma was a princess, and my prince's chivalry would always ensure she was home safe and sound well before midnight. I was tender and solicitous, like grandpa must have been; and she was light-footed, beautiful and appreciative in return. We didn't need anyone else, but reflected

*each other's attention back to one another in a timeless loop as I whirled her
around and around and around.*

My attachment here to my mum's story, the affects it generates, allow me to
develop a desiring scene of my own that crosses generations and gendered
roles. They allow me to imagine a different relationship both to grandma herself and to the idea of gendered and sexual inheritance than the heteronormative orderings that usually mark such tales.[2] Mum's telling of grandma's story
gives me the chance to inhabit a romance narrative crafted from the detail of
movement, sequins, and light, and to try out different ways of bringing the
past into the present, calling on grandma to recognize her queer granddaughter as a potential suitor. This is a tactic that resonates with the recent scholarship on queer temporality, too: work that starts from queer desire's capacity
to disrupt linear, familial time and suggest alternative narrations.[3] Listening
to my mum's tall tale in the 1970s and now in the 2020s, I still want both to
participate in these reassuring narrative arcs of gender and sexuality, and to
imagine other ways of telling and experiencing those same stories. History
can't keep me from playing all the different parts.

I am not the only child listening to my mum's stories of her mother.
My brother is there, too, and we work together to embellish the stories my
mum gives us. I recreate this rare intimacy between my brother and me in
"Grandma . . ." as follows:

*Over time my brother and I grew bored with mum's tale, frowning at the some-
what strained narrative that saw grandma arrested with that drink in her hand,
and grandpa so innocently falling for her that very night. We allowed that she
would indeed have been the belle of the ball, waiting for the right tall handsome stranger to rescue her. Grandma was a fabulous dancer with those eyes
and those legs. But we reset grandma's story at the shadowy edges of this historic
Welsh scene: less airy public houses with enthusiastic young women wanting a
bit of fun; more filthy dark corners of working men's clubs and the opportunity
to make a bit of extra cash. Or we moved grandma to a set of private rooms in
the nearest town, owned by wealthy Londoners: heavy red velvet curtains and
shabby ornate corner lamps casting salacious shadows. These gentlemen, with
their expensive cravats and smiles, paid well for a personal dance performance
but they easily turned nasty. On a good night, our grandma would make enough
to give a week's rent to her mum, handing over what was left after paying off the
bartender or the security out front, and keeping just enough back for a couple
of feet of silk. Julian and I unrolled our story out over the top of mum's version,
rolling our eyes at each other when she started on again with what a fabulous
dancer Grandma had been.*

My brother and I forge our counternarrative together at my mum's expense, returning Grandma's knowing wink or, perhaps more violently, putting "dancer" in heavily ironic inverted commas without her consent. We craft our own stories from the raw material of our mum's, just as I did when wooing grandma. We work with the restlessness of the original tale, pulling brutally on its frayed edges. While my own childhood storytelling imagined me grandma's beau, my brother and I tell a perhaps equally queer tale of generational poverty and sexual labor. We fashion our grandma into a call girl rather than a chorus girl, a "dancer" whose navigation of the English predates her move to the south of England. We try this out on one another and on neighborhood friends, playing the turn for laughs even though we don't fully know what we are describing. Yet, grandma and grandpa always end up together no matter the narrative routes they take. I am beginning to be schooled in the significance of affect as the motor that drives and temporarily resolves competing stories of the past that generate the complex presents we live within. And of course in queer disappointment as well as hope, in the relentlessness of the heteronormative script, despite the other stories of LGBT rights and recognition that surround me in 1980s' Brighton.

"Grandma Was a Dancer" is part of a larger project in which I work with my immediate family's "memory archive" to tell different stories about gender, class, and national belonging than those we are typically presented with.[4] In earlier work on storytelling and feminist theory, I sought to map—and then interrupt—the dominant narratives of progress, loss, and return that restrict the possibilities for innovation and political transformation.[5] Through tactics of "recitation," I meddled with the citation traces so central to these narrative forms. By inserting different, equally plausible antecedents, and thus by unearthing minor threads, I tried to playfully reimagine the past and future of feminist theory. I continued that effort to tell different stories—or tell stories differently—in a project on Emma Goldman's significance for queer feminist theory and politics.[6] The ways in which her legacy has been reclaimed to provide a specific past, present, and future for feminist queer writers tend to domesticate or even abandon the unruly (and often more interesting) complexity of her thinking. I longed instead to hear resonances of her raw sexual and gendered courage and to imagine her archive as a queer feminist one filled with contradiction and disappointment as well as pleasure. As part of that project, then, I wrote the love letters we do not have from Goldman to her lover Almeda Sperry: Goldman must have written them, but they are nowhere to be found. This speculative intervention into the archive has steered me toward my current project of tracking a memory archive, bringing together storytelling and family archives to explore the fissures and contradictions that make up the complex and contradictory plots that are my complex inheritance. In line with the aims of this volume, I am interested in recovering the half-hidden truths and unknowable secrets that emerge in the *ways* family stories are told, even if not in the stories themselves. And I experiment with telling tall tales as part of recasting the past as newly resonant with those truths and secrets.

It is the intersubjective nature of history—and the ways that stories shared within families make the relational character of inheritance plain—that attracts me to this archival work. Hearing, as we all do, competing stories about our own lives and those of our families, we learn ways of navigating the differences among them. We learn early on to make sense of past and present and then develop the skills necessary to imagine a future that differs from the present we inhabit. A memory archive thus foregrounds the subjective and desiring nature of *adjudication*—which story one settles with or embellishes—at the heart of how history is experienced and embodied. Marianne Hirsch's work on generational transmission is instructive here: She invites us to embrace family memoir and storytelling as deeply affective forms of connection and disconnection that have the capacity to make rather than only respond to history.[7] I take up her invitation, albeit in the very different context of my white class-transitional family, to draw out the unsettled nature of the past and hence open up possible though as yet unrecorded futures both within and beyond the family.

The embellishment of the tales I am told is thus central to my memory archive not just because of the limits of the formal archive, although that is a key issue, as Saidiya Hartman so richly demonstrates.[8] What she terms "critical fabulation" is an essential part of her desire to engage pre- and postslavery Black life as more than its brutal representation.[9] My interventions take a very different track: It is the sexual and gendered feelings and plots through which the white, class-transitional aspirations of my family are expressed that are the central focus for this project. I fictionalize to draw out of the memory archive the underbelly of progress narratives of class and whiteness in the United Kingdom, foregrounding forms of displacement and violence that stories of aspiration tend to obscure. And I fictionalize, as I did with Goldman's letters, to explore the possibilities for emphasizing multiple histories as a serious feature of inheritance. I fictionalize because this is how families navigate their relationships to one another, within and across generations. I fictionalize, in other words, because I always have, we always do; it feels impossible to gather the stories that form the fabric of the present otherwise.

I repeat "fictionalize" here to distinguish this speculative work from the actual writing of fiction. I am working with the imaginative threads that I believe are necessary to provide a fuller picture of the ways all of us navigate the family tales and histories we inherit. I am not writing either fiction or history outside of this investment in challenging dominant narratives of sexuality, gender, and class that an engagement with my memory archive enables. I have come to think of this method as generating what I call "empirical fictions": I make things up as a way of characterizing how the past enters the present in narrative form, and how we spin yarns of our own to find ways of living with the past.

II. Searching for Reg

Growing up, my maternal grandma and grandpa were a consistent presence in family life. My parents would drive my brother and me up to their Croydon bungalow in their red Ford Fiesta at least once a year to drop us off while they went on a two-week holiday to France, and we always saw them at Christmas and Easter. We saw my paternal grandparents much less frequently, and when we did I could never quite shake the sense that we were a noisy interruption into the quiet life they had made for themselves in Kent. Despite that, when starting this family archival project, I had to confront the fact that the most visible evidence in the archive was related to my paternal grandparents' history. My dad's father, Bill, had saved birth and death certificates, job references and war memorabilia, photographs and receipts in a small leather suitcase. My mum's family fortunes were less carefully preserved: residing in the repeated stories my mum told, in the tales that gestured and buried as well as revealed. So, too, in the extensive census data, parish and court archives, probate or military archives, the evidence base privileges my dad's family. They stayed in one place. They were more established in their class transition. They did everything properly. The archive, then, pushes me firmly toward telling the history of my paternal legacy, precisely because of that respectability that brooked no rowdy interruption, while my body memories are of my maternal family and the stories my mother told us about them.

So I started this project already suspicious of the archive: not only for its absences, but also for its *transparent detail* that does little to help me grapple with or understand the embodied attachments, smells, and tastes of family that are a primary mode as well as outcomes of affective inheritance. That suspicion of archival presence works in another way too. While the stories my mother and her grandmother told were vibrant ones of economic migration, war survival, and bitter sadness as well as increased respectability, these stories are also gendered. Grandma ruled her household roost, my brother and I soon realized in our visits, while grandpa was a more distant, less loquacious presence, always at the edges of the scene. The tales told about my grandma Flo are myriad, too, while those told about my grandpa Reg are scant. In thinking with stories of grandma I was presented with an excess of possibility, much of it contradictory: I resolved the differences within and across competing tales by letting the stories swell. Applying the same method to grandpa would have meant Reg barely got a story at all.

I tried to characterize that half-formed sense of grandpa as I wrote "Grandma Was a Dancer" by edging as close as I could to the images of him that were passed on, but it was difficult:

> Grandpa's story always lurked behind Flo's; he played the supporting role in mum's original tale, and in my brother's and my re-writes. Grandma was always the heroine, even if we weren't sure of which sub-plots. Grandpa was more an ill-drawn figure helping to propel the narrative than a fully fleshed out character in his own right. My own young desire to be grandpa was always confined to his role as protector, aggressor, or rescuer. When I played him, he wore my face; when I played grandma, she kept her own face, and I became her.

My grandpa was not forthcoming about himself, and what we heard about him rarely moved beyond minutiae. And anyway, my brother and I liked the stories about Flo more because she was the one who captured and held the light. He was a policeman. He had an argument with his brother that he took to the grave. He liked making macaroni and cheese. He spent a lot of time in the basement with his tools. Fragments barely numerous enough to make a story arc. Yet despite the appeal of staying with grandma's rich narration, I came to want Reg there too. While "not knowing much about Reg" has its feminist pleasures, especially with such a glamorous protagonist at our stories' heart, that unevenness also reinforces gender's heteronormativity: Wives tell stories, as we know, while their husbands put up with them. I wanted to flesh out the bare bones of these stories about my maternal grandparents and make Reg responsible for his own script for once, forcing him out of his role as Flo's sidelined and put-upon foil in the misogynist histories we more usually inherit. I wanted to know what Reg was doing in that basement, and what he was thinking when he boiled the pasta and rummaged around for the cheese grater. I needed more character development for Reg if he was to be more than a straw figure whose place I imagined I could take in wooing Flo.

So as Flo and Reg's romance narrative wore thin, I pieced together a gritty story for grandpa drawn from 1970s' and 1980s' social realist dramas rather than the historical romances of my youth. These fictionizations draw on labor history and the brutal treatment of the Welsh working classes by English landowners, as well as the small details that resonate from within the stories I inherit.

> *Reg was a policeman, a good job for a man from a poor South Wales family whose inter-war alternative was the brutality of coal or metal mining. His dad had lost a leg in 1913, the result of an ultimately lucky mine accident since it likely saved him from death in the trenches. . . . Reg's dad was a hero among the local men, as he'd organised effectively to keep Sunday prohibition intact, knowing the English envoys who spoke so easily of the right to pleasures for the working man were talking out of the wrong side of their mouths. Union busting and strike breaking were more like it, he insisted, recoiling instinctively and politically from oily Tory speechifying. Reg's dad knew of course that coal mining would kill them all in the end, and before his accident he had dreamed of moving the family north to the Dolgellau gold belt, hoping Reg would pick up the mantel. But Reg had always been such a bloody disappointment.*
>
> *Reg was happy above rather than underground; his lanky frame was better suited to it, too, and he relished the cold, damp air he could walk into warmth. The steel in his boots rang out his rhythm as he walked around and between neighbouring villages. He liked being a policeman: it gave him the unearned authority he was otherwise refused. Reg's job was mostly to break up brawls between men who drank their pay checks the weekend they got them. Usually his uniform was enough of a deterrent, but if it wasn't he happily joined the fray. He thought of these fights as a valve for letting off steam, and rarely arrested anyone. It was the same story Reg told the women who asked him for help after a domestic. Give him time, love; he loves you really, pet. Don't make him feel small, he said (because he already does, he added silently). Reg took the pay-outs from the public house or club owners to turn a blind eye to Sunday booze, and came down hard when the cash flow was interrupted. One of the policemen would order a whiskey, drink it down in one, and then make the signal for the others to descend with a show of force. A few punches, some broken chairs and the pouring out of liquor into the drain was usually enough to ensure the right attitude next time they came round.*

Social realism as a genre allows me to give a context for Reg, situate him in a family of his own as well as temperance and union history in industrial and rural Wales; it allows me to give a sense of the harsh environment of that Welsh earth above and below. This fictionalization resonates with tales my mum told me about Reg's right-wing politics and conservative commitments that departed from his father's but were far from unusual in the white suburbs of postwar London. Indeed, one of the abiding themes of my memory archive is the importance of right-wing, class- and land-dominant politics for our white, Welsh, class-transitional family to belong. So, too, there is a sense here of the Reg who is most himself in his enjoyment of a solitary task: here, walking the Welsh hills in all weathers; later, patrolling the streets of London.

When I am in my late teens, my mum tells me and my brother a story that centers Reg's need for solitude: his retreat to the basement of their childhood home, the basement that she alone was allowed to penetrate. I recreate that story in "Grandma . . ." to allow Reg the intimate attachments that memory tends to strip from him:

> "Tell us about the war, daddy" mum told us she used to beg him, and by all accounts Grandpa always answered the same way: it's not something you should concern yourself with, pet. Mum was his favourite and she used to sit on the stool by his workbench in the basement, as close to him as he let her be while he cleaned his carpentry tools. She liked the smell of the oil, and watching his fingers move easily to complete this familiar task; she liked the stillness that rustled between them. One evening when they sat together, her hand in his, she asked again: What did you do in the war, daddy? She waited for the nothing you need to know about, Annie, and a ruffle of his hand on her head; but instead he looked at her as if from far away and said quietly, I pulled out the bodies. I pulled out what was left. And then unaccountably, he blushed. . . . When mum told us this story, I could see my tall thin grandpa, a spare shadow picking his way through stone: on his own, slow and deliberate, head bowed. Every now and then he'd turn his head to one side like a crow, listening for the noises or silences, keeping away from the lights.

Characteristically, my retelling of mum's story of her dad is about the dangers of speech. Mum always framed his reticence as a way of protecting his family (and his favorite, Annie) from the grim horror of war. The blood rushing to his face is as much in shame at breaching his long silence as it is a bodily reaction to remembered horror, helplessness, or survivor guilt. Either way, of course, it's the blush of a hero, of a family man doing what he had to during the Blitz and long afterward.

The secrets shared in the basement also resonate with my social realist setting through the threads and threats of violence: the harshness of Reg's father, his own enjoyment of the policeman's authority, and the cautioning of women not to make a fuss. These threads are entangled with questions of national duty: the sanctioned violence and regulation of the state's representative, Reg's confrontation with the devastation of bombing raids on London, the wartime conversion from policeman to undertaker. These stories of violence are hard to tell. They slip in Gothic horror so easily because they are whispered and, or because, they are bound up with questions of respectability that have to be safeguarded for the family's own good. I have heard and overheard all my life stories of violence that never quite interrupt the main narratives of family. They remain undocumented either because they mirror (or are) the law or were buried by other more sanctioned narratives of classed progress or loss. And they are gendered stories, too, of course, because of the different ways in which women and men are expected to hold together nation and family. "Grandma . . ." continues:

> War and loss were stitched into Flo's story too. Her three older brothers were killed in the Great War, including the dashing but profligate Uncle Charles. He had run away to London when he was just 15, lived hand to mouth until he got lucky; then blown it all on a motor car that Flo's dad described as bloody ridiculous. Charles would drive up to them at the weekend sometimes, back seat filled with presents, all store-wrapped and tied off with string. Toot toot and a booming laugh, that's how I'd know he'd arrived, Flo would declare, delighted all over again! Charlie was always all smiles and Flo beamed ear to ear too as she remembered how he'd be fussed into the kitchen, usually horribly drab but now lit up by his presence. Charlie would bounce her on his knee until she was nearly sick and Flo's mum had to whisk her off with a disapproving tut. Charlie was all hands as well as smiles: 'sausage fingers' his mum called him when he smacked her arse and tickled the kids even though they didn't like it. Flo only had a vague memory of Charles' dad chasing him out of the house with a shovel one weekend when he'd spent a bit too long tucking her up in bed; she overheard her mum following behind them crying, shouting that he'd better not think about coming back any time soon or she'd put his dirty fingers in the mincer. The army will be the making of him, Flo's dad had said, and that was the end of the conversation. Everything was forgotten when the policeman came to their door. The memory of Charles all smiles was restored: there he was, lying dead in a ditch, rictus grin at the end of a bayonet.

I remember my grandma talking about her uncle Charles in such saccharine tones that even my earliest memory of her pleasure was suffused with discomfort at its overblown repetition. Charlie the charismatic one who drew everyone in, Charlie the generous, wild, seductive one—like Flo, larger than life. Charles the one whose wartime death was framed as rehabilitation, that swift page turned through the family album accompanied by pursed lips and a sigh every time. How to write into my archive of sexual and gendered inheritance a sense of its burial rituals, the memory loss protecting more than its dead? How to write a history of two world wars and their devastation in the United Kingdom that highlights gendered labor and the consistent presence of obscured, routine violence? How to think a history of gender and class that foregrounds the importance of respectability and ties grandpa's blush with Charlie's bonhomie? We need the blush and the bravado to continue to fantasize a Britishness favoring the brave; it helps us paper over the cracks that threaten to reveal more foundational horrors at the heart of nationalism.

Women do the telling, and their folding in of heroism with the secrets that it consigns to dust with a sigh of relief offers no surprises from a feminist perspective. A whole area of scholarship devotes itself to the gendered and heteronormative as well as racialized scripts of militarism and nationalism. It tracks the effort required of women to preserve the "home front." In the case of Charlie, though, this is a "home front" from which men's violence can and must be excised precisely because he does not return. Yet, of course, while longing for their return, many women benefited financially from widow's pensions and may have breathed secret (or shared) sighs of relief at the space that men's absence opened up. How might we tell stories of the gendered ambivalence about men's return from the war or its cleanup operations? How might we represent our inheritance of women's relief as well as sadness when men failed to return. I have grandma preparing in her imagination:

> *Flo had the meters of black silk for her funeral dress ready. . . . She would cut it plainly but to flatter her, a top-layer of tulle adding texture without too much cost. And of course a hat, plain too but with a thicker net veil, that she would lightly bead in the early hours of her sorrow. But though he went out night after night during the Blitz, Reg came home night after night too, and by the end of the war she had added his survival to the long list of reasons she resented him.*

Reg continued to disappoint Flo in this strand of my family story. While the war she lived through was marked by "men's failure to return," Reg kept turning the key in the suburban domestic lock. I write their relationship in wartime as marked by Flo's resentment, and perhaps it is me who, more than Flo, likes imagining her guilty pleasure at grandpa's demise. My fictionalizing seeks to foreground the disappointment that feels like the shared bottom line of this period of their family life, a disappointment that is overwrought as well as unrepresentable in dominant histories. But I also want to protect my grandma from the critical gaze that saw Reg as hen pecked and depicted her as an insatiable nag in ways that threatened to break through that prized respectability. This is another reason why violence bubbles through my social realist depiction and why Reg's blush can't quite protect his favored daughter. Because violence also took more palpable and present forms in the Croydon family home my mum grew up in, and it's the only violence that forms a direct part of her storytelling:

> *Affable grandpa beat his son Glyn thoroughly and carefully for most of his youth. He would take his belt off when he got home and chase him around the house till he had him cornered. If it took a long time to catch him, it was the buckle end.*

*The twins and grandma told him not to run, but he always did. The one respite
was when the children were evacuated to second cousins in Wales during the
Blitz. There were of course plenty of explanations for grandpa's violence if you
looked for them. Anyone could see that he lived a life where he felt humiliated at
every turn: no one at work to recognise his talents; no one at home to big him up
so he wouldn't have to do it himself. Maybe he looked at Glyn and couldn't bear
to witness the lost promise of boyhood; or perhaps he felt he needed to train him
to expect to be obliterated in the world (may as well start now). We could give
Reg a wounded heart, a youth where he had got used to the same banal brutality,
give him the unconscious daddy complex he's been denied. Certainly, that was
the way mum told the story, searching for an explanation that absolved grandpa,
that let him still be hers. . . . But the truth that both Reg and Glyn knew, even
if the others didn't, was that grandpa beat his son because he could. Because he
liked it; he was good at it; it was his due.*

We have to imagine the scene because its banality is beyond official documentation. None of the explanations I include in my retelling of my mum's
story stretch the truth: They're all plausible and echo the histories of pride
and sorrow etched into masculinity, its successes and failures across aspirant
generations. There are many ways to retell violence, to limn its place and its
status as an open secret within families. Reg is both diminished and dimin-
ishing; Flo is both vengeful and compliant. Violence and fantasies of violence
suffuse my familial stories, but the ways in which I receive these tales are also
shot through with my own queer feminist desires. I narrate Flo's telling of her
uncle Charlie's tale to highlight the sexual violence that lies at its heart, and at
the heart of a gendered nation and its ways of memorializing. I try to flesh out
Reg's embodied uncertainty in his relationship to his favored daughter. But I
am brought up short by tales about Reg's violence toward his son, a violence
I simply don't want to give a history, don't want to allow to slip into *justification* or fanciful fictionalization. I receive these stories as the girl who wants
to have and to be grandma, the girl who wants to be and to console grandpa,
the woman (perhaps the girl, too) who refuses to mystify violence as part of
a historical narrative and wants instead to revisit the multiple scenes of its
repetition. I want to be left with its brutal truth.

III. The Genre of Inheritance

Giving Reg a story fleshes out his bare bones with what I hope can be read as
empathy, while still holding him to account for familial violence. The story I
give Reg suggests a context he otherwise lacks, a social history of economic
migration and insecure nationalist participation. I recounted grandma's

ambivalence with elements of the Gothic, a touch of the melodramatic, and told of my desire for grandma as a historical romance. I play with genre because that feels true to the ways I was told these familial stories, and thus true to the memory archive I am charting. My mum's tale of her parents meeting and moving to England is told from deep within the satisfactions of the romance. I tell the story of wooing grandma through fairy tales I otherwise find alienating. Readers of a similar age and location to me might also recognize the oblique allusion to the children's story of an ice queen offering (orientalized) Turkish delights in the world behind the back of the cupboard when I describe sitting among grandma's dresses. Toward the end of "Grandma Was a Dancer," I introduce a dash of holiday farce to humanize Flo and Reg, to give them a relationship bound by their children's choices in turn:

> Flo and Reg would arrive [in Brighton] the day after mum and dad had left, just in case the Newhaven to Dieppe ferry was cancelled. They'd get the bus from the station and walk up the steep hill to the house, laughing like naughty children as they fumbled with the keys, saying shhh shhh to each other for no reason. They quickly established a routine. If the weather was fine they'd get the bus to the beach for the day, making a picnic from the things mum had left for them in the larder. Or they'd read in my dad's study and then have tea on the back patio, with a slice of vanilla sponge. This is the life! It doesn't get better than this! Reg would say every time, and Flo found she didn't mind. They brought their own sheets to put on the double bed, and made sure that they left the house exactly as it had been when they arrived (that was a challenge for Flo, who would have loved to scrub that kitchen with bleach and clear out the cupboards). Do you really think dad didn't know, I asked mum? If he did, he never said anything.

Nancy K. Miller has written persuasively of memoir as genre, and this has helped to legitimate memoir as a form of literary or historical evidence that should not be dismissed or minimized.[10] But this rehabilitation of an otherwise feminized form has come at the expense of exploring what it means to write history through memory and fiction in a range of *different genres*. Initially, I experimented with form to find a fictionalizing voice (something that continues to both elude and please me). But as my empirical fictions have grown increasingly central to a complex memory archive, the question of genre has emerged as a central mechanism for developing fuller, more accurate family histories. Telling the story of Flo's move from Wales to England as a romance narrative—rather than, say, a horror story—produces a distinctive history that folds in the heteronormative with ease. The story of Flo and Reg staying at the family home in Brighton without leaving any traces generates humor as well as the cringe and anxiety that so often comes with the sitcom. No one is innocent within its world. But that genre also allows a certain rapprochement between Reg and Flo, a getting along as rubbing along, one excised by melodrama, realism, or horror.

Such stories have been told before. When Flo and Reg move to the south of England, we can anticipate the realism of repetition or disappointment in one genre, yet long for a happy ever after in another. And despite Flo being such a wonderful dancer, with those long legs, there is *no version* of my memory archive that comes into being as a musical. Perhaps I will need to get over my antipathy to that genre and write Flo! Genre allows me to convey tone and affect in the juxtaposition of the stories that make up my archive. Genres are not equal; some are more unreliable than others. The romance narratives of a teenager are likely to fade, as are the love stories of the young married couple hoping for fortunes to open up as they head for the disaffections or banalities of middle age. Genres have a tone that insists, that tells us how we are supposed to read the story (as comedy or tragedy): They give us advance warning of how the story will end and how we are supposed to feel about it. Genre thus generates expectations that can be satisfied or thwarted. Genre proffers an open narrative secret—how the tale will turn out—that allows the reader to share in the knowledge of where the tale is going.[11] The war story and the realist drama are expected to linger, describing history and the present in more verifiable ways, while melodrama is by definition overwrought, suffused with untrustworthy femininity, open to being discredited.

"Grandma Was a Dancer" thus not only dramatizes different ways of telling family stories, it also asks what kind of reader receives them. Their answer to that question marks their own understanding of histories of gender, class, and sexuality. Readers also have genre preferences: In other words, a good war story or a travelogue may keep one person turning the page; another might be unmoved by melodrama, while secretly enjoying a bodice ripper. Yet another reader might be disturbed by my use of the romance genre to introduce my queer desire for grandma, or, on the contrary, may wish that it occupied a more central place in the story. A reader might be enraged at my tinkering with a heroic war story or relieved that otherwise hidden violence seeps through all the genres. Those "reading protocols," to use Samuel Delany's phrase, including the affects that guide the reading of a disappointing farce or an inauthentic travelogue, are interpretations in their own right of Reg and Flo's stories.[12]

Genre also informs my queer feminist position on the stories I am passing on. If drawing on particular genres allows me to rely on convention, it has also allowed me to try and scupper expectations while highlighting the intersubjective nature of genre as an uneasy agreement between author and reader. It has allowed me to stage interruption through juxtaposition (forcing the reader to pick a favorite story, perhaps), or by combining features of more than one genre. Combining a war story with melodrama unearths the former's half buried knowledges and challenges its heroic arcs. The Gothic or horror genre, with its hidden truths a reader anticipates, opens up space for bringing buried sexual and gendered violence to the fore without interrupting the plot. Adding a touch of the uncanny—Charlie's too brittle laugh and our readerly knowledge that *something is amiss* that will most certainly come to light—can force a reconsideration of plot and thus also received history. And even as a child, I wanted to interrupt the romance tale of Flo and Reg that my mum told, to mark myself as a desiring subject and reject the heteronormative gendering that can so easily remain unquestioned in accounts of sexual progress over the last century. My desire for grandma highlights the queerness of the past as well as the queerness of the present, even if I have to time-travel through the wardrobe to rescue her.

If, following Mikhail Bakhtin, genre transformations are always representations and interventions into social meaning, my memory archive explores multiple pasts and presents.[13] To play with genres is thus to refuse singular histories, singular affects, and singular modes of reading. Working across genres, I can inherit a past that refuses to move on from the misery of marriage, the stoicism of survival, the enduring capriciousness of male violence and its cover-ups. But that is also a past in which the pleasures of walking or dancing are folded into their plot's uneven rhythms. I can give Flo a story of her own that doesn't stop at the genres through which she is remembered or imagined. Indeed, I like to think that my fictionalizing can allow Flo to make use of genre in her own right. At the end of the story, Flo takes a boat to New Zealand on her own, some ten years before going with Reg, to visit their daughter Sheila. Her travelogue refuses the previous genre attempts to pin her feelings down, as I finally allow her to demonstrate knowledge of other people's stories and a creative relationship to her own past:

> The Suez Canal was open, and she took all the port trips along the way (Casablanca had been her favourite film and now she got to go there herself). Flo kept to herself for the most part, devouring novels, wandering along the decks in all weathers, cooped up in her cabin only when there was no other choice. There was an after dinner dance on Saturday night, and Flo always got dressed up. She let herself be twirled from first to last dance, remembering the pleasure of moving her long legs, but was surprised to find she missed grandpa's easy rhythm.
>
> At dinner, Flo liked to play a game and become someone she was not. No point in trying to spin a yarn about being a doctor or a writer, for which she had no reference points. But she knew enough about being a teacher (because Ann and Sheila were both teachers), and about wartime ambulance driving (as

she'd heard other women talking about it), to be able to tell a convincing tale about who she wasn't. She was careful to cover her boasts about rescues of the injured, or the reformation of difficult children with the right amount of self-deprecation—such accomplishments were always team efforts, she reassured her listener. She found she liked telling these stories, that other people's lives felt closer to hers in the telling; in pretending to be an exhausted teacher, she finally empathised with her daughters' choices. In her newfound role as wartime rescuer, Flo pulled out bodies from the rubble along with Reg, felt both his and her necessary dissociation in her body as an unsentimental bond.

Flo had always been persuasive at being someone else, and these not so tall tales were no exception: at points she really did have the feeling of having been a teacher or a driver. These weren't uncertain memories, dangerous fantasies, or outright lies; they were part of the making of possibility that took the past and made it something new and vibrant in the present tense of storytelling; honoring the work she had always done to create space for the accomplishments of others, whether they appreciated it or not (she remarked to herself wryly). Her sincere falsehoods—her reward for all those years of making do and mending—opened up a space and time in which she got to be whoever she wanted, for as long as she liked.

Beyond Taboo, Worship, and Irony:
Tracing the War in My Family History

MARNIX BEYEN

History can prove dangerous—even in a liberal democracy such as Belgium. That's what I was thinking in the spring of 2012, in the Antwerp police office, as I reported a threatening letter from a man I did not know. Its author was outraged about an op-ed I had written on the annual pilgrimages to the IJzer Tower, one of the most iconic places of Flemish nationalism. It was erected in 1930 to commemorate the Flemish soldiers who had fallen during the First World War. Pilgrimages to their graves had been organized since 1920. From the start, two different, partly contradicting ideologies coalesced in the messages that were conveyed during pilgrimages that, during the 1950s and 1960s, gathered more than 50,000 people. One of these messages was pacifist ("Never Again War"); the other, sprung from a conservative and catholic strand of Flemish nationalism, took on virulently anti-parliamentary, anti-Belgian, and xenophobic forms. During the Second World War, the pilgrimages became showcase moments of the massive collaboration of Flemish nationalism with the Nazi occupier. My op-ed objected to the organizing committee's decision to change the pilgrimage date to November 11, Armistice Day. This, I argued, obscured the pilgrimages' history of right-wing radicalism and collaboration during the Second World War.[1] This was reason enough for the letter-writer, who presented himself as a relative of a Flemish veteran of the First World War, to call me an extreme left-wing activist, a KGB agent even. He invited me to visit his grandfather's grave on November 11, 2018. There, he promised to "knock on my extreme-left face until it bled."

This writer also called me a "falsifier of history," a "denier," and—in red ink—"stemming from a Nazi nest." This formula unsettled me. Whereas the other allegations were patently false, the last one contained some truth. I have always known that my paternal grandfather, August Beyen, had been imprisoned for acts of collaboration with the Nazi occupier. Strangely, I had never connected this part of my family history to my involvement in Belgian history. Yes, investigating right-wing tendencies in Flemish nationalism has formed the heart of my research, but I attributed this to fascination with the complexities of Belgian history and politics, or sheer coincidence. In many ways, I had tried to escape the history of the Second World War by moving to other periods, regions, and fields.

In this respect, I saw myself as different from those colleagues who, as many of us saw it, were addressing the collaborationist politics of their ancestors through their scholarly work. This seemed obvious to me: Their ancestors had been prominent SS figures or had grown up in typically "black families" (as they were called), steeped in nostalgia for a war period during which Flemish nationalists had—with the help of the Nazis—taken over power from the Belgian state at several levels.[2] Seeking distance from their familial past, these historians either wrote demystifying histories of Flemish nationalism or highlighted the positive role of the Belgian resistance. They broke from the hagiographic historiography that had been dominant within Flemish nationalist circles.

None of this was true in my family. I was only four when my grandfather died (in 1975), so my acquaintance with him rested entirely on the stories I heard from my father, who was five when Nazi Germany occupied Belgium. In these stories, my grandfather appeared as a prototypical figure of the hardworking, popular hero of the coastal city of Nieuwpoort. Born in 1912, he was a fisherman—the last in a multigenerational line—who spent most of his time at sea, but he also loved bicycle races and playing cards. My father depicted him as good-hearted yet emotional and impulsive. Even if he cherished a populist form of Flemish nationalism—depicting the "artificial" Belgian state that betrayed the Flemish people—he was anything but an ideologue or a militant. My father said that, in spite of his pro-German stance, my grandfather entertained positive relations with individual resistants during the war. I assumed that he had not been a radical collaborator.

After the war, moreover, my family looked askance at right-wing Flemish nationalism and the legacy of collaborationism. My parents' worldview was progressive and universalist—they accepted Belgium as a state without embracing Belgian nationalism—and they bequeathed this mindset to their four children. All of this to say: I had nothing from which to make a break.

Being accused of "stemming from a Nazi nest" made me question these certainties. Had I underestimated my grandfather's implication in collaborationism? Could he have been a true Nazi? Was our family story steeped in silencing, or even lies? Was my trajectory as a historian a subconscious attempt to deny my own background? Perhaps this had been obvious to everyone but me.

At the very least, it was strange that I did not know what exactly my grandfather had done during the war. Having read dozens of postwar prosecution (or epuration) files of collaborators in the course of research projects, I knew how to investigate the whereabouts of individuals during the war. And yet. What did this reveal about my position in a complex historiographical field: memories of the Second World War in Belgium? I certainly grasped the specific mixture of taboo and idealization that tended to reign within "black families" in Flanders. Outside the home, the family history of collaboration was most often silenced for fear of social exclusion by neighbors, colleagues, and friends. Within the families or during gatherings of like-minded people—such as the pilgrimages to the IJzer Tower—former collaborators were, on the contrary, worshipped as idealists who had risked (or even given) their lives for Flanders before suffering disproportionate punishment by a merciless postwar state. This Flemish nationalist culture of idealization found powerful allies among Christian Democrats, who dominated political and cultural life in Flanders until the end of the twentieth century.[3] They had been close to Flemish nationalism before the war, and their condoning of acts of collaboration increased during the "Royal Question" (between 1945 and 1951, mainly Francophone left-wing parties prevented King Leopold III from returning to power due to his wartime behavior). The justification of collaboration by Flemish cultural and political elites (along with the downplaying of Francophone collaboration in the southern part of the country) remains one of the forces of division between Belgian Francophones and Flemings. It deepens the divide between "right-wing Flanders" and "left-wing Wallonia" that has taken form since the end of the nineteenth century.

To some degree, this combination of taboo and worship characterizes August Beyen's postwar life. Upon returning home in February 1946 after seventeen months of captivity, he never explained what he had done. My father did not even know that his father had been sentenced. Nostalgia for "Flanders's finest hour" (as the collaboration was sometimes called) had no purchase in his house—his wife would never have allowed it. Though he maintained a lifelong grudge against the Belgian state and politics in general, August did not turn this resentment into political activism. According to my father, he simply grew more religious and silent. At certain moments, though, he did participate in the culture of idealization. More precisely, he venerated Irma Laplasse, a resident of an adjacent village who was imprisoned in the same jail as him during the first months of his internment. She was executed in

May 1945 for betraying a group of resistance fighters to the retreating German troops. Flemish nationalists turned this allegedly guiltless woman into a symbol of Belgian injustice.[4]

In spite of his deep love for his father, my father's way of dealing with the history of the Second World War and its aftermath has been different. As a small child, I heard him talk abundantly about the conflict. He accompanied his mother to prison, where guards allowed his father to leave for some hours to see his kin. After such visits, my grandmother would explain to my father that he had to remain close to her because she didn't want his father to make her pregnant again. She would be suspected of adultery.

I also remember my father watching with rapt attention a seminal 1982 documentary series about collaboration. I remember how much my father appreciated that, as an eleven-year-old boy, I watched it with him. At that moment, I could not grasp the series' provocative nature. Through years of research by a team of historians and inquisitive interviews by the Flemish journalist Maurice De Wilde, it exposed how the Flemish nationalist collaboration had fundamentally been driven by fascist tendencies and sheer power aspirations. Only much later did I understand the anxiety my father must have felt. The series' harsh judgment on Flemish collaboration cast a shadow on his father's behavior.[5] Years later, we watched with similar intensity the televised adaptation of the most famous Flemish war novel, Hugo Claus's *Het verdriet van België* (*The Sorrow of Belgium*, 1983). In his typically lavish and often hyperbolic language, this iconic author—one of the country's leading left-wing, anti-nationalist intellectuals—dealt with the demons of his own collaborationist past as well as, indirectly, what he viewed as the true "sorrow of Belgium": its undigested war.[6] My father kept repeating that the autobiographical story of the main character, Louis Seynaeve, was partly his story: a young boy living near the Flemish coast, torn between an Anglophile mother and a Germanophile father. He emphasized one important difference, however: Unlike Hugo Claus, he had refused to join a collaborationist youth movement during the war.

Also, my father never worshipped Flemish nationalist collaboration after the war. He often returned to a symbolic event: When his father asked him to read the manuscript version of Irma Laplasse's diary—which she had written in prison—he refused. Though he was only twelve, he presented this gesture as an early act of resistance against idealization. His later life distanced him even more from his father's ideals.[7] Instead of becoming a fisherman, my father studied French language and literature, the language and literature of those whom Flemish nationalists saw as their hereditary enemy. He did so at the Catholic University of Leuven, which at that time was still half

Francophone. During the 1960s, Flemish students successfully "Dutchified" it, but my father did not engage in this struggle. Instead of screaming *"Walen buiten!"* (Out with Walloons!), he embraced the struggle for sexual liberation. After the scission of the university in 1968, he became a professor at the Flemish university in Leuven, but remained in close contact with some of his Francophone colleagues, who had moved to the new, Francophone university in Louvain-la-Neuve. In other words, he did everything a staunch Flemish nationalist would not do.

In 1994, my father became the first Flemish member of the Académie royale de langue et littérature françaises de Belgique, an institution created in 1920 by a socialist minister who embraced Walloon regionalism. This election rewarded his research on Michel de Ghelderode, a Francophone playwright of Flemish descent—and hence a prototypical "traitor" for Flemish nationalists (a so-called *fransquillon*).[8] Like many Francophone Flemish authors, De Ghelderode combined a deep love for an idealized Flanders with a strong suspicion of those who wanted to make Flanders unilingually Dutch. The singer Jacques Brel, whom my father admired, likewise sang the praise of his flat country (*"mon plat pays/mijn vlakke land"*) while deriding *Flamingants* as "Nazis during the wars, Catholics between the wars."

My father discovered during his research that De Ghelderode had been sued for wartime talks he had given about his love of Flanders, talks given on *Radio Bruxelles*, the Francophone radio station of leading collaborators. This is why, after the war, he fervently distanced himself from *Flamingants*. My father's family history was thus entwined in complex ways with his literary research. But this was neither idealization nor a cult of a martyr. If my father idealized his father, it was only for a generosity that bordered on naivety. He told me stories about unpaid loans his father made to relatives, which prevented him from leading a comfortable life. As a child, I came to believe that this naivete, rather than political conviction, led my grandfather to collaborate with the Nazis. It also led him, so I assumed, to render certain services to the Resistance. Looking back, it is easy to detect a pattern of justification in my version of the past.

Discovering the Humanity of History

Is this why I refrained from investigating my grandfather's wartime history? Did I fear shattering this relatively positive image? Perhaps, although I believe that something else was at play: irony. I belong to a generation and a social group—white middle-class men born in the 1970s—for whom irony was the primary mode of being. From a self-assured position in life, we believed we could consider most things from a complacent distance. Though I did not lack political awareness, I took for granted the values for which our parents had struggled: secularism, anti-racism, anti-colonialism, cosmopolitanism, sexual and other freedoms. These values were so obvious that they required no activism. This ironic posture was reinforced by the historiographical current that prevailed as I entered academia. Some of the leading theorists in the 1990s advocated an uncommitted way of practicing history, without any justification besides sheer fascination before aspects of the past.[9] This fascination could be triggered by historical sensations—moments of direct contact with the past— but historians were also expected to radically liberate the past from the present and the future. Understanding the present or creating a better future could not constitute the driving force of historiography. As a consequence, historians should feel neither empathy with nor abhorrence toward choices made by historical actors. If these actors warranted investigation, it was neither because historians felt a personal connection with them nor because these actors cast a shadow over the present. Studying the past in its strangeness, for its own sake, had intrinsic value. Family history was hence too close for the young historian who sought strangeness. It was entangled with memory, whereas postmodern historians maintained a strict separation between memory and history.

In the course of my doctoral research, I began to understand the limitations of this postmodern paradigm for the study of the Second World War—a war whose imprint on Belgian society was still considerable at the end of the twentieth century. It still weighed—and weighs—heavily on the relations between the left and the right, and also between Flanders and Francophone Belgium. I tried to resolve that paradox by adopting a cultural rather than political approach to the conflict. Instead of reducing historical actors to their position vis-à-vis the occupier, I paid attention to the continuities and discontinuities of their artistic, literary, and intellectual endeavors. One of my inspirations was the prominent Dutch historian Hans Blom, who, in his inaugural lecture at Leyden University, urged us to study the Second World War "beyond right and wrong." Blom became my co-supervisor once I broadened the scope of my project from Flanders to Belgium and the Netherlands.[10] This transnational, comparative framework would enable me to escape ongoing Belgian political discussions of the war.

In the early 2000s, having completed my doctoral studies, I came to believe that this postmodern, ironic stance—for all its merits—reflected the arrogance of a privileged social group that believed in the end of history. It underestimated the weight of the past on many people, especially subaltern and dominated groups. Memories mattered. They could not simply be replaced by detached historical writing. Obviously, I was not the only one to view things this way. Moving beyond the cultural turn and even postmodernism was the order of the day. Emotions and experiences were not mere representations but phenomena that historians should try to uncover. As a Belgian historian, I was also influenced by developments in colonial historiography. If Belgian colonial atrocities—especially those committed during the personal rule of King Leopold II, between 1885 and 1908—had been largely revealed in the 1980s and 1990s, a new generation of—often nonacademic—historians started considering the transgenerational suffering of oppressed populations. In this context, family history obtained a new meaning and urgency. The traumas experienced by colonial subjects and their descendants often provided an incentive for historical research. In recent years, professional and nonprofessional historians have conducted such research about their own families. Nadia Nsayi, for example, received wide acclaim for her book on her grandfather, a white colonial who conceived a child with a Congolese woman.[11] In the Netherlands, Suze Zijlstra wrote an even more ambitious book in which she traced the history of Asian and Eurasian women in her own family back to the seventeenth century.[12] In a similar vein, a growing number of Belgian historians from migrant backgrounds are recovering their personal and family histories.[13]

Although colonial suffering and migration are foreign to my own experiences, personal loss and trauma did play an important role in my turn to family history. In June 2011, my mother died. Though she is largely absent in this essay, her passion as a history teacher had a greater impact on my decision to study history than my father's struggle with his family history. Her death made me aware that my father, too, was growing older; it made me keener to know about his father's war story. I increasingly felt a duty, as a son-historian, to formulate answers to his own questions with regard to this past. A much bigger catastrophe occurred on January 30, 2017, when our fourteen-year-old daughter Fleur died. This shook not only my certainties about the present and the future, but also my attitude toward the past. I grew aware, in ways I had not been before, of the humanity of history and memory. History was about actual people, with their vulnerabilities, their doubts, their pleasures, their grief. As a historian, I became less interested in the large patterns of human action or representation, and more so in emotions. While I had until then believed that historians should deconstruct memories, I now grew convinced that they also had to construct them. They should protect the dead against oblivion through careful empirical research and precise writing—not with the blind veneration of statue builders but as honest relayers of voices that can no longer be heard. These voices, in turn, should find their place within the choir of human society. Through this interplay, individual experiences, emotions, and broader societal or discursive patterns acquire their full meaning.

This drew me toward family history. So did the people (outside academia) who showed empathy after the death of our daughter and asked me to help them explore the war activities of ancestors who had been involved in collaborationist activities. They, too, wanted to listen to their ancestor's voices, even if these voices prove discordant today. They convinced me just a few years ago to pay closer attention to the stories I heard about my grandfather—neither to put him on a pedestal nor to debunk him, but to recover his full humanity.

Sources to engage in this quest were scarce. My family has preserved little personal correspondence or ego documents relating to my grandfather. I hence combined juridical documents with lived memories or, to use Sarah Wagner's language, *forensic* and *individual or narrative truths*.[14] In the Belgian State Archives, I consulted the record of my grandfather's trial. Confronted with these documents, my father told stories I had never heard and also endowed the ones he had previously shared with new, sometimes unsettling meanings. The people about whom he spoke acquired names in archival sources, and from their formal language, human beings emerged. All of this was possible thanks to my father's stories. I was able to reveal part of the history of August Beyen and provide at last some answers to the questions that had been haunting my father for decades, the same questions that had started to obsess me.

Tracing Inconvenient Truths

My archival research quickly made three things clear. First, in early 1942, August Beyen joined the *Vlaamsch Nationaal Verbond* (Flemish National Union), the prewar Flemish National Party that from the start of the German occupation collaborated with the Nazis and, from 1941 onwards, recruited men for the *Waffen-SS*.[15] Without minimizing ideological kinship, the VNV sought above all a form of Flemish autonomy. One-sided, apologetic though they are, postwar depictions of VNV members as misguided "Flemish idealists" did apply to some of them. Finding out that my grandfather had belonged to the VNV fitted within my horizon of expectations.

Second, I found out that August had *also* joined the *Deutsche Arbeitsgemeinschaft* (DeVlag), an organization that, in the 1930s, promoted German-Flemish academic relations and, under the occupation, became a Flemish wing of the SS.[16] For DeVlag, the triumph of the German Empire trumped guarantees of Flemish autonomy. Belonging to DeVlag leaves little space, therefore, for justification in terms of Flemish idealism. In fact, August joined at the end of 1942, that is, after the first roundups of Jews and the proclamation of compulsory work in Germany for young Belgian men and unmarried young women. It would be very difficult to rationalize his late decision to join an extreme party as somehow beyond good and evil.

The third revelation made this impossible. Beginning in June 1944, August had been a member of the DeVlag Security Corps (*Veiligheidskorps*), with permission to carry arms.[17] Founded in late 1942 to "protect" collaborators, the *Veiligheidskorps* became notorious for its brutal assaults against Jews and resistance fighters. Its leader, Robert Verbelen, remains the face of the most extreme collaboration in Belgium.

Confronted with this information, my father did not try to mitigate. He disclosed that an aunt had told him in the 1980s that, on more than one occasion, August had chased Jews in the woods around Bruges. While this story is not confirmed in his file, a police inspector concluded from the information he gained in Nieuwpoort at the end of May 1945 that August "did participate in raids, among others in Beverlo [in Limburg, the most eastern province of Flanders, where the Security Corps was very active]," and that, in the summer of 1944, he was sometimes away for two or three days. The most incriminating testimony came from a fisherman from the neighboring village of Koksijde, who asserted that August had been a "fanatic propagandist" of DeVlag. August's wife, Marie-Louise Coulier, did very little to refute this incrimination. She confirmed to investigators that her husband had often left for days, traveling to unknown destinations in the summer of 1944. She mentioned a ship being built for them in Boom (in the province of Antwerp), but did not confirm that he visited it during his absences.[18] My father, for his part, does remember accompanying his father during his visits to the shipyard—hoping that these trips, rather than roundups of Jews, accounted for his absence.

The allegation that August had participated in roundups was taken very seriously by military justice. It was the main reason why the authorities rejected many of his requests for temporary liberation. This changed only when a former *gendarme* cast doubt on the Koksijde fisherman's testimony. During an interview months earlier, this fisherman had not referred to August's alleged participation in the roundups. The *gendarme* concluded that the witness had offered a "false accusation," which was all the more credible given that he had also confessed to being an enemy of August. Partly on this basis, August was set free on February 18, 1946. Following his conviction in March 1947, it was decided that his seventeen months of internment would suffice because he "had not exercised any activity" in the Security Corps.[19] In September 1946, the military court of Bruges had already judged that the sequester on his ship could be levied because of "the minor nature of the offences with which he is charged."[20] For that same reason, August recovered most of his civil rights on December 13, 1949. Military justice determined, in other words, that no evidence supported the worst accusations against him.

This was a relief for my father. Yes, his father had been deeply implicated in Nazi organizations, but he was most likely not a Jew hunter. However, my father also revealed—unwillingly, no doubt—that his mother had shared that a police officer had promised to testify in her husband's favor if she agreed to have sex with him. Was this the officer who turned the trial in favor of August?

The files contained another revelation: August had testified against Alphonse Dumon, the secretary of the Central Organisation of the Coastal Fisheries in Nieuwpoort, who in 1943 was sentenced to death for usury by German justice but survived in prison. Dumon's imprisonment would have allowed August to become head of that organization, created by the occupying forces in 1940 to ply the fishermen's corporation to their wishes. Again, August's wife did not help his cause. She declared that her husband would have "turned in Dumon to the Germans" because the latter had "practised usury with the Germans." In his postwar testimony, Dumon depicted August as an overt Germanophile, who always looked "to strike against me at the right moment."[21] Dumon's denial that he muddled with German officers seems not to have been convincing. This is probably one of the reasons why August's actions against him were not mentioned in the final verdict.

From the military justice files, a persistent image of August surfaces: a man deeply embedded in the collaborationist milieu for both ideological and pragmatic reasons, but a follower rather than a leader. This was the reasoning he presented in his defense, and which—following her first, imprudent testimony—his wife upheld in letters she sent to the president of the military court.[22] August depicted himself as "a poorly developed fisherman" who, according to his wife, was persecuted "solely out of jealousy" and had only sought to help others.[23] The narrative he set forth is broadly speaking as follows.[24] When the German forces occupied Belgium in May 1940, he escaped with his family to France. When the French government capitulated on June 18, he tried to return home, but his ship was seized by the German army. Only in September 1940 was he able to recover the said ship, with the help of a befriended member of the VNV and another man who would become the local leader of DeVlag. In return for this favor, August joined the VNV and then DeVlag, "a merely cultural association." He insisted that, in 1943, fishermen elected him president of the Central Organisation of Coastal Fishery, a mandate he accepted "to help everyone." He became a member of the Security Corps for the same "humanitarian" (menschlievende) reasons: to help members of DeVlag in the first place, but also "to help anyone" in case of emergency. After learning as a member of the Security Corps that, in 1944, the German occupiers were about to destroy the quays of the Nieuwpoort harbor to prevent an Allied invasion, he convinced the German commander of the harbor to evacuate all the fishermen's ships before the explosions.

Hoping to strengthen his case, August referred to two members of a left-wing resistance organization (the Independence Front) who confirmed this version. They may have been the same men who, according to my father, had come to their house to listen to radio London, along with a German officer. His friends in another resistance organization (the White Brigade) would have warned him after the Normandy landings that he should join them to avoid dramatic consequences. August refused to do so—still according to my father, who had witnessed the conversation—because he was not a *kazak-draaier*, a colloquial Flemish term for a person who changes their mind out of convenience. One of these White Brigade members arrested August at the moment of Liberation, but also sheltered his family in his house. This story, too, contributed to the image of August as a man who, in spite of his obvious collaboration, was well respected by the Resistance.

Situating Family History in War Historiography

From my family's perspective, my archival research was both disturbing and comforting. But what did it mean for me as a historian? At first sight, it seemed to support the paradigm I had always defended when studying the war. The case of August Beyen confirms the limits of Manichaean categories of interpretation. As I wrote in the conclusion of my dissertation, it did not suffice to insert the then fashionable concept of "accommodation" between collaboration and resistance. Many actors, indeed, did not simply try to adapt to the new circumstances, but eagerly combined "partial support and partial rejection [of the German occupier]."[25] In retrospect, these words might have been inspired by the history of my own grandfather, more so perhaps than I could accept or even understand at the time. Had I adopted the "beyond right and wrong" paradigm because it corresponded so well to my family history?

Recent discussions of this paradigm among Dutch historians and intellectuals make this question pertinent. The historian Rudolf Dekker has criticized the "grey turn in the historiography of the Second World War" as "whitewashing" (*nivellering*).[26] By stressing complexities and halftones, historians are blurring the atrocities that collaborators had made possible, as well as the extreme suffering they had caused. Others point out that advocates of the "grey turn" are often offspring of collaborators.[27] Their strategy differed from that of earlier Flemish historians, who had debunked collaboration or put the spotlight on the resistance to break with their family history. Would my own trajectory resemble that of the Dutch "whitewashers"?

However that may be, I came to understand that the "beyond right and wrong" paradigm has justified some war crimes while obscuring the heroism of men and women who had risked and often given their lives against Nazi oppression. I began to look into resistance in my own village of Wijgmaal, twenty miles outside Brussels.[28] I did so in the same post-ironic spirit that has been drawing me to my family history. A study of street names (a typically postmodern research object) opened onto one of human experiences. In the course of this research, I talked with descendants of resistants who had been deported and never returned. One of them was a former neighbor, whose mother had died in Ravensbrück in 1945. Never before had I been so intimately connected with one of my historical actors. Thanks to this research, the municipal authorities renamed a public square in my village after this woman, Jeanne Dormaels.[29] Here, too, I felt a sense of duty to save people from oblivion and recover their memory for their families—while trying to understand the broader mechanisms behind their fates.[30] This did not mean that contributing to public monuments became my sole mode of historical practice. Historians should, in my view, urgently engage in archival work and conduct the oral histories required to recover the more than 150,000 individual stories of resistance in Belgium—not out of blind veneration, but to restore these men and women in their humanity.

Engaging with my grandfather's war history and exploring resistance in my village are part of the same thrust, anything but gray. This is not about whitewashing my grandfather's war history. If his files had confirmed that he had chased or denounced Jews, I would not have kept it under wraps. Nor do I privilege August's self-justificatory narrative over the critical ones that emerge from the archives. Though his narrative may be coherent and plausible in certain ways, by remaining a member of DeVlag and even the Security Corps during the last months of the occupation, he was complicit with the cruelties of Nazism—even if their massive character was not fully known at the time. Likewise, August had not seized the opportunities that presented themselves to resist the occupying forces. My loyalty as a grandson of a grandfather I have barely known cannot lure me into denying these facts.

But can I divorce the historian from the grandson? Following Michael Rothberg, I argue that my status as relative magnifies my position as "implicated subject," the position of any historian with regard to violent periods of the recent past.[31] Being a grandson of the main character of my story prevents me from embracing a postmodern vantage point; it leads me to participate in his humanity, to try to understand the choices he made in specific contexts.

I have come to believe that is what we historians should do, without losing our moral sense—regarding the victims, the bystanders, the accomplices, and the perpetrators of war violence. It would be wrong to conclude this essay by minimizing my grandfather's choices during the war. Freeing a member of the Security Corps from the Nazi label because of his lofty justifications is to forsake the historian's critical duty. Stressing the complexities of a life finds its place, however, within my ethical framework. Yes, my grandfather was a Nazi during a certain period of his life. No, he does not seem to have been repentant. But he was *also* a fisherman who cared for his ship, his corporation, and his harbor; he was also a father who cared for his children; he was also a member of his urban community. None of these facets should negate the others.

Jack in the Fog

CHRISTINE BARD

FOR JACQUELINE BARD (1935–2022), *my mother*

If there is anything free, anything necessary, it is related to memory. I can feel it.
ANNIE ERNAUX[1]

Every day I set less store on intellect. Every day I see more clearly that if the writer is to repossess himself of some part of his impressions, reach something personal, that is, and the only material of art, he must put it aside. What intellect restores to us under the name of the past is not the past.
MARCEL PROUST, *By Way of Sainte-Beuve*, Prologue

My father, Jack Bard, died in 2015. The grief I felt initiated a project, vague at the time, to preserve my family memory. I imagined the "free" and "necessary" writing of one book at first, and then several: a quartet. The first volume, *L'histoire traverse nos peaux douces. Jack* (*History Runs through Our Soft Skins. Jack*) (2022)[2] will be followed by *Fernande* (my paternal grandmother and her world), *Jacqueline* (my mother's side of the family), and *Retours à Maubeuge* (Returns to Maubeuge).[3] This hybrid genre breaks with the academic practices that have been familiar to me for forty years. Its stakes revolve around the balance between history and memory, analysis and emotion, expository and literary writing.[4]

Jack is not a biography. For this reason, I begin this essay by providing an overview of his life. In doing so, I fulfill my role as a historian, well versed in the practice, and also my familial role given that, at several burials, I was the one who summarized the life of the deceased, providing what the Catholic church calls "life paths," concise and nonhagiographic.[5] Jack's life story from the cradle to the grave fits on one page here, but it could have become a book. Sensing that the memorial I wanted to build with words should evoke and suggest rather than describe and explain, I chose a different approach. Instead of writing a social history of a man across the twentieth century, I would be present as a daughter and invent a style to approach the edge of the inexpressible, where his poetic legacy resides.

FIGURE 10.1. Jack Bard at the age of twenty (1957).
Courtesy of the author.

Jack Bard was born in Jeumont, a small town near the Franco-Belgian border, on February 22, 1937—nine months after the start of the left-wing Popular Front government and ten years after his parents' wedding. He was the only son of Fernande Moreels, born in 1907 in Thuin, Belgium, described as "unemployed" in administrative records (but, in reality, a worker, a milliner, and a housewife), and Georges Bard, a metalworker from Neuves-Maisons, near

Nancy, son of Gabrielle, who gave birth to Georges, her first child, at age sixteen.

The outbreak of the Second World War separated Jack from his father, who was taken prisoner in 1940. After the Liberation, Fernande and Georges split up and then divorced, in 1951. Jack was raised with his cousin Guy, son of Fernande's brother, Robert, a Belgian resistance fighter with communist sympathies who was killed by the Germans in September 1944. Jack grew up surrounded by the love of his grandparents, Belgians from Thuin who had moved to France in 1909: Fernand, a union member who made sand molds at the Baume & Marpent steel company, and Julienne, an anti-clerical housewife who, alone among her kin, converted to Protestantism. All three generations shared a small house on the Franco-Belgian border, at the edge of a wood frequented by smugglers. The large garden and surrounding countryside were an unforgettable paradise for Jack.

A good student whose mother would do anything to help him move up the social ladder, Jack became a teacher. Like others in his generation, he was conscripted and fought in Algeria between 1960 and 1962. In 1963, he met Jacqueline Monnier, a twenty-eight-year-old social worker, at a summer camp in Concarneau (Brittany). He was assistant director, and she worked as a nurse. They married the next year. For Jacqueline's family, this was an unsuitable match. Her parents were (very) Catholic and politically active storeowners; her father, René Monnier, was a populist (*poujadist*) member of parliament elected in northwestern France.[6] Madeleine Monnier, her mother, was enraged to see her daughter marry an unbaptized man, the son of a divorced couple who taught in a secular public school. Fernande, for her part, worried so much about losing her cherished son that she fell ill. The wedding, which took place in Paris, midway between northern and western France, was a nightmare, though not as tragic as *West Side Story* (1959). The lovers savored their wedding night and delighted in becoming parents nine months later. Jack had three children: Christine in 1965, Marie-Emmanuelle in 1966, Jean-René in 1971.

Jack became a primary school special education teacher and, in 1970, director of a Special Education Section in Maubeuge's new Épinette neighborhood. The family lived in housing provided by the national education system across from a supermarket parking lot. Jack was a passionate educator, creative and imaginative, whose superiors gave him the highest marks. He also wrote poetry. Two of his collections have been published: *Effilure* (Shred) followed by *Le Chant de nuit des sentinelles* (The Sentinel's Night Song) with the Éditions Saint-Germain-des-Prés in 1976, and *La part du feu* (The Fire's Share) with José Millas-Martin in 1978. He was also a devoted father, who cared deeply about his children's upbringing and schooling.

Around 1975, he stopped going on vacation with his family and children; shortly afterward, he set up an office-workshop in a house near the train station. An apartment for the family was purchased in the center of Maubeuge, facing the futurist church designed by the architect Jean Lurçat. A second apartment on the same floor housed "Mémé" (Fernande), whose later years, spent in financial and emotional security, close to her family, were the happiest of her life. It took Jack ten years to overcome his mother's death in 1994.

Sunday leisure time was taken up with antiquing, walks in the woods, and collecting plants for Jack's herbarium and collages of dried flowers. He also painted hundreds of "flower pictures." He enjoyed reading—Stefan Zweig was his favorite author—and television. Nearly pathologically sedentary, he loved his little-known region (the Avesnois) and suffered from seeing it so scorned. He was also attuned to deindustrialization and its environmental ravages. He gave literacy classes to newly arrived North African youths, voted for Socialist candidates, read the regional daily *La Voix du Nord*, subscribed to the left-wing weekly *Nouvel Obs*, and received *L'école libératrice*, the teacher's union's periodical.

In 1995, Jack retired from the national education system. His leisure activities evolved little. As Jacqueline grew increasingly invested in Socialist politics, winning several elections, their roles changed at home. Jack was now the one who cooked on a daily basis. His seven grandchildren brought him much joy. Always willing to lend an ear, he was close to his three children. Lymphoma subjected him to painful months in 2012. Seemingly cured, he succumbed to a sudden bout of pneumopathy in 2015. Though it left a permanent mark on his family, Jack did not experience his impending death as a tragedy. He had never wanted to grow old and "ugly."

When we write personal family histories, are our motivations as unique as our stories?[7] Beyond the differences, several shared tropes recur: taboos, secrets and shame, sociological anomalies, journeys of migration and social ascent, extreme situations, and unbearable pain. For the sociologist Anne Muxel, family memory—the primary material of my story, alive and sensual—has three main purposes: transmission, resurrection, and reflexivity.[8] All three are central to this project.

I have always been curious about my family and its history. Writing about it thus builds on this initial interest while prolonging my psychoanalysis in a different but equally effective way. I write to understand, not to judge—that goes without saying. History is useful because it offers a wellspring of explanations, because it "runs through our soft skin" and shapes us in a thousand and one ways. Like many of my contemporaries, I am intrigued by "family prehistories," these transgenerational influences that partly determine who we are.[9] From my family comes my taste for French contemporary history and everything that has shaped it: conflicts, controversies, taboos.[10] From my family comes my revolt against what the novelist Annie Ernaux calls "the unjust world order" and my interest in my paternal family's working-class world, in feelings of marginalization (distance from Paris and regional urban centers), and in people who move between social classes (I am interested in their neuroses as well).[11] The modest middle-class status my father attained strikes me as undeservedly underrepresented in nonfiction and literature.

At some point, a form of inquiry becomes necessary. It allows us to sort through "family sagas," myths, and the compromises we make with the truth. I understand the excitement an investigation stimulates and the narrative benefits it provides: As readers, we are trained to appreciate all of this. Investigations also enable us to recover the lives and deaths of the "lost."[12] Historians who write about their family often seek to document its history This is the case in many French works, by among others Mona Ozouf, Ivan Jablonka, Camille Lefebvre, and Stéphane Audoin-Rouzeau.[13] The same holds true for sociologists as well as writers such as Danièle Sallenave.[14] Annie Ernaux's interest revolves around "memory that becomes history"—*l'histoire* as a story, *l'histoire* as a historical investigation.[15] The works of the Nobel laureate explore her memories of childhood and life as a woman in all their dimensions, including shame about her working-class background, her abortion, her life as a young wife, and her first, nonconsensual sexual experience. Ernaux embraced what she calls "flat writing": "If I wish to tell the story of a life governed by necessity, I have no right to adopt an artistic approach, or attempt to produce something 'moving' or 'gripping.' [. . .] No lyrical reminiscences, no triumphant displays of irony. This neutral way of writing comes to me naturally. It was the same style I used when I wrote home telling my parents the latest news."[16]

Ernaux's style comes close to the factual, event-based narration that constitutes one way of writing history. The quotidian events woven throughout her body of work bring to light relations of domination, class, and gender. Ernaux's autobiography accordingly takes on a collective dimension—readers identify with it—and carries a political message, echoed in her commitments to feminist struggles and progressivism.

Though I have been deeply influenced by Ernaux, a spokeswoman for the voiceless and those who have journeyed from one social class to another, I believe I have taken the opposite path, moving from history to memory. As a historian, my predispositions lead me toward a vision of my family's past structured by chronology and corroborated by sources. I cannot avoid it. Yet, I am not "investigating" my father. Instead, I am sketching an impression, a portrait; I do not unravel a mystery. In writing these words, I am already confronting the difficulty of reconstituting *Jack*'s creation. Intertwined as it is with my path as a historian, my poetic intention is also connected to a specific emotional state: the loss, the death of Jack.[17] This led me to experiment with a form of writing freed from numerous constraints, a form of writing that differs from academic prose. Though I begin with my feelings, though I write freely, I remain committed to an "autobiographical pact": the writer-narrator, at once Jack's daughter and a historian, holds the reins of a true story.[18]

This is the tension I am trying to capture: on one hand, a letting go; on the other, conscious narration of the admittedly deconstructed, fragmentary, emotional story through which I fashion my narrative identity. To quote the sociologist Vincent de Gaulejac, "the individual is the product of a story of which he is trying to become the subject."[19] Writing is a privileged way of becoming a subject.

The portrait of my father—"*ma père*" to cite one of my common slips of the tongue—also suggests another type of blurring, this time of the feminine and the masculine.[20] Jack's almost ineffable difference and his outside status in the patriarchal order have both fascinated and shaped me. He lived as a poet in a world of flowers brightened by his reading, very far from the archetype of virility. In 1954, at the age of seventeen, he cried at the death of his cherished author Colette. Later, this sensitivity was his legacy to me. So was my name, Christine, after Queen Christina of Sweden, a bisexual rebel who changed religions, abandoned her throne, and was personified on screen by Greta Garbo, a bisexual actress whose performances drew the attention of Roland Barthes. So many signs, undetectable for those satisfied by statistical averages: There were at least four "Christines" in each of my primary school classes.

Gender subversion pleased my father. I turned not toward literary studies, as he wished, but toward history, albeit the history of gender and sexuality. In doing so, I could draw from my familial background. Very early on, I also encountered an existential feminism that would shape my views on the norms of family life. Toxic, pathogenic families; families at the heart of patriarchal reproduction; families as cocoons for incestuous crimes; families as pillars of the social and political order ("work, family, country");[21] families as guardians of the heterosexual order and gender orthodoxy:[22] There are many enlightening memoirs on such questions.[23] The impetus to write *Jack* responds to a contrary impulse, so much so, in my view, that I questioned my legitimacy. I wanted to capture the ease of living with my father, to give an idea of alternative ways of experiencing masculinity and fatherhood, without fanfare, in a generation born before the war.

In 1964, Jack chose to have a family ("I got married to have children," chap. 26); I have not chosen motherhood. Given as examples among others, these biographical facts matter, though how and to what extent I do not exactly know. That the "I" in *Jack* belongs to a feminist historian inevitably shapes the story.

I believe that writing from this critical point of view is necessary on political grounds.[24] This will influence one's reading of *Jack*, all the more so because the book was published by a feminist press, iXe. The focus on gender became less central as I wrote, however. Acutely aware of the dangers of reductionism, I sought to create a complete portrait of Jack—including, for example, his childhood and his work life. Gender is everywhere in this book, but not necessarily front and center.

Writing about my family has led me to confront my family tree: I will go as far back as my great-grandparents, for they are present within the memories passed down by my parents. Still, truth be told, I do not like genealogy. Though I understand the excitement of the quest, its results strike me as disappointing, lacking flesh and spirit. Geography is thus the only thing I have in common with the novelist Marguerite Yourcenar, who wrote about her ancestors near the Franco-Belgian border. Her aristocratic lineage gave her a perspective that is not mine: the property holdings, the castles, the names with noble particles spoke to her.[25] I do not have the same relationship to the land, my ancestors, or history. I never say "my people." There is a tenant's way and a property owner's way of writing historical intimacies. Whereas Yourcenar could draw from geography, history, and even geology, it took me years to understand that Jack's life could inspire the "paternal geography" of a tiny area straddling the border. A thick fog surrounded his family tree. Nobody had taken an interest in it until I did so—a statistical anomaly in a country that cannot get enough of genealogy. On my mother's side of the family, the work had been done and passed down in the form of a photocopied, detailed family tree that left me indifferent. Connecting genealogy to emotion is one of my ambitions.

Writing raised the question of readership. Though I struggled to discern my readers—anonymous, unclear, but potentially visible in comments, reviews, and emails—I had to grow comfortable with sharing facets of our private lives. Before seeking a publisher, I allowed myself a resting period after the writing process, not unlike the preparation of dough. *Jack* sat for seven years. I needed time to read and reread my manuscript and, especially, have others read it. Through their encouragement and suggestions, relatives and friends gave me permission (sort of) to publish. About thirty of them read and commented on *Jack* while it was still a word-processed document. The number of people I approached revealed my eagerness to share the text, to discover its impact on readers, and, no doubt, to appease my doubts as I ventured onto a new terrain and put myself on display. The quality of the writing was particularly important to me. I needed reassurance.

Though she was not my primary audience, my mother turned out to be an essential reader. No one (except for me) beat her record of twenty-five readings (accompanied each time by expressions of approval and new revelations). While reconnecting with her Jack, she assured me of the fairness and accuracy of my observations, cherished the poems I included, questioned anew the nature of her marriage, and felt my deep affection for my father. She read Jack first and foremost through the lens of respect for the truth.

I have already said it: Jack comes out of mourning. Writing this book was necessary: I had to hold onto memories while "emptying" the places where my father had lived.[26] I had to make hundreds of decisions: what to sort, donate, sell, destroy, or keep. This last choice, so appealing, would result in an overcrowding of my "interior space" with my parents' memories and objects from previous generations.[27] After my father's death in 2015, my mother moved into a smaller apartment and sold the house that served as his office-workshop. In 2021, she decided to enter a retirement home, where she died the following year. I handled these four moves, which yielded yet more papers, family photos, and souvenirs. In 2016, my maternal grandmother's death had also enriched my archive and—very modestly—my jewelry box. In 2015, the death of the last of my uncles had therefore launched a cycle in my life, marked by death, disappearance, loss. Nearing the age of sixty, I am now the oldest person in my family. Age clearly played an essential role in the decision to begin a personal family history.[28] As I age, what I write about my ancestors is also the trace that I wish to leave behind. My personal life-course encounters broader intellectual current trends, the normalization of autobiography, and the multiplication of personal family narratives.[29]

Sources of a Life

In the beginning, I did not plan to rely on documentation. I preferred delving into my memory—the memory of a witness and protagonist in this story—and the memories that relatives and friends had shared with me. There were many such memories: fifty years of life "with" my father, under my parents' roof until I was seventeen and then intermittent encounters, particularly during my "returns to Maubeuge." We had always been close though we did not—alas—exchange letters (this deprives me of a wonderful source). There is so much to say about this closeness. At its core: fatherly love, daughterly love. Jack is a love story, which I want to anchor in a regional class culture. In the north of France, family solidarity is a strategy for survival and resistance, a strategy that my father inherited.[30] Our closeness was also physical: my most precious memories are related to my father's body.[31] One chapter, *"Papa par corps"* (Papa by Body but also Papa by Heart, *Papa par coeur*), is written in the style of Georges Perec's *I Remember*.[32] His fragmentary autobiographical writing, with its recurring leitmotif "I remember," matches the stream of consciousness of a daughter in mourning. This repetition has a musical quality that echoes my father's poems; it also resembles a mantra, a secular prayer that keeps alive memories that were in danger of being erased (a frequent concern after the death of a loved one). In the end, I sought out, as writing prompts, traces of my father's life that proved moving after his death. "I cherish all of his papers, even the flimsiest," I wrote at the time.[33] The sources often took on the flavor of my tears.

My father did not create or keep many documents related to his ordinary existence.[34] He was not the kind of man to construct a personal archive. But he died suddenly, without sorting through what he would leave behind. For this reason, I found much more than I could have imagined.

First, the photographs. He kept them religiously, in old frames. I have in my possession about 400 photographs of my paternal family, many of which I had noticed before. I had of course read Roland Barthes's classic essay on photography and mourning, *Camera Lucida*. Using photos was also a professional practice in my research on bodies and appearances. In the early 2000s, I conducted a study of working-class clothing in northern France and Brittany based on family photographs. I had interviewed my father about the way he had dressed throughout his life. In writing *Jack*, I learned to reconcile a nostalgic approach with rigorous analysis of the photos. I learned to look at them with care, to look at them for a long time, sometimes individually, sometimes as part of a series, and to consider inscriptions on the back of snapshots. Suddenly, I grew aware of what, in some distant fashion, I had already known: this collection of family photos failed to include my parents' and paternal grandparents' weddings. I had to write about this odd fact.

The body was a source. So were settings. Objects created or found at flea markets, his images of dried and painted flowers, his calligraphed poems, his herbarium. I know, through a kind of atavism, that an inkwell, a drawing, a vase constitute archives. My father approached them through a gaze that was both emotional and learned. He shared this gaze with me for the way I consider familial objects is immediately "biocentric."[35] I did not anticipate how much his bookshelves would teach me. I found his favorite works, observed the bookmarks, the wear and tear, the occasional annotations.

And then there are diplomas; birth, marriage, and death records; along with institutional reports on his teaching. I long resisted coaxing information from military papers and photo albums devoted to my father's military service in Algeria, during the war of independence. I mostly wrote about silence, the postmemory of the event, and the veteran's hidden trauma. At my editor's request, and that of several readers, I explored these questions in an afterword.[36] Deeming my two chapters on Algeria to be sufficient ("Jack at the Machine Gun" and "The Algerian Ghost"), I did not want to skew my portrait. On the other hand, the questions raised were legitimate: What did Jack do, exactly, in Algeria? How long did he stay, and where? At what point in the war? There was a series of rather factual historical questions to which it was easy to find answers. Beyond the ostensible banalities of his military life between 1960 and 1962, I uncovered distinctive features, such as his ubiquitous smile in the photos sent to my mother or the inappropriate way he wore his beret and regimental insignia.[37]

My interest for place and movement developed gradually, but in time it generated a "paternal geography." Still, nothing in my documentation has as much depth or value as my father's poems.

In *Atelier 62*, historian Martine Sonnet sketches a portrait of her father, Armand Sonnet, a metalworker in the Renault factory of Boulogne-Billancourt, west of Paris. Her book ends with a double loss: the death of her father and the closing of the industrial site in 1986. It ends with this sublime conclusion:

> But in the palm of my hands, channeled, the energy of all those
>
> who had one day opened the black gate.
>
> *Writing with*[38]

I situate myself within a history that is written *with* rather than *about*. I make a number of voices exist; mine does not prevail. I go as far as entering into fictional conversations with my late father. Sometimes I mention memories of discussions. Shared characteristics—our class trajectories, our taste for history, for a women's history that has always sought to give a voice to those who did not have one, or have been forgotten—undoubtedly explain why, like Martine Sonnet, I spontaneously followed the path of intertextuality. The structure I gave *Jack* comes naturally to a historian who, like me, appreciates citations and uses them to the limit of what could be considered reasonable.

I did not want to write about Jack, but with him.

To write with a poet who sought to delight the world, decorate it with his flowers, save it from its dehumanizing transformations.

To write with his words interlaced with mine.

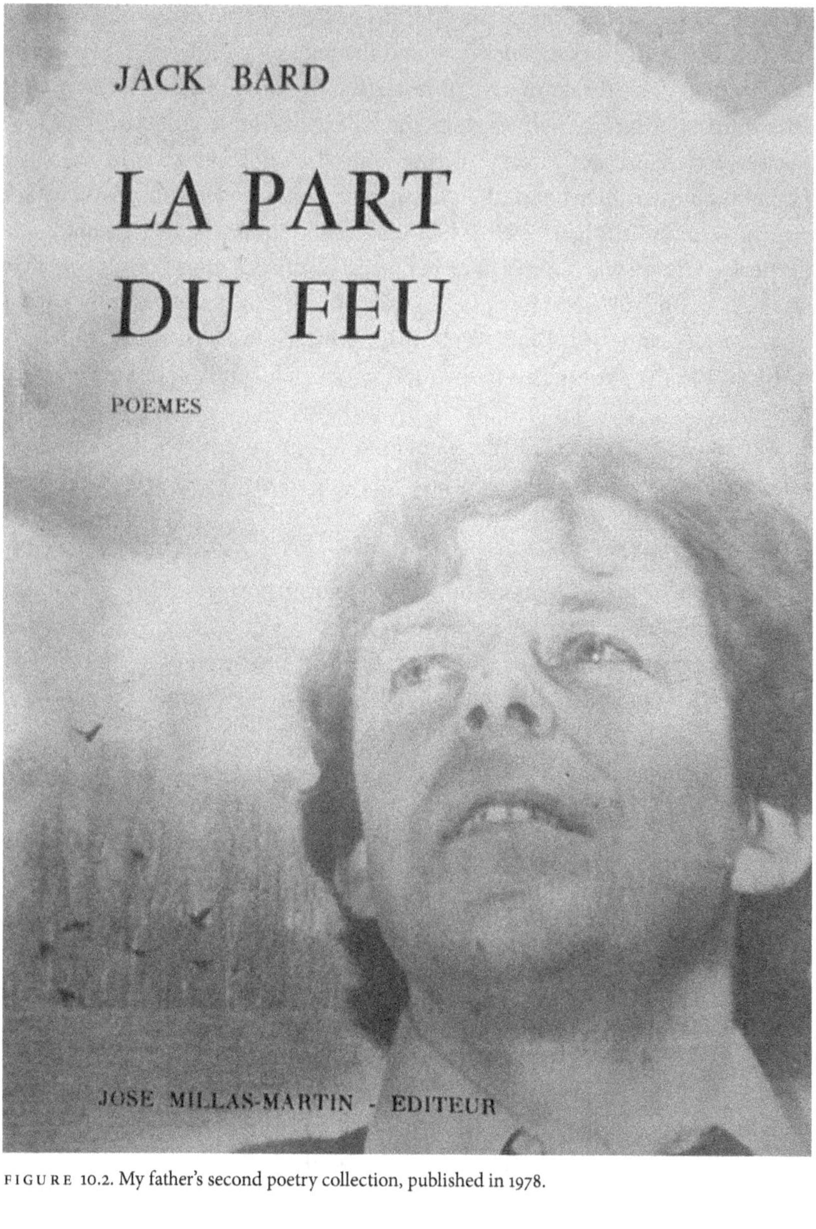

JACK BARD

LA PART
DU FEU

POEMES

JOSE MILLAS-MARTIN - EDITEUR

FIGURE 10.2. My father's second poetry collection, published in 1978.

In the Fog

I had let my heart
Run across the fog.
Suddenly, I lost it
And I did not look for it,
In the fog.
*

Then, I said: "Good!
No more heart, no more sorrow!"
And I sang, danced,
In the fog.
*

Afterward, I don't know anymore,
My heart was no longer in it,
My head was struggling,
In the fog.
*

So, I decided
To lose my mind as well
And quickly, I ran,
Into the fog.
*

But the fog disappeared,
My heart quickly recognized me,
My mind became obvious to me,
My memories returned,
Without the fog.

Jack Bard

TO GET A LITTLE LOST

I reread the poem sadly now that my father is no longer here, and I admire his ability to synthesize. The memories, the "heart" and the "head" constrain an "I" that aspires to dance and sing; "I" frees itself as a result of uncontrollable, outside circumstances, but the party cannot last forever and the fog clears.

Fog: his last name, Bard, is written in the word *brouillard*.

Fog: the weather of my fading memory.

Preceding my father in the fog was Maurice Carême (1899–1978), a famous Belgian poet and, like my father, a primary school teacher from a humble background, son of a building painter and a grocery store owner. His poems were taught in schools. One of them was also titled "The Fog."

"The fog puts everything / In its cotton bag; / The fog took everything / Around my house / No more flowers in the garden, / No more trees along the drive; / The neighbor's greenhouse / Seems to have flown away. / And I really do not know / Where might have landed / The sparrow that I hear / Calling so sadly."

Carême remained on the outside of the fog he described, whereas my brave father threw himself into the unknown. He returned to the original meaning of the word. Before becoming a weather phenomenon in the sixteenth century, fog designated a physical and mental disorder, a moment of confusion that drew my father in, like the fog for which he searched in glasses of whisky and good wine. Jack imagined himself in this fog, "out of sight, out of mind" in a space of incredible freedom, symbol of the indeterminate. Lost without a map. Concealed.

His poem speaks to fundamental fears. Fog evokes a funeral pall, a shroud, the winding sheet. Still, my father returned from this space haunted by the dead.

The fog alludes to the feminine universe of Jack's mother and grandmother. Veils, curtain, threads, tassels, muslin, cotton, ribbons: textile metaphors abound.

What did I think when, as a child, I read this poem? How old was I when the fog triumphed? Eleven. The rhythm was pleasing to children.

Jack sought to lose himself, he dared to do so. My father was a hero who committed himself, body and soul, heart and head, to this cloudy area, but returned to find us.

He would have approved of the poet Ismaïl Kadaré: "because the sights and facts of this universe are too scary for our eyes and our conscience. They need a veil. So that the truth reaches us broken [...] . Otherwise, it would risk destroying the fragile fabric of our souls and bodies" (*The Legend of Legends*).

Later, I discovered other appearances of his "fog."

In 1981, he wrote in "My Land": "I am from a land of clouds / Where, slowly, the heart scatters / And tears in the wind, / Where dreams spin without respite / In the fogs that birth them, / Land of overly vague expectations / Where we get drunk on departures / When the rainy season comes / To inundate the cracked earth."

The fog is also an attachment to Mother Earth. Of incredible strength.

Jack entitled his last collected poems "Private Fogs." In a 2007 poem, the fog made people "lose their memory"; "days" "hid" in their midst, but, no matter, the fog slipped away as do all weather phenomena, all the moments that endow our life with rhythm.

Fog is strange. It conceals, but poorly; a discreet sketch, it leaves us to surmise. Averse to therapy, sheltered against intrusions, protected by his solitude, Jack nonetheless revealed himself in poems that ran from child-like candor to a celebration of the senses.

My immersion in my father's poetry has influenced my style. There is nothing surprising about that. Historical writing often bears the traces of a "contamination by sources."

The inclusion of poems creates a contrapuntal structure that places father and daughter on equal planes, between the dead and the living. My words alternate with poems Jack wrote between the 1960s and 2010. I selected thirty-eight of them, a significant number, and made him my posthumous coauthor.[39] This is not anodyne. My father was pained by the nonpublication of much of his poetic output, and so was I. He would have liked my help. But my scholarly publications did not enable me to crack the codes that govern the poetry market, on a downfall in France. My "assistance" was thus ineffective, much to my regret. My guilty conscience explains, at least in part, why I include many of my father's poems. It is a compensation. Needless to say, I hope that this type of poetry, so removed from twenty-first-century literary trends, will be read and appreciated, beyond the indifference and deprecation of critics.

To be completely honest, I cannot repress an uncomfortable memory about this poetry. I was a child at the time, a fan of her father's art. I was given the following assignment at school: write a poem (about a specific theme). I had trouble, the words would not come, and a double shame lay in wait: mocking judgments from my father as well as the school, the institution to which my father also belonged. Paralyzed, probably in tears, I resolved to ask him for help. Forgetting for once his absolute respect for the teacher's authority and the ethics of schoolwork, he wrote before my eyes a wonderful poem about a bird eating cherries. My guilt kept me from boasting. *Jack*'s "poetics" carry the secret shadow of my dishonesty: I would have loved to be a poet. By publishing my father's poems, am I appropriating them? At the very least, doing so is an homage that does not conceal daughterly pride.

In *Fernande* (my paternal grandmother) and *Jacqueline* (my mother), I quote other documents: administrative records, old romance novels, guides for Christian women, and the fiction series *Brigitte* (written for adolescent girls) to understand Jacqueline's upbringing. Also: direct and indirect memories. Jacqueline provided an authentic life story in answer to my questions. I conveyed her point of view and the limits of her medical condition (What does this reoccurring sentence mean: "I have a bad memory"?). Within this polyphony of voices, I am surrounded by support, beyond the confines of my own perceptions.

It was also the reader in me who wrote. *Jack* bears the imprint of all of the readings that have made me who I am.[40] Countless personal stories that please me, touch me, upset me.[41] To be sure, legacies are difficult to discern once one reaches my age. Nonetheless, I find it important to say that writing follows reading. I am thinking above all of the many female authors who have written stories of liberation. Feminist and lesbian literatures have given meaning to my life and my desires. Liberation is both life and the hope for a better life, a "*survie*" (over-life) that is at once survival and transcendence of life.[42] The idea of "creating one's life," to borrow an aphorism from Natalie Clifford Barney, the American writer and salon hostess who shaped Parisian sapphic culture in the first half of the twentieth century, has become almost tritely obvious to me.[43]

I am also writing "with" daughters who write about their fathers: Paule du Bouchet's poet father, Yaël Pachet and Marie Nimier's writer fathers, Anne Pauly's struggling father, Virginie Linhart's mute Maoist father, Martine Sonnet's working-class father, Colombe Schneck's secret father, and Leïla Sebbar's, Danièle Sallenave's, and Mona Ozouf's primary school teacher fathers.[44] Is the portrait of a father by his daughter a literary genre nowadays?

Facing the Secret

Writing with is not a writing workshop concept. The memory of its gradual development has already vanished. It is partly inaccessible to me. What I felt, deeply, was the need for an original and appealing structure, reflecting what my father valued to the point of excess. While it is true that the form given to a subject allows us to "think the unthought,"[45] I have not finished my work: Each rereading provides new discoveries. Indeed, *writing with* means writing with the secret, writing about the secret. This is why I chose to include passages from *Jack* that allude to my father's homosexual life.

A PATH WITHOUT A NAME

Taking care of "its flights and its wanderings" went without saying between us. It was enough not to ask questions that would not yield answers. Not to be surprised about his after-dinner outings "to take a walk." About his comings and goings between our family's apartment and his house. The latter was not a bachelor pad but a refuge where he painted and wrote, where the hours passed, often without inspiration. On my return trips to Maubeuge, I would ask, "Have you written any poems?"

No. Sometimes, for a long time, no.

Surrounding him, a veil protected his private life like a "fog." This invisible wall separated us: father on one side, daughter on the other. Did I really try to break through this wall? I remember the respect and a distance that asserted itself naturally. He did not need words to protect his secrets. The measures he took sufficed. As did geography. The house-workshop-office avenue de la Gare was a fifteen minutes walk from the apartment place de la Concorde, in the lower part of town.

I sometimes feel retrospective fear. What if something terrible had happened to him? An encounter gone wrong or a blackmailer. Impossible: To imagine my timid, sensitive father manage situations according to codes about which I knew nothing. Papa Jekyll and Mister Hyde? Why? What an absurd question!

[. . .] My experiences as an adult did not change anything; I remained on the threshold of his ramparts. At the same time, I would enter the fog of others, in search no doubt of more explicit joys in the history of gender and sexuality or in love affairs and friendships in which we share everything, or almost. I would see films, read books, seek an unveiling, instinctively, only to find myself on familiar ground.

For the secrets were but half secrets. Jack could not exclude from his poetry the "embracing shadows" or the people who "leave, weary from expectations." In "Evening," he outlined with modesty the "shadows / and furtive moons / that make up a world / where we lose ourselves a little."

Must I put into words the desire that governed "The Getaway"?

> It is but a day withdrawing,
> Why speak to say nothing?
> Soon the zippers will settle down.

A handful of poems, allusions, so many tiny stones that trace a stippled path without a name. Like "the love that does not dare say its name"?

This was the only chapter to undergo a sort of censorship—which became self-censorship—and a partial rewrite. This inconvenience turned into a stroke of luck, for I now prefer the second version.

I did not wish to ignore or upset my mother if *Jack* were published: This was a delicate and painful subject for her. My brother, for his part, indicated that he did not want to know anything (which, incidentally, demonstrated that he knew without knowing). My sister did not react to my offer to read the text.

This facet of my father's life was most significant to me. I was twenty years old when my mother shared with me the secret she had recently grasped, and then asked me to remain silent. I alone, and neither my sister nor my brother, became the keeper of this specific knowledge, a secret that I could not discuss with the primary protagonist, my father.

In the studies about sexual health that developed at the end of the twentieth century, my father would have been labeled "MSM": a man having sex with men. The term has the advantage of naming a group without taking questions of self-identification into consideration. As for me, unconstrained by the taxonomies of sociodemographers and harboring a dislike of acronyms, I alluded to Jack's secret homosexual life in conversations with people with whom I was close. My yearning to name stood in contrast to my father's refusal to do so, which he justified through a universalist discourse about the futility of identity ("I can't stand labels").

In doing so, I was shaping a character, my gay father, my queer father (a notion that pleased him in its rejection of strict homo/hetero categories).[46]

Inventing: is that not what we do to others, dead or alive, and to our own selves, to the extent that our identity is narrative? Is invention not what memory generates as the years pass? "When we have passed a certain age," Marcel Proust writes in *The Captive*, "the soul of the child that we were and the souls of the dead from whom we spring come and bestow upon us in handfuls their treasures and their calamities, asking to be allowed to cooperate in the new sentiments which we are feeling and in which, obliterating their former image, we recast them in an original creation."[47]

My readings have played an important role in my filial approach to my father's sexual orientation. I will not discuss my scholarly work on the history of sexuality or the homosexual authors whom I have read throughout my life, but instead the recent, moving discovery of works that daughters have written about their homosexual fathers. I do not know exactly what role these sisters-in-writing have played, but they must have encouraged me in this venture. They have also opened a comparison between the lives of homosexual men from approximately the same generation and the lives of their writer daughters. I feel particularly close to Alison Bechdel, the well-known chronicler of lesbian life in San Francisco, because her father was closeted and obsessed with decoration, and because she is herself lesbian. (For all that, *Jack* is not at all similar to *Fun Home*, a humorous graphic novel.) Alysia Abbott's story about her gay, poet father cut down by AIDS also impressed me. Then, in the order of my reading, came two French women, Isabelle Carré and Constance Joly, who wrote with admirable sensitivity about their fathers' marriages and their lives after coming out.[48] I also sought out books and testimonies by homosexuals who, born between the two world wars, described the transition between the worlds that preceded and followed the coming out of the closet.[49] I even found a book about the wives of homosexuals.[50]

At that point, an ethical question surfaced: What do I do with Jack's secret? If I decided to write about my father, it was at first quite certainly because I wanted to approach this secret. The chapter comes at the end of my narrative; everything—hints dropped throughout the preceding chapters—leads toward this revelation.

Would my father have appreciated this revelation? I grappled with this ethical question, and so in a way did my mother, in Jack's name. I told her that my father's death had lifted certain constraints. When I asked her to read the manuscript, she told me gently, carefully, diplomatically that this chapter made her a little uncomfortable. She did not like the allusion to the ramparts, my father's "cruising area," an ill-famed place. She admitted that she was embarrassed by her acquaintances' potential reactions. This request, wrapped in respect for my work and its political and emotional stakes, requires contextualization. Though it can seem timid nowadays, we can just as equally say that it speaks to advances in sexual freedom made over the past fifty years, notably, though, not only for someone like my mother.

Was my mother's request completely explicit? I tend to think not. Though she mentioned the ramparts, the most shocking word—fag—came a bit later in my passage. I felt unease myself while writing, and dealt with it by using a quote from Bechdel, as if to say that this experience was not so special.

To avoid upsetting my mother, I removed the chapter's most explicit passages about homosexuality and introduced a certain amount of fog. Of course, I was relinquishing my own desire for homosexual visibility, but fictional dialogue allowed me to retain at least part of it, to continue the fight by other means.[51]

Rereading the deleted passage now, I find my words rather benign:

> The ramparts form a semi-circle around the town center. Their massive rock- and plant-covered presence shapes the town. Considered dangerous, this is a forbidden zone for children and unaccompanied women. It is at once solidly constructed (built by the famed engineer Vauban) and wild (nature reasserting its presence). These ramparts are a border, but what must be understood is that here, "one goes into the ramparts," into their passageways, their staircases, their paths, their thickets—not on the ramparts but inside. The defensive wall is lost among all the green, and countless hiding spots present themselves to those looking for secret sex. My father, a cross-border child, was certainly destined for this disreputable area.
>
> [. . .] I did not tell myself that, like Alison Bechdel's, "my father was a fag," for as a child I likely knew nothing of the word and the concept. It was also inconceivable that my father could be described by an insult. What to say, then? Because he did not say anything.

In the second version, I invented a dialogue with my mother that showed our opposing points of view about the allusion to a "secret life." What ultimately won my mother's support, however, was the daughterly love that gave life to my book, a love that, in her eyes, gave me the right to write about my father. For ethical reasons, I resorted to a *mise en abyme*, a double mirroring effect that would respect the wish of a living person, my mother, while giving her a place in the story of Jack, her husband. The pertinence of this gesture seemed confirmed by the question that my first readers most asked: "And what did your mother think?"

Soft lighting captures my father's sensibility with greater acuity than a spotlight. I now reveal the veil, not what it hides.[52] I embrace my father's fog, echoing the beautiful, evocative metaphor in which he couched his secret.[53] I accept what remains unsaid and realize that I cannot say everything I know. Nor do I want to.

This differs from the position I embrace as a historian. But respect for privacy is at stake, and I do not want to resemble those writers who fall out with their families or, in some cases, are dragged to court.

This forced rewriting ultimately proved enriching to someone who, like me, is obsessed with transparency, someone who was looking for healing, someone who sought to say something without saying it. "Homosexual" is the missing word in chapter 27. As a historian, this experience has led me to think in new ways about the historization of identities: How best can we describe a sexual identity situated in a specific time and place? This experience also reminds me that, as a historian, I have not always "said everything." I have censored myself while tapping oral sources and writing biographical texts.[54] This is something I have come to accept.

> It is not merely that intellect can lend no hand in these resurrections; these past hours will only hide themselves away in objects where intellect has not tried to embody them. The objects which you have consciously tried to connect with certain hours of your life, these they can never take shelter in. What is more, if something else should resuscitate those hours, the objects called back with them will be stripped of their poetry.
>
> MARCEL PROUST, *By Way of Sainte-Beuve*, Prologue

The same holds true of Jack's objects, his poems, his flower scenes, my memories of him. If understood only through what Proust called "intellect," everything would wither and what is essential—the charm—would elude us. For Jack the poet, for the literary effect I sought, I needed to find a distinctive poetics.

My writing has resembled a dreamy journey in which the road materializes as one walks, without any goals but evocation, the pleasure of writing, tenderness toward the sources, encounters with the dead while anticipating the pleasure of sharing all of this with readers. The questions got a bit lost along the way, as if I had moved beyond that stage, into one of resignation and consolation—my own, and that which helped my father live. The "secret life," the silences—about evening outings or memories of Algeria—hence occupy a modest place in the final manuscript; the same is true of the trace this writing experience has left within me. The intense and worrisome relationship Jack maintained with time became the central connection between the book's chapters. I only understood this at the end of my work.[55]

Evoking my father is an encounter with difference—of gender and generation, above all—and with my own self. My fog has dissipated a little; I have come to understand that I, too, have taken a (writing) path without a name, between the memoir, the book of mourning, the book-poem, the filial narrative, the septentrional book, the floral book. It is a work of history, too, in its own way. I am attached to this word, which is present in the series title (*History Runs through Our Soft Skins*), balanced by a vocabulary that is less common within the discipline: "our soft skins," we fragile humans, designated by a blurry pronoun that is open to interpretation.[56]

I now understand differently the lesson my father imparted about desire. In the following poem, I cannot help but hear a criticism he often leveled at me.

> *Shh!*
>
> Your secret garden
> No longer has a secret.
> When you confide in someone
> It is without restraint
> And then you are surprised
> At being laid bare,
> Without shadows and without a veil
> To protect you
> And without mystery
> To desire you.

What if the same were true of books, especially the ones we write?

Do I want to be laid bare?

No.

Translated from the French by Hilary S. Handin

Afterword

MARIANNE HIRSCH AND LEO SPITZER

Readers encounter many intriguing questions in this volume of essays. Should scholars be present in their work, and in what ways? In the context of scholarly inquiry, what is the personal and, especially, the autobiographical for? What does it *do*? Does it further the scholarly project, or is it significant in its own right? Must the personal academic voice always be autobiographical, or can scholars be situated, located, even embodied, revealing the stakes and commitments of their work, without autobiographical details and anecdotes?

In the early 1990s, we and other like-minded scholars organized a seminar to explore the promises and pitfalls of an increasingly engaging "personal turn" in academic writing. At the time, the two of us were working on scholarly books that, we each thought, had a great deal to gain from a personal voice. In our projects, moreover, the personal was also the familial. That increased our caution; in fact, we were grateful to the skeptics who slowed us down with their misgivings. But we also discovered the stakes and seductions of combining scholarly inquiry with life writing. This hybrid scholarly writing acquires a greater geographical and historical scope, and thus more expansive dimensions, in the present volume.

Importantly, we each came to personal writing—and specifically to personal family history—with different stakes and hesitations and from different scholarly and intellectual traditions specific to our fields of history and cultural studies. Authors in this volume emerging from additional fields such as anthropology, sociology, and environmental studies add different genealogies yet.

LEO SPITZER

I was working on Hotel Bolivia: The Culture of Memory in a Refuge from Nazism *(1998), a book examining the displacement of Jews and others from Nazi-dominated* central Europe and their resettlement in Bolivia, one of the few remaining places to accept such refugees in the late 1930s. Over twenty thousand found a haven and attempted to remake their lives there, a land that for almost all of them was alien, unknown.

I was born in La Paz, Bolivia, ten days after the outbreak of World War II in September 1939. As a child of Jewish immigrants who had fled Austria only months before, I had a privileged connection to the refugee experience about which I was writing—one that allowed me to combine a long-standing scholarly interest with an insider's perspective. While my book-in-progress was thus the work of a historian, personal memory was not only a component of its overall makeup but a key factor in its creation. As a work of history, it was grounded in many of the traditional sources of historical reconstruction: in documentary materials found in archives, repositories, and libraries in the Americas, Europe, and Israel. It made extensive use of written memoirs, letters, photographs, family albums, artistic representations, newspaper articles, and advertisements. But it was also based on videotaped oral history accounts I collected from the immigrants and witnesses, including persons in my family. These recordings held more than 150 hours of oral history interviews with surviving refugees (by this time, widely dispersed throughout the world), with Bolivians, and with members of the "second generation" who either were born in Bolivia or had entered the country as young children.

My personal and familial presence in the larger refugee survival story I was relating, and my historical and critical engagement with that fact—the conjoint relation and interconnection between historian, kin, and subject—formed a central conceptual feature of Hotel Bolivia. The completed book was thus refracted through lenses of my Bolivian childhood memories and the shadowed presence in my life of my family's and their fellow refugees' "lost Europe." I aimed to apprehend and respond to the advantages and possible pitfalls of my special relationship to the places, subject, and people about whom I wrote. But I also wished to uncover and reveal my dual role, as participant and historian, and to make this fact a visible element throughout the book.

My intellectual and cultural formation as a historian gained immensely from the civil rights and Vietnam war eras in the United States, where I was attending graduate school. New and imaginative comparative and multidisciplinary approaches were developing to non-European culture areas, especially Africa and Latin America. During my graduate study and my fieldwork in West Africa, I received training in the collection and analysis of personal oral histories—"life histories"—and remembered and performed oral traditions.

In the early 1970s, I decided to pursue my intellectual interests and historical training through a comparative, cross-cultural approach that focused on life histories of several generations of post-enslavement West African and South American families—Sierra Leone Creole (Krio) and Afro-Brazilian. I initially intended to study persons who were experiencing social ascension over the course of the avowed "Century of Emancipation" that followed the French Revolution, roughly from the 1780s into the early twentieth century. But I discovered another interest while examining some of these life history accounts and analyzing them comparatively (or, as I would now term it, "connectively") to gain clearer insights into assimilationism, exclusion, and the predicament of marginality. While I certainly was interested in understanding aspects of African and Afro-Latin American experiences, I was also trying to comprehend experiences of European Jews like those in my family. My research and analysis thus expanded to include a comparative study of the Zweig-Brettauers, Central European Jewish families that had intermarried with members of my extended Spitzer family in the late eighteenth and nineteenth centuries. Eventually this research yielded my book Lives in Between: The Experience of Marginality in a Century of Emancipation (1989).

Like Saul Friedlander, a historian whom I greatly admire and who had survived the Holocaust as a hidden child in France, I have long acknowledged that my perspective as a historian—the orientation from which I examine the nature of individual and group confrontations with forms of exclusion and domination—is interpretive. And, as interpretation, it is in no way neutral. I abhor omniscient narratives in which historians claim to stand above the fray. Like Hayden White, I acknowledge that the telling of history is shaped by narrative conventions, and, like Dominick La Capra, I believe that the relationship of historians to their materials is inflected by structures of transference.

I fully admit that I am an engaged historian who uses a personal interpretive voice. Indeed, for me, the voice of the historian, as well as the voices and memories of the participants, are as much part of the fabric of history as are written records and other archival materials. To take into account subjectivity and affect complicates and restores a measure of contingency to history. Considering what is remembered as well as forgotten, feared as well as imagined, apprehended as well as misapprehended deepens our historical understanding and helps us resist interpretive closure.

Only in the 1990s with Hotel Bolivia, however, did my located interpretive presence begin to include autobiographical and familial accounts.

MARIANNE HIRSCH

I was writing the book that would become Family Frames: Photography, Narrative, and Postmemory (1997), an exploration of the genre of family photographs and the cultural work they do. I engaged both vernacular images and family pictures as they appear in literary works, memoirs, and photo-based art works. To account for the power that family photos hold in our imaginary, for the ways in which they shape memory and identity, I found that, in addition to reading memoir-essays like Roland Barthes' Camera Lucida or Annette Kuhn's Family Secrets, I had to delve into my own images and family albums and their many lives and afterlives. I was particularly interested in how family photographs *undergird the family as an institution and how these objects might be used to critique and undermine its ideological stronghold. Looking at my own photos, however, I also experienced, viscerally, the strong affective ties they spawn and the nostalgia they elicit.*

Feminist scholarship offered inspiring models, paradigms, and theorizations for personal writing and scholarship—ranging from the 1970s' "The Personal Is Political," to Lee Edwards's insistence on "the authority of experience," Adrienne Rich's influential "politics of location," the idea that knowledge needs to be "situated" (Donna Haraway), and Nancy K. Miller's account of "Getting Personal," to the often playful but also deadly serious critiques of scholarly objectivity and neutrality by Hélène Cixous, Luce Irigaray, Jane Gallop, Audre Lorde, Gloria Anzaldúa, and, of course, the queer theoretical work Eve Kosofsky Sedgwick inspired. The family as an institution and specific family relationships, including mothers and daughters, were often the objects of these personal interrogations and critiques, especially for British Marxist feminists such as Annette Kuhn, Valerie Walkerdine, Jo Spence, and others who also inspired Clare Hemmings's essay in this volume. When in the early 1990s I joined the seminar on personal scholarly writing at the National Humanities Center, I had already written The Mother/Daughter Plot: Narrative, Psychoanalysis, Feminism *(1989). But my personal voice and my perspective as a daughter and a young mother appeared only briefly in one section of the introduction. Later, that personal and anecdotal voice merged with my scholarly voice to serve as a hybrid vehicle of academic, personal, communal, and generational inquiry. In fact, my first cautious and somewhat skeptical attempts at personal writing became my entry into memory studies and specifically my work on the postmemory of the Holocaust.*

The permission we claimed to acknowledge our own situatedness and write a hybrid scholarship in the personal voice led us to family archives and family photographs that now spoke to us with urgency. We came to discover not only the strong affective ties these ego documents can spawn, not only the nostalgia they can elicit, but also the uncanny traps they can set.

We experienced the seductions of family history and memory and felt the thrills and risks of uncovering family secrets. Subsequent projects, such as our coauthored *Ghosts of Home: The Afterlife of Czernowitz in Jewish Memory* (2010) and *School Photos in Liquid Time: Reframing Difference* (2019), only deepened the pleasure and frustration, the urgency and dangers of researching and writing personal family histories. But we had already learned that, for us, personal and familial stories needed to serve a larger communal and collective narrative for which we came to feel a sense of responsibility. The fact that the histories we were researching were those of destroyed Jewish communities, of survivors and descendants who rebuilt their lives during and after the Holocaust, amplified the stakes.

What, as familial and communal descendants, do we owe the victims? How can we carry their stories forward without appropriating them or allowing them to overshadow our own experiences? In *Between Vengeance and Forgiveness*, a study of South Africa and its Truth and Reconciliation Commission hearings, legal scholar Martha Minow argues that direct victims and survivors of mass violence and historical trauma need, first, a venue to "tell [their] story and be heard without interruption or skepticism"; and, second, a "commitment to produce a coherent, if complex, narrative about the entire nation's trauma, and the multiple sources and expressions of its violence."[1] These two dimensions reinforce one another. Each individual story helps to shape a larger history by providing detail, depth, and nuance. In turn, each story is enhanced and given broader meaning through its contextualization within a larger historical matrix. Like several authors in this volume, we find that, as members of a post-generation haunted by communal histories that have not been adequately acknowledged or worked through, we owe the victims this act of attentive listening, as well as this work of historical repair. And yet, we also worry that the historiography of Holocaust victimization has become such a powerful template of extreme violence that it risks overshadowing other histories and the possibilities of telling them otherwise.

The range of stories about racialized and gender-based persecution and violence included in this volume offer welcome experiments with different kinds of narrative possibilities, different forms of telling. The "putative" in Tao Leigh Goffe's account of Afro-Asian families; the imagined account of her grandmother's life in Clare Hemmings's essay; the speculative accounts of a Harlem obstetrician in Martha S. Jones's contribution or a rescuer in Nice in Stéphane Gerson's; the motivations for downward mobility among Leslie Harris's Creole grandparents in New Orleans: All these exhibit forms of imaginative investment motivated by a sense of responsibility to enlarge and deepen family and communal histories even while providing careful historical context. They delve not only into *what was*, inasmuch as that can be known, but also into *what might have been*, into what Ariella Aïsha Azoulay calls "potential history."[2] In this sense, some of this work constitutes an attempted act of repair.

For us, as for this volume's authors, the stakes are therefore as high as they are tricky to gauge and control. Familial descendants enjoy privileged access to family and communal documents and stories—and they may, perhaps, deserve greater trust as interlocutors in oral history interviews. Inherited knowledge also gives us a better chance of capturing the specificities of the past worlds we research, the textures of everyday lives, and both the desire and possibility of imagining the conversations, fantasies, hopes, dreams, and fears of our ancestors. Empathy and identification can aid in the work of post-memory and imagination. Writing about people we care about and love, we have both felt the intense responsibility to be as true as possible to what we understand their experiences to have been.

At the same time, as family members, scholars may have access to family secrets. Information that is kept hidden from some or most family members demands considerable responsibility and restraint. Family secrets are often unsettling, shameful to reveal, embarrassing to hear. They can prove transgressive by crossing the ethical boundaries of privacy, especially across generations. They can wound, or even kill. Apparently the fact that her youngest daughter had died of suicide was kept from one of Leo's grandmothers for fear that the news would "kill her." But we have found, like some of the personal family historians in this volume (Bard, Détrez, Harris), that life events deemed so momentous that they require secrecy over long periods of time, generations even, can reveal a great deal about historical circumstances—when contextualized and told with sensitivity and care. They can serve as portals to larger transpersonal stories that illuminate individual and familial lives in moments of extremity. Exposure, done thoughtfully and with restraint, can thus serve a larger cause.

In histories of racialized persecution, such as the Holocaust and enslavement, moreover, the family is sometimes depicted as a potential haven. The realities of its own violence and inequalities can be submerged within the mythology of familial protectiveness . Such idealizations of family can inhibit scholars from engaging in systemic and critical analyses of its patriarchal, heteronormative hold. It is difficult, moreover, to criticize the private or public failings of family members who are victims or survivors. Tellingly, the essays that expose the effects of familial and social gender-based violence (Bard and Détrez, for example) emerge from ordinary histories rather than times of enslavement, war, or genocide.

Similarly, our subject positions—as children of Holocaust refugees and Holocaust survivors in wartime Romania—endow our personal scholarly voices with particular authority, one we have approached with no small amount of hesitation. Speaking from a position of extreme victimization can endow an author with a legitimacy that may appear exclusionary while delegitimizing voices that are less closely connected. Yet what drew each of us to writing in the personal and familial is precisely the opposite: the opportunity to foreground the process of research and discovery; to acknowledge all we don't know and need to know; to make space for contingency, potentiality, and our own vulnerability as scholars and as characters within the stories we tell.

It is not surprising that personal family histories follow similar structures and strategies, separating the historical past from the present level of research.

Most of us writing in this mode expose our research strategies along with our questions and hesitations; we second-guess our conclusions. What is more difficult to reveal and analyze, what commonly remains in the background or acted out, is the way in which family relationships are subject to often un-conscious processes of transference, projection, investment, and attachment as well as ambivalence, disidentification, and disavowal.

These unconscious structures help to explain why it is difficult, perhaps impossible, to strike a balance between too much or too little personal in-quiry or revelation. We can easily get caught up in life-writing passages and become bored with the scholarly inquiries that build on them. We become curious, want more life writing, additional details and stories. We want a nar-rative arc. At other moments, we find the personal stories self-indulgent and overly granular. We want greater streamlining and discipline, a more direct segue to the larger story to which the personal should, we believe, serve as a springboard.

As Stéphane Gerson specifies in his introduction, we are all dealing with shame and guilt, fear and betrayal. Even as we welcome memories transmit-ted to us across generations, we also resist them. For these complex psycho-logical investments, our accounts remain partial, in continual need of revi-sion. This sense of contingency and vulnerability endemic to personal family history is present throughout this volume—a testament to the ways in which this mode of writing can serve as a more general model for the contingencies of scholarly inquiry.

Contributors

CHRISTINE BARD is professor of modern history at the University of Angers and senior member of the Institut universitaire de France. She has published many books on the political, social, and cultural histories of women and gender. Bard presides the association *Archives du féminisme*, edits an eponymous collection at the Presses universitaires de Rennes, and oversees the virtual museum on the history of women and gender MUSEA. She is currently working on a tetralogy focused around her familial memory: *History Runs through Our Soft Skins (L'histoire traverse nos peaux douces)*. Its first volume, *Jack*, came out in 2022.

MARNIX BEYEN teaches modern political history at the University of Antwerp, where he is a member of Power in History—Center for Political History. His research focuses on the cultural and political representations of nations and other collectivities in Western Europe during the nineteenth and twentieth centuries. With Judith Pollmann and Henk te Velde, he recently published *De Lage Landen. Een geschiedenis voor vandaag* (Ons Erfdeel, 2021).

CHRISTINE DÉTREZ is professor of sociology at the École normale supérieure de Lyon. She specializes in the sociology of gender, culture, and emotions. She is also a novelist. Her latest books are *Nos mères: Huguette, Christiane et tant d'autres. Une histoire de l'émancipation féminine* (La Découverte, 2020); *Pour te ressembler* (Denoël, 2021); and *Le crush: Fragments du nouveau discours amoureux* (Flammarion, 2024).

STÉPHANE GERSON is professor of French, French studies, and history at New York University. His scholarship explores questions of place and memory, disasters and their aftermaths, and modes of historical writing. His publications include the prizewinning *The Pride of Place: Local Memories and Political Culture in Nineteenth-Century France* (Cornell, 2003) and *Disaster Falls: A Family Story* (Crown, 2017). His contribution to this volume is part of a broader relational history of survival, aid, and postwar storytelling in Belgium and France: *Les gestes de notre guerre, 1994–1942. Une histoire en contrepoint* (La Découverte, forthcoming).

TAO LEIGH GOFFE is associate professor of literary theory and cultural history at Hunter College, City University of New York. Her writing, which includes histories of geology, European colonialism, photography, and debt, has been featured in *South Atlantic Quarterly, Women & Performance*, and *New York* magazine. She has received grants supporting her research from the National Endowment for the Humanities, the Ruth Foundation, and the Mellon Foundation. She is the executive director of the Dark Laboratory, where theorists use creative technology to explore the nexus of stolen land and stolen life in the Americas. Goffe recently published *Dark Laboratory: On Columbus, the Caribbean, and the Origins of the Climate Crisis* (Doubleday, 2025).

LESLIE M. HARRIS is professor of history and Black studies at Northwestern University. A specialist in pre–Civil War African American history, she has authored or coedited five books, including the award-winning *In the Shadow of Slavery: African Americans in New York City* (Chicago, 2003), and, with James T. Campbell and Alfred L. Brophy, *Slavery and the University: Histories and Legacies* (Georgia, 2019). She is currently completing *Leaving New Orleans: A Personal Urban History*, a book that combines memoir with family, urban, and environmental histories to explore the multiple meanings of New Orleans from its founding through its uncertain future amid climate change.

CLARE HEMMINGS is professor of feminist theory at the London School of Economics, where she has worked in the Department of Gender Studies (formerly the Gender Institute) for twenty-five years. Her work concerns histories of queer and feminist studies and their institutionalization and translation within and across national and international contexts. She has been particularly interested in how participants tell stories about these fields and those stories' resonance with broader political agendas. Recent work concerns family memoir and genres of storytelling across competing narratives: *Why Stories Matter: The Political Grammar of Feminist Theory* (Duke, 2011), and *Considering Emma Goldman: Feminist Political Ambivalence and the Imaginative Archive* (Duke, 2018).

MARIANNE HIRSCH is William Peterfield Trent Professor Emerita of Comparative Literature and Gender Studies at Columbia University. She writes about the transmission of memories of violence across generations, combining feminist theory with memory studies in global perspective. She is a former president of the Modern Language Association of America and a member of the American Academy of Arts and Sciences. Recent books include *The Generation of Postmemory: Writing and Visual Culture after the Holocaust* (Columbia, 2012); the coedited volume *Women Mobilizing Memory* (Columbia, 2019); and, with Leo Spitzer, *School Photos in Liquid Time: Reframing Difference* (Washington, 2020). She is working on a book about reparative memory.

MARTHA HODES is professor of history at New York University. Her most recent book is *My Hijacking: A Personal History of Forgetting and Remembering* (HarperCollins, 2023). She has been awarded fellowships from the Guggenheim Foundation, the Cullman Center for Scholars and Writers, the National Endowment for the Humanities, the American Council of Learned Societies, Harvard University, the Fulbright Program, and the Whiting Foundation. She is also the author of *Mourning Lincoln* (Yale, 2015); *The Sea Captain's Wife: A True Story of Love, Race, and War in the Nineteenth Century* (Norton, 2006); and *White Women, Black Men: Illicit Sex in the Nineteenth-Century South* (Yale, 1997).

MARTHA S. JONES is the Society of Black Alumni Presidential Professor, professor of history, and professor at the SNF Agora Institute at Johns Hopkins University. She is a legal and cultural historian whose work examines how Black Americans have shaped the story of American democracy. Her publications include the prizewinning books *Birthright Citizens: A History of Race and Rights in Antebellum America* (Cambridge, 2018) and *Vanguard: How Black Women Broke Barriers, Won the Vote, and Fought for Rights for All* (Basic, 2020). She is also the author of a family memoir, *The Trouble of Color: An American Family Memoir* (Basic, forthcoming), from which this essay is derived.

AMY MORAN-THOMAS is associate professor of anthropology at MIT and teaches in the Program in History, Anthropology, and Science, Technology, and Society (HASTS). Her ethnographic writing focuses on the ways technologies and ecologies are designed and materially embodied—often inequitably—by people in their ordinary lives. Her first book, *Traveling with Sugar: Chronicles of a Global Epidemic* (California, 2019), received several awards, including one from the caregivers in Belize whose work it describes, one from the Diabetes Foot Care Group with the Caribbean Diabetes Association, and the Victor Turner Prize for Ethnographic Writing. Moran-Thomas's current research about oil, planetary health, and generational embodiment centers the approach of "kinship as critical method"—this time writing from her own family histories.

LEO SPITZER is Vernon Professor of History Emeritus and research professor at Dartmouth College. He writes about responses to imperialism, Jewish refugee memory, and traumatic witnessing and its transmission. His books include *Lives in Between: Assimilation, Marginality, Exclusion in the Era of Emancipation* (Cambridge, 1989); *Hotel Bolivia: The Culture of Memory in a Refuge from Nazism* (Hill & Wang, 1998); the coedited volume *Acts of Memory: Cultural Recall in the Present* (Dartmouth, 1998); and, with Marianne Hirsch, *School Photos in Liquid Time: Reframing Difference* (Washington, 2020). He recently edited a doctor's memoir from the Romanian Holocaust (Rochester, 2024) and is currently writing a family memoir about ethnic cleansing in a small Austrian town after the Anschluss.

Notes

Introduction

1. LaToya Ruby Frazier, *The Notion of Family* (New York: Aperture, 2016 [2014]), 42; LaToya Ruby Frazier, "A Creative Solution for the Water Crisis in Flint, Michigan," in her *Flint Is Family in Three Acts*, ed. Michal Raz-Russo (Göttingen, Germany: Steidl, 2022), 10. Other photographers have likewise delved into their family lives and histories: see, for instance, Gay Block, *Bertha Alyce: Mother ExPosed* (Albuquerque: University of New Mexico Press, 2003); Mitch Epstein, *Family Business* (Göttingen, Germany: Steidl, 2003); Deborah Willis, *Family History Memory: Recording African American Life* (New York: Hylas, 2005).

2. Frazier, *Notion of Family*, 152; Teju Cole, "The Living Artist," *New York Times Magazine*, February 10, 2016.

3. Dennis C. Dickerson, "Black Braddock and Its History," in Frazier, *Notion of Family*, 140; Laura Wexler, "A Notion of Photography," in ibid., 143.

4. Claire Zalc, *Z ou souvenirs d'historienne* (Paris: Éditions de la Sorbonne, 2021), 11, 115. Unless otherwise indicated, translations from the French are mine.

5. Charles Dew, *The Making of a Racist: A Southerner Reflects on Family, History, and the Slave Trade* (Charlottesville: University of Virginia Press, 2016), 2. Other disciplines in the social sciences, including anthropology, have also equated scholarly authority with distance. See Paper Boat Collective, "Archipelagos, A Voyage in Writing," in *Crumpled Paper Boat: Experiments in Ethnographic Writing*, ed. Anand Pandian and Stuart McLean (Durham, NC: Duke University Press, 2017), 13.

6. Carla L. Peterson, *Black Gotham: A Family History of African Americans in Nineteenth-Century New York City* (New Haven, CT: Yale University Press, 2011), 30. On this longer history, see Kendra T. Field, "The Privilege of Family History," *American Historical Review* 127, no. 2 (2022): 600–633. On archival absence and personal family history, see Thulani Davis, *My Confederate Kinfolk: A Twenty-First Century Freedwoman Rediscovers Her Roots* (New York: Basic Books, 2006), 65–66. I take stock of personal family history as a genre, in France and beyond, in "A History from Within: When Historians Write about Their Own Kin," *Journal of Modern History* 94, no. 4 (2022): 898–937. I draw from this article at various points in this introduction.

7. Carolyn Kay Steedman, *Landscape for a Good Woman: A Story of Two Lives* (New Brunswick, NJ: Rutgers University Press, 1987), 8. A few years later, Richard White published another

important book about class and familial storytelling: *Remembering Ahanagran; Story-Telling in a Family's Past* (New York: Hill & Wang, 1998).

8. Tiya Miles, *Ties That Bind: The Story of an Afro-Cherokee Family in Slavery and Freedom* (Berkeley: University of California Press, 2015 [2005]), 3. On family history, see Nara Milanich, "Whither Family History? A Road Map from Latin America," *American Historical Review* 112, no. 2 (2007): 439–58; Malcolm Allbrook and Sophie Scott-Brown, eds., *Family History and Historians in Australia and New Zealand: Related Histories* (New York: Routledge, 2021); Tanya Evans, "Secrets and Lies: The Radical Potential of Family History," *History Workshop Journal* 71 (2011): 49–73.

9. Michel Winock, *Jeanne et les siens* (Paris: Éditions du Seuil, 2003); Joanna Brooks, *Why We Left: Untold Stories and Songs of America's First Immigrants* (Minneapolis: University of Minnesota Press, 2013).

10. Françoise Vergès, *Monsters and Revolutionaries: Colonial Family Romance and Métissage* (Durham, NC: Duke University Press, 1999); Benjamin Stora, *Les trois exils: Juifs d'Algérie* (Paris: Stock, 2006).

11. See, among others, Susan Rubin Suleiman, *Budapest Diary: In Search of the Motherbook* (Lincoln: University of Nebraska Press, 1999); Leo Spitzer, *Hotel Bolivia: The Culture of Memory in a Refuge from Nazism* (New York: Hill & Wang, 1998); Marianne Hirsch and Leo Spitzer, *Ghosts of Home: The Afterlife of Czernowitz in Jewish Memory* (Berkeley: University of California Press, 2012); Ivan Jablonka, *A History of the Grandparents I Never Had*, trans. Jane Kuntz (Chicago: University of Chicago Press, 2016 [2012]); Monika Sznajderman, *Fałszerze pieprzu. Historia rodzinna* (Wołowiec, Poland: Czarne, 2016). Daniel Mendelsohn's *The Lost: A Search for Six of Six Million* (New York: HarperCollins, 2006) has spurred many similar ancestral quests.

12. A nonexhaustive bibliography, in chronological order: Mark Mazower, *What You Did Not Tell: A Russian Past and the Journey Home* (New York: Other Press, 2017); Miroslava Chávez-García, *Migrant Longing: Letter Writing Across the U.S.-Mexico Borderlands* (Chapel Hill: University of North Carolina Press, 2018); Adele Logan Alexander, *Princess of the Hither Isles: A Black Suffragist's Story from the Jim Crow South* (New Haven, CT: Yale University Press, 2019); Mikhal Dekel, *Tehran Children: A Holocaust Refugee Odyssey* (New York: Norton, 2019); Martine Segalen, *Destins français: Essai d'auto-ethnographie familiale* (Grâne, France: Créaphis, 2022); Annette Wieviorka, *Tombeaux. Autobiographie de ma famille* (Paris: Éditions du Seuil, 2022); Blair LM Kelley, *Black Folk: The Roots of the Black Working Class* (New York: Liveright, 2023); Michael Roper, *Afterlives of War: A Descendant's History* (Manchester, UK: Manchester University Press, 2023); Simukai Chigudu, *When Will We Be Free? Living in the Shadow of Empire and the Struggle for Decolonization* (New York: Crown, 2024).

13. *History Workshop Journal* has published consistently in this vein. See, among others, Norma Clarke, "Family Matters," *History Workshop Journal* 85 (2018): 315–21; Joe Moran, "The Scattering: A Family History for a FloatingWorld," *History Workshop Journal* 92 (2021): 4–28. See also "Family History Workshops" (organized by Julia Laite), https://historianscollaborate.com/family-history-workshops/; "Inheriting the Family" (spearheaded by Joanne Begiato and Katie Barclay), https://inheritingthefamily.org/; "The Stories in *Our* Histories: Historians Confront Themselves" (conference organized by Leslie M. Harris, Northwestern University, Evanston, IL, May 9–10, 2024), https://historicalstudies.northwestern.edu/events/conferences/Conference%201.html.

14. Christine J. Walley, *Exit Zero: Family and Class in Postindustrial Chicago* (Chicago: University of Chicago Press, 2013), 5. On historians and self-writing, see Jaume Aurell, *Theoretical Perspectives on Historians' Autobiographies: From Documentation to Intervention* (New York: Routledge, 2015); Jeremy D. Popkin, *History, Historians & Autobiography* (Chicago: University of Chicago Press, 2005).

15. Gregory Crewdson, quoted in Zoë Lescaze, "LaToya Ruby Frazier, American Witness," *New York Times Style Magazine*, March 1, 2021.

16. Atina Grossmann, "Family Files: Emotions and Stories of (Non-)Restitution," *German Historical Institute London Bulletin* 34, no. 1 (2012): 62; Martine Sonnet, "Atelier 62: un récit littéraire du travail en friction avec les sciences sociales," *Intercâmbio* 2nd ser., no. 5 (2012): 205, 214. Sonnet's personal family history is *Atelier 62* (Bazas, France: Le temps qu'il fait, 2009).

17. Dinah Birch, "The Iron Way," *London Review of Books*, February 19, 2015. See also the recent reflections in Marion Clerc et al., "L'intimité des sociologues. Retour réflexif sur une enquête collective sur des proches," *Genèses* 131, no. 2 (2023): 133–34; and the critique by Enzo Traverso, *Singular Pasts: The "I" in Historiography*, trans. Adam Schoene (New York: Columbia University Press, 2023 [2020]).

18. I am quoting from the paper Tao Leigh Goffe gave at the symposium, "Scholars and Their Kin," New York University, March 2020. In France, too, personal family history "comes at greater risk for non-white scholars," writes Audrey Célestine. The same is true, of course, in other disciplines, where mistrust of female colleagues, "suspected of philosophizing with their bodies and emotions," can still run high. See Audrey Célestine, "A French Family: Navigating Racial Realities, Academic Imperatives and Political Stakes," *EuropeNow*, December 8, 2020, https://www.europenowjournal.org/2020/12/07/a-french-family-navigating-racial-realities-academic-imperatives-and-political-stakes/; Manon Garcia, "Qu'est-ce que la philosophie?" *Libération*, June 16, 2023. Célestine's personal family history is *Une famille française: Des Antilles à Dunkerque en passant par l'Algérie* (Paris: Textuel, 2018).

19. Alison Twells et al. make this point regarding all forms of experimental writing: "Undisciplined History: Creative Methods and Academic Practice," *History Workshop Journal* 96 (2023): 169.

20. Doctoral students are beginning to tap personal family histories in their dissertations. See, for instance, Kendra T. Field, *Growing Up with the Country: Family, Race, and Nation After the Civil War* (New Haven, CT: Yale University Press, 2018); Yvonne Horsfield, "A Ballarat Chinese Family Biography: An Intergenerational Study" (PhD diss., Federation University Australia, 2020); Natalie Fong, "Chinese Merchants in the Northern Territory, 1880–1950: A Translocal Case Study" (PhD diss., Griffith University [Australia], 2021); Madina Thiam, "Seeking Freedom in the Sahel: Frontiers of Liberation and Geographies of Belonging in an Atlantic-Saharan Crossroads" (PhD diss., UCLA, 2022); Malik Al Nasir, "Kinship Networks and Mercantile Hegemony in the Latter Days of British Slavery: The Case of Sandbach Tinne, c. 1790–1840," (PhD diss., University of Cambridge, in progress).

21. This event received logistical support from Isabelle Genest and Mariah Harvey, to whom I am grateful. In addition to the volume's contributors, I also want to thank the other speakers, respondents, and panel chairs: Edward Ball, Ed Berenson, Carolyn Dinshaw, Kendra T. Field, Ivan Jablonka, Claudio Lomnitz, and Frédéric Viguier. A few months earlier, Kendra T. Field had organized another conference that brought together historians of the US and the African diaspora who are writing about their families: "Writing Family, Reconstructing Lives" (Tufts University, Medford, MA, November 15, 2019), https://politicsofkinship.tufts.edu/events.

22. One participant elected not to contribute an essay. Clare Hemmings, an attendee that day, has joined the ranks of contributors, and so have I.

23. Claudio Lomnitz, *Nuestra América: My Family in the Vertigo of Translation* (New York: Other Press, 2021), 18.

24. Siegried Krakauer, "Photography," trans. Thomas Y. Levin, *Critical Inquiry* 19 (Spring 1993): 422, quoted in Afsaneh Najmabadi, *Familial Undercurrents: Untold Stories of Love and Marriage in Modern Iran* (Durham, NC: Duke University Press, 2022), 57.

25. Simone Weil, *The Need for Roots: Prelude to a Declaration of Duties towards Mankind*, trans. Arthur Wills (London: Routledge 2005 [1949]), 96.

26. Clémentine Vidal-Naquet, "Habiter l'intime?," *Sensibilités* 6 (2019): 6–9.

27. See, for instance, Vinciane Despret, *Our Grateful Dead: Stories of Those Left Behind*, trans. Stephen Muecke (Minneapolis: University of Minnesota Press, 2021); David Charles Sloane, *Is the Cemetery Dead?* (Chicago: University of Chicago Press, 2018). On genealogical writing and mournful consolation during an individualistic age, see Alexandre Gefen, *Réparer le monde: La littérature française face au XXIe siècle* (Paris: Corti, 2017), 240–41.

28. Rejecting tropes of pathology and dislocation, other African American personal family historians have depicted lives full of "tenderness and humor, family unity and affection . . . inner conviction, resilience, and inventiveness." See Ronne Hartfield, *Another Way Home: The Tangled Roots of Race in One Chicago Family* (Chicago: University of Chicago Press, 2004), xvi.

29. On family and "violent transactions," see Hazel V. Carby's profound *Imperial Intimacies: A Tale of Two Islands* (London: Verso, 2019). Also: Irene Kacandes, ed., *On Being Adjacent to Historical Violence* (Berlin: De Gruyter, 2022).

30. Personal family histories of complicity constitute a subgenre of their own: see, among other recent works, Edward Ball, *Life of a Klansman: A Family History in White Supremacy* (New York: FSG, 2021); Lucas Bessire, *Running Out in Search of Water on the High Plains* (Princeton, NJ: Princeton University Press, 2021); Cécile Desprairies, *La propagandiste* (Paris: Gallimard, 2023).

31. Christine Bard, *Jack* (Donnemarie-Dontilly, France: Éditions iXe, 2022), 179. On sites of forgetting: Philippe Artières, "Lieux d'oubli," in his *Rêves d'histoire: pour une histoire de l'ordinaire* (Paris: Prairies ordinaires, 2014), 116–20.

32. Renato Rosaldo, *Culture and Truth: The Remaking of Social Analysis* (Boston: Beacon Press, 1993), 181; James Davies and Dimitrina Spencer, eds., *Emotions in the Field: The Psychology and Anthropology of Fieldwork Experience* (Stanford, CA: Stanford University Press, 2010); Deborah B. Gould, *Moving Politics: Emotion and Act Up's Fight Against AIDS* (Chicago: University of Chicago Press, 2009).

33. Shobana Shankar, "Emotions as the New Ethical Turn in Social Research," SSRC *Items*, June 2020, https://items.ssrc.org/covid-19-and-the-social-sciences/social-research-and-insecurity /emotions-as-the-new-ethical-turn-in-social-research/.

34. Françoise N. Hamlin, "Historians and Ethics: Finding Anne Moody," *American Historical Review* 125, no. 2 (2020): 492; Alisse Waterston and Barbara Rylko-Bauer, "Out of the Shadows of History and Memory: Personal Family Narratives in Ethnographies of Rediscovery," *American Ethnologist* 33, no. 3 (2006): 405.

35. Marianne Hirsch, "The Generation of Postmemory," *Poetics Today* 29, no. 1 (2008): 104; "Difficult Stories and Ethical Dilemmas in Family History," History Workshop Podcast (2021), https://www.historyworkshop.org.uk/podcast/difficult-stories-and-ethical-dilemmas-in -family-history/.

36. Patrick McGuinness, *Other People's Stories: A Journey into Memory* (London: Vintage, 2015), 178. Scholars of family photography have set the agenda: Marianne Hirsch, ed., *The Familial Gaze* (Hanover, NH: University Press of New England, 1999); Marianne Hirsch, "Space, Materiality, and the Social Worlds of the Photograph," in *Imagining Everyday Life: Engagements with Vernacular Photography*, ed. Tina M. Campt et al. (Göttingen, Germany: Steidl, 2020), 279,

283; Petra Rau, "The Future Imperfect: Memoir and the Family Photograph," *European Journal of Life Writing* 12 (2023): 9–20. See also Solène Billaud et al., eds., *Histoires de famille. Les récits du passé dans la parenté contemporaine* (Paris: Éditions Rue d'Ulm, 2015); Hannah Holtschneider, "Narrating the Archive? Family Collections, the Archive, and the Historian," *Shofar* 37, no. 3 (2019): 331–60. Historians Caroline Muller and Nicolas Guyard recently organized a pathbreaking conference on family archives: "Des vies mémorables. Archives familiales ordinaires et sciences sociales" (Université Rennes 2, Rennes, France, May 2022).

37. Aaron Sachs, "Letters to a Tenured Historian: History as Creative Nonfiction—or Maybe Even Poetry," in *Artful History: A Practical Anthology*, ed. Aaron Sachs and John Demos (New Haven, CT: Yale University Press, 2020), 241; Pandian and McLean, prologue to *Crumpled Paper Boat*, 3; Lucas Bessire et al., "Reflections on Ethnographic Writing Today," October 16, 2017, https://culanth.org/fieldsights/reflections-on-ethnographic-writing-today.

38. Arlette Farge, *The Allure of the Archive*, trans. Thomas Scott-Railton (New Haven, CT: Yale University Press, 2013 [1989]), 123.

39. Nicole Lapierre, *Sauve qui peut la vie* (Paris: Éditions du Seuil, 2015), 184; "New Approaches to Writing History" (roundtable sponsored by the Royal Historical Society, London, UK, May 9, 2019), https://royalhistsoc.org/calendar/new-approaches-to-writing-history/. See also Kate Brown, *Dispatches from Dystopia: Histories of Places Not Yet Forgotten* (Chicago: University of Chicago Press, 2015), 1, 13, 145; *Parler de soi: Méthodes biographiques en sciences sociales* (Paris: Éditions de l'EHESS, 2020).

40. Michael Jackson, "After the Fact: The Question of Fidelity in Ethnographic Writing," in *Crumpled Paper Boat*, 48.

41. Renato Rosaldo, *The Days of Shelly's Death: The Poetry and Ethnography of Death* (Durham, NC: Duke University Press, 2014); Michael Jackson, *The Genealogical Imagination: Two Studies of Life Over Time* (Durham, NC: Duke University Press, 2021).

42. Frazier, *Notion of Family*, 64.

43. David A. Bell, "Ego-Histories," *New York Review of Books*, June 22, 2023

44. Frazier, conversation with Dawoud Bey, in *Notion of Family*, 153.

45. Nathalie Léger, *The White Dress*, trans. Natasha Leher (St. Louis: Dorothy, 2020 [2018]), 40. On family secrets and shame: Sherene Seikaly, "How I Met My Great-Grandfather: Archives and the Writing of History," *Comparative Studies of South Asia, Africa and the Middle East* 38, no. 1 (2018): 12.

46. Brett L. Walker, *A Family History of Illness: Memory as Medicine* (Seattle: University of Washington Press, 2018).

47. Angelika Bammer, "Mother Tongues and Other Strangers: Writing 'Family' Across Cultural Divides," in *Displacements: Cultural Identities in Question*, ed. Bammer (Bloomington: Indiana University Press, 1994), 105.

48. Field, "Privilege of Family History," 631. See also Saidiya Hartman, *Lose Your Mother: A Journey along the Atlantic Slave Route* (New York: FSG, 2008).

49. Frazier, "Creative Solution," 19; Frazier, untitled contribution to *Kinship*, ed. Dorothy Moss et al. (Munich, Germany: Hirmer, 2022), 49.

Chapter One: What's in a Name?

Thank you to my collaborator, Alex Trapps-Chabala, without whom I would have been unable to write this history; and to Emily Clark for her perceptive edits and suggestions.

1. Spike Lee, *When the Levees Broke: A Requiem in Four Acts* (New York: HBO, 2006), DVD. Cheryl Harris and Devon Carbado, "Loot or Find? Fact or Frame?" in *After the Storm: Black Intellectuals Explore the Meaning of Hurricane Katrina*, ed. David Dante Troutt (New York: New Press, 2007) details some of the ways in which media coverage constrained our understanding of those most harmed by Hurricane Katrina. In contrast, Michael Eric Dyson's *Come Hell or High Water: Hurricane Katrina and the Color of Disaster* (New York: Basic Civitas, 2006) only briefly discusses the specifics of New Orleans as an entrée to a larger, albeit necessary, argument about the failures of government action in the early 2000s. Andy Horowitz's *Katrina: A History, 1900–2015* (Cambridge, MA: Harvard University Press, 2020) effectively pushes back against the limits of many of the early books published soon after 2005 by carefully combining attention to the local political and economic context with the larger national framework.

2. Kent Germany, *New Orleans After the Promises: Poverty, Citizenship, and the Search for the Great Society* (Athens: University of Georgia Press, 2007); Arnold Hirsch, "Simply a Matter of Black and White: The Transformation of Race and Politics in Twentieth-Century New Orleans," in *Creole New Orleans: Race and Americanization*, ed. Arnold Hirsch and Joseph Logsdon (Baton Rouge: Louisiana State University Press, 1992), 262–320; Gavin Wright, *Sharing the Prize: The Economics of the Civil Rights Revolution in the American South* (Cambridge, MA: Harvard University Press, 2013).

3. Hirsch and Logsdon, *Creole New Orleans*; Gwendolyn Midlo Hall, *Africans in Colonial Louisiana: The Development of Afro-Creole Culture in the Eighteenth Century* (Baton Rouge: Louisiana State University Press, 1992); Jennifer Spear, *Race, Sex, and Social Order in Early New Orleans* (Baltimore: Johns Hopkins University Press, 2009); Kimberly S. Hangar, *Bounded Lives, Bounded Places: Free Black Society in Colonial New Orleans, 1769–1803* (Durham, NC: Duke University Press, 1997).

4. Ira Berlin, *Slaves Without Masters: The Free Negro in the Antebellum South* (New York: Pantheon, 1974).

5. On myths about plaçage in New Orleans, see Kenneth Aslakson, "The Quadroon-Plaçage Myth of Antebellum New Orleans: Anglo-American (Mis)interpretations of a French-Caribbean Phenomenon," *Journal of Social History* 45 (Spring 2012): 709–34; Emily Clark, *The Strange History of the American Quadroon: Free Women of Color in the Revolutionary Atlantic* (Chapel Hill: University of North Carolina Press, 2013). On the realities of intimate interracial relationships, see Spear, *Race, Sex and Social Order*; Hangar, *Bounded Lives, Bounded Places*, 90–94; quote on 92; Kimberly Welch, "The Stability of Fortunes: A Free Black Woman, Her Legacy, and the Legal Archive in Antebellum New Orleans," *Journal of the Civil War Era* 12 (December 2022): 479–80. On relationships within the community of free people of color, see Clark, *Strange History*. On intimate relationships throughout the South, see Joshua Rothman, *Notorious in the Neighborhood: Sex and Families Across the Color Line in Virginia, 1781–1861* (Chapel Hill: University of North Carolina Press, 2003), esp. 204–34; Annette Gordon-Reed, *The Hemingses of Monticello: An American Family* (New York: Norton, 2008), esp. 80–90, 120–21, 536–40; Feay Shellman Coleman, "Salley and Her Children: Maria, Emma and John Charles Gibbons," in *Slavery and Freedom in Savannah*, ed. Leslie M. Harris and Daina Raney Berry (Athens: University of Georgia Press, 2011), 89–90; Michael P. Johnson and James L. Roark, *Black Masters: A Free Family of Color in the Old South* (New York: Norton, 1984); Kent Leslie, *Woman of Color, Daughter of Privilege: Amanda America Dickerson, 1849–1893* (Athens: University of Georgia Press, 1995).

6. Aslakson, "Quadroon-Plaçage Myth," 715–18; Kenneth Aslakson, *Making Race in the Courtroom: The Legal Construction of Three Races in New Orleans* (New York: New York University Press, 2014), 109–17; Clark, *Strange History*.

7. Leonard P. Curry, *The Free Black in Urban America, 1800–1850: The Shadow of the Dream* (Chicago: University of Chicago Press, 1981), 22–26, 29, 39–44.

8. Kimberly S. Hanger, "Origins of New Orleans's Free Creoles of Color," in *Creoles of Color of the Gulf South*, ed. James H. Dormon (Knoxville: University of Tennessee Press, 1996), 1–23; Hanger, *Bounded Lives, Bounded Places*, 17–54; quote on 17–18.

9. Hangar, *Bounded Lives, Bounded Places*, 55–87.

10. Richard Wade, *Slavery in the Cities: The South, 1820–1860* (New York: Oxford University Press, 1964), app., "Free Negro Population by Sex," 329; Curry, *Free Black in Urban America*, tbl. A-10, "Ratio of Females to Each Male in the Populations of Fifteen Cities, 1820–50," 253.

11. Hangar, *Bounded Lives, Bounded Places*, chap. 2; Aslakson, *Making Race in the Courtroom*, 108ff. Welch, "The Stability of Fortunes," details the ways in which Eulalie Mandeville, a free woman of African descent, was a more successful businesswoman than Eugene Macarty, her common law white husband. Through a series of court cases, she was able to argue that she had built the wealth of their household.

12. On the sexual myths surrounding the New Orleans Creole community, Clark, *Strange History*. On skilled labor among Creoles of African descent, Hangar, *Bounded Lives, Bounded Places*; Jonn Ethan Hankins, Steven Maklansky, and New Orleans Museum of Art, *Raised to the Trade: Creole Building Arts of New Orleans* (New Orleans: New Orleans Museum of Art, 2002); Darryl G. Barthé, *Becoming American in Creole New Orleans, 1896–1949* (Baton Rouge: Louisiana State University Press, 2021). On sexual myths about enslaved Black people, especially Black women, Deborah Gray White, *Ar'n't I a Woman? Female Slaves in the Plantation South* (1985; New York: Norton, 1999), 27–62; Jennifer L. Morgan, "'Some Could Suckle Over Their Shoulder': Male Travelers, Female Bodies, and the Gendering of Racial Ideology, 1500–1770," *William and Mary Quarterly* 54 (January 1997): 167–92; Stephanie M. H. Camp, "Early European Views of African Bodies: Beauty," in *Sexuality and Slavery: Reclaiming Intimate Histories in the Americas*, ed. Daina Ramey Berry and Leslie M. Harris (Athens: University of Georgia Press, 2018), 9–32.

13. Keith Weldon Medley, *We as Freemen: Plessy v. Ferguson* (Gretna, LA: Pelican, 2003).

14. Joseph Logsdon and Caryn Cossé Bell, "The Americanization of Black New Orleans," in Hirsch and Logsdon, *Creole New Orleans*, 204–15; Arnold R. Hirsch, "Simply a Matter of Black and White: The Transformation of Race and Politics in Twentieth-Century New Orleans," in Hirsch and Logsdon, *Creole New Orleans*, 262–319; Barthé, *Becoming American*; Angel Adams Parham, *American Routes: Racial Palimpsests and the Transformation of Race* (New York: Oxford University Press, 2017); Audrey Elisa Kerr, "The Paper Bag Principle: Of the Myth and the Motion of Colorism," *Journal of American Folklore* 118, no. 469 (2005): 271–89.

15. Clark, *Strange History*; Mary Bernard Deggs, Virginia Meacham Gould, and Charles E. Nolan, *No Cross, No Crown: Black Nuns in Nineteenth-Century New Orleans* (Bloomington: Indiana University Press, 2001); Shannen Dee Williams, *Subversive Habits: Black Catholic Nuns in the Long African American Freedom Struggle* (Durham, NC: Duke University Press, 2022), 25–26, 34–42.

16. Berlin, *Slaves Without Masters*.

17. Daniel H. Usner, *American Indians in Early New Orleans: From Calumet to Raquette* (Baton Rouge: Louisiana State University Press, 2018); Daniel H. Usner, *Indians, Settlers and Slaves in a Frontier Exchange Economy: The Lower Mississippi Valley Before 1783* (Chapel Hill: University of North Carolina Press, 1992); Gwendolyn Midlo Hall, *Africans in Colonial Louisiana: The Development of Afro-Creole Culture in the Eighteenth Century* (Baton Rouge: Louisiana State University Press, 1992).

18. Claudio Saunt, *Unworthy Republic: The Dispossession of Native Americans and the Road to Indian Territory* (New York: Norton, 2022).

19. Alice Dunbar-Nelson, "Brass Ankles Speaks," in *The Works of Alice Dunbar-Nelson*, vol. 2, ed. Gloria T. Hull (New York: Oxford, 1988), 311–21; essay quoted in Tara T. Green, *Love, Activism and the Respectable Life of Alice Dunbar Nelson* (New York: Bloomsbury, 2021), 1–2. With thanks to Martha S. Jones for alerting me to these sources.

20. Jordan B. Noble, Declaration for an Original Invalid Pension, Orleans Parish, Louisiana, June 15, 1880. War of 1812 Pension and Bounty Land Warrant Application Files, Record Group 15, Records of the Veterans' Administration, National Archives, Library of Congress, Folder 3, p. 12, https://catalog.archives.gov/id/187122184.

21. Sister Dorothea Olga McCants, trans. and ed., *Our People and Our History*, by Rodolphe Lucien Desdunes (Baton Rouge: Louisiana State University Press, 1973), 14. Although the title of the book is *Nos Hommes*, which is usually translated as "Our Men," there is a chapter on women, translated as "The Creole Women of Color in the Catholic Churches—The Generosity of Madame Bernard Couvent."

22. Roland C. McConnell, *Negro Troops of Antebellum Louisiana: A History of the Battalion of Free Men of Color* (Baton Rouge: Louisiana State University Press, 1968), 56–90; Gerard T. Altoff, *Amongst My Best Men: African-Americans and the War of 1812* (Put-in-Bay, OH: Perry Group, 1996), 144–60.

23. Allyson Hobbs, *A Chosen Exile: A History of Racial Passing in American Life* (Cambridge, MA: Harvard University Press, 2014), 11–13; quote on 13.

24. Toni Morrison, *Beloved* (New York: Knopf, 1987), 274–75.

Chapter Two: What Did I Do with the One I Lost?

1. Sophie Calle, *Que faites-vous de vos morts?* (Arles, France: Actes Sud, 2019).

2. Pierre Michon, *Small Lives*, trans. Jody Gladding and Elizabeth Deshays (Brooklyn, NY: Archipelago Books, 2008); Jean-François Laé, *Une fille en correction* (Paris: CNRS Éditions, 2018); Arlette Farge, *Vies oubliées* (Paris: La Découverte, 2019).

3. Camille Lefebvre asks the same question regarding history: *A l'ombre de l'histoire des autres* (Paris: Editions de l'EHESS, 2022).

4. I will address the last questions below. Regarding the first two, see Christine Détrez et Karine Bastide, *Nos mères. Huguette, Christiane et tant d'autres. Une histoire de l'émancipation féminine* (Paris: La Découverte, 2020); Christine Détrez, *Pour te ressembler* (Paris: Denoël, 2021).

5. Translator's note: *Coopérants* were public employees whom the French state assigned to medical, engineering, and, in the case of the author's father, teaching positions in former French colonies and protectorates. They would promote socioeconomic development in the postcolonial period.

6. Translator's note: The documentary was originally released in French as *Histoire d'un secret* in 2003.

7. Translator's note: The film's title translates as "Plot 35," a reference to a burial plot.

8. Ivan Jablonka, *A History of the Grandparents I Never Had*, trans. Jane Kuntz (Stanford, CA: Stanford University Press, 2016); Daniel Mendelsohn, *The Lost: A Search for Six of Six Million* (New York: HarperCollins, 2006); Philippe Sands, *East West Street: On the Origins of Genocide and Crimes against Humanity* (New York: Knopf, 2016).

9. Marguerite Yourcenar, *Dear Departed*, trans. Maria Louise Ascher (New York: FSG, 1991), 52.

10. Translator's note: Copies of French birth records can be requested in either an abridged version or as a *copie intégrale*, a complete record that lists the parents' names, birthdates, and places of birth. When applicable, the individual's wedding and death dates are recorded in the *mentions marginales*, or marginal notes.

11. The *écoles normales d'instituteurs et d'institutrices*, also called *écoles normales primaires*, were teacher training schools created in France at the beginning of the nineteenth century (1810 for the first men's school, 1838 for the first women's school). They prepared students for careers in primary schools.

12. Since 1959, middle schools have welcomed all the children of the same age category, from sixth grade (age eleven) to ninth grade (age fourteen).

13. Before beginning this research, I had only ever briefly met my maternal grandparents. I did not know my uncles (my mother's brothers) nor their children, my cousins.

14. Georges Perec, *L'infra-ordinaire* (Paris: Éditions du Seuil, 1989).

15. Dominique Memmi, "Mai 68 ou la crise de la domination rapprochée," in *Mai-juin 68*, ed. Dominique Damamme et al. (Paris: Éditions de l'Atelier, 2008).

16. Françoise Picq, *Libération des femmes, les années mouvement* (Paris: Éditions du Seuil, 1993).

17. Francine Muel-Dreyfus, *Le métier d'éducateur. Les instituteurs de 1900. Les éducateurs de 1968* (Paris: Minuit, 1983).

18. Sue Fischer and Kathy Davis, eds., *Negotiating at the Margins: The Gendered Discourses of Power and Resistance* (New Brunswick, NJ: Rutgers University Press, 1993); Nancy Fraser, *Unruly Practices: Power, Discourse, Gender in Contemporary Social Theory* (Minneapolis: University of Minnesota Press, 1989).

19. Janice Radway, *Reading the Romance* (Chapel Hill: University of North Carolina Press, 1984).

20. Eleni Varikas, "Subjectivité et identité de genre. L'univers de l'éducation féminine dans la Grèce au XIXe siècle," *Genèses* 6 (1991): 29–51.

21. Catherine Achin and Delphine Naudier, "L'agency en contexte: Réflexion sur les processus d'émancipation des femmes dans les années 70 en France," *Cahiers du genre* 2, no. 55 (2013): 109–30.

22. For an analysis of these investigations as a literary genre, see Laurent Demanze, *Un nouvel âge de l'enquête. Portrait de l'écrivain contemporain en enquêteur* (Paris: Corti, 2019).

23. Mendelsohn, *The Lost*, 73.

24. Anne Muxel, *Individu et mémoire familiale* (Paris: Nathan, 1996), 197.

25. Roland Barthes, *Camera Lucida: Reflections on Photography*, trans. Richard Howard (New York: Hill & Wang, 1981), 65.

26. Georges Perec, *Things: A Story of the Sixties*, trans. David Bellos (Boston: Godine, 1990 [1965]).

27. Vinciane Despret, *Our Grateful Dead: Stories of Those Left Behind*, trans. Stephen Muecke (Minneapolis: University of Minnesota Press, 2021 [2015]), 47.

28. Françoise Waquet, *Une histoire émotionnelle du savoir: XVIIe–XXIe siècle* (Paris: CNRS Éditions, 2019).

29. Despret, *Our Grateful Dead*, 11–12.

30. In addition to the two books cited above, I will also mention my daughter's documentary: Lilia Mercklé-Détrez, *Filatures* (Paris: Cinéfabrique, 2021).

Chapter Three: The Diary of a Twelve-Year-Old Hostage

Text excerpted and adapted by the author, from *My Hijacking: A Personal History of Forgetting and Remembering* by Martha Hodes. Copyright © 2023 by Martha Hodes. Used by permission of HarperCollins Publishers.

1. The PFLP, founded in 1967, had become an influential militant minority faction within the Palestine Liberation Organization by September 1970. With a strategy of armed resistance, its goal was a secular, democratic state for Jews, Muslims, and Christians, along with "modernization" and women's liberation. On the origins and aims of the PFLP, see, for example, "First Political Statement Issued by the Popular Front for the Liberation of Palestine," *Al-Hurriyah*, November 12, 1967, in *International Documents on Palestine, 1967*, ed. Fuad A. Jabber (Beirut: Institute for Palestine Studies, 1970), 723–36; *The Military Strategy of the PFLP* (Beirut: Information Department PFLP, 1970); As'ad AbuKhalil, "Internal Contradictions in the PFLP: Decision Making and Policy Orientation," *Middle East Journal* 41 (1987): 361–78; Paul Lalor, "Black September 1970: The Palestinian Resistance Movement in Jordan, 1967–1971" (PhD diss., Saint Anthony's College, Oxford University, 1992). More generally, see Helena Cobban, *The Palestinian Liberation Organisation: People, Power and Politics* (New York: Cambridge University Press, 1984); Alain Gresh, *The PLO: The Struggle Within; Towards an Independent Palestinian State* (London: Zed, 1985); Yezid Sayigh, *Armed Struggle and the Search for State: The Palestinian National Movement, 1949–1993* (New York: Oxford University Press, 1997).

2. David Phillips, *Skyjack: The Story of Air Piracy* (London: Harrap, 1973), 140 ("remarkable"); June Haesler conversation with author, New York, October 14, 2019, recalling Kiburis ("news").

3. "Airstrip of the Guerrillas Was Once R. A. F. Field," *New York Times*, September 10, 1970; "Situation Report as of 0600 Hours EST," September 7, 1970, Near Eastern Affairs Working Group, State Department, folder 2, box 330, Subject Files: Hijacking, National Security Council Files, Nixon Presidential Materials Staff, Richard Nixon Presidential Library and Museum, Yorba Linda, CA (hereafter RNL) (thirty miles); Statement of First Officer J. A. Majer, p. 2, Trans World Airlines Records, box 168, KO453, Manuscript Collection, State Historical Society of Missouri, Columbia (hereafter TWA) ("greaser"); Carroll D. Woods, "Hijacking Report of TWA Flt. 741 of September 6, 1970," Prairie Village, Kansas, October 16, 1970, TWA (no damage); Rodney C. Campbell, "TWA Flight 741—Hijacked September 6, 1970," *TARPA Topics*, November 2007, p. 58 (celebration); Jim Majer, "Black September, 1970," *TARPA Topics*, November 2009, p. 13 (triumphant); Sylvia R. Jacobson, "Individual and Group Responses to Confinement in a Skyjacked Plane," *American Journal of Orthopsychiatry* 43 (1973): 460; Majer statement, p. 2; "Combined Statement of Hostesses: B. McCarthy, R. Metzner, V. McVey, L. Jensen," p. 2, TWA (People).

4. Sylvia R. Jacobson, untitled notes, folder 10, box 1, Jacobson Papers, MS-681, Jacob Rader Marcus Center of the American Jewish Archives, Cincinnati, OH (hereafter SRJ-AJA) ("safe and welcome"); Bassam Abu-Sharif and Uzi Mahnaimi, *Best of Enemies: The Memoirs of Bassam Abu-Sharif and Uzi Mahnaimi* (Boston: Little, Brown, 1995), 83 (sorry); Statement of Flight Engineer A. Kiburis, p. 2, TWA (passports); "Combined Statement of Hostesses," p. 2 (milk and water); Statement of Hostess J. Haesler, pp. 2–3, TWA (ambulance, doctor, cabin crew).

5. Jacobson, "Individual and Group Responses," 463 (cat's cradle); Sylvia R. Jacobson, "Children's Attitudinal and Behavioral Responses to Skyjack and Hostage Experiences," draft ts., 1976, folder 9, box 1, p. 11, SRJ-AJA ("Don't cry"); David Raab, *Terror in Black September: The First*

Eyewitness Account of the Infamous 1970 Hijackings (New York: Palgrave Macmillan, 2007), 30, quoting 1970 recollections ("one lady").

6. Rudolf Swinkels crew report, courtesy of June Haesler, p. 4 (weapons); Vicki McVey, quoted in Campbell, "TWA Flight 741," 60 ("catch"); William Montgomery, "Mrs. Burnett Recounts Her Ordeal," *Albuquerque Journal*, September 16, 1970 ("bullets"); deposition in lawsuit brought by hostage against Trans World Airlines, citation redacted for privacy ("trust"); Fran Chesler, "The Saga of a Flight: TWA Flight 741, September 6–September 28, 1970," unpublished ms., Fall 1970, part II, 1 ("Zoo").

7. Paul Martin, "Biscuits and Water Diet for Hijacked Britons," *London Times*, September 11, 1970 ("manned"); Intelligence Information Cable, "Government of Jordan intentions regarding hijacked TWA and Swissair airliners," September 8, 1970, folder 2, box 330, Subject Files: Hijacking, National Security Council Files, Nixon Presidential Materials Staff, RNL (surrounded).

8. Abu-Sharif and Mahnaimi, *Best of Enemies*, 85 ("colleagues"); Statement of Flight Engineer A. Kiburis, p. 2, TWA (watched); June Haesler conversation, New York, NY, October 14, 2019 ("Don't").

9. United Press International-Cairo, September 7, 1970, folder 2, box 330, Subject Files: Hijacking, National Security Council Files, Nixon Presidential Materials Staff, RNL ("guerrilla leaders").

10. "First Women and Children Freed—'Well Treated,'" *Egyptian Gazette*, September 13, 1970 ("threats"); William Lewis Burmeister, *Sky-Jacked by PFLP Pirates: To Nowhere and Back* (self-pub., 2011), 28 ("cannot wait").

11. Interview by Jeremy Cole and A. J. Sullivan, New York, September 20, 1970, original tape.

12. Stuart Hodes interview by John Gruen, New York, April 27, May 4, 1976, Jerome Robbins Dance Division Oral History Project, New York Public Library for the Performing Arts ("heading," Graham).

13. Eric Pace, "Released Hostages Tell of Their Ordeal in Desert," *New York Times*, September 13, 1970; "Quotation of the Day," *New York Times*, September 13, 1970.

14. Jacobson, "Individual and Group Responses," 459–69.

15. "Messages pour les otages transmis par la Croix-Rouge américaine," September 11, 12, 1970, B AG 226-004, Archives of the International Committee of the Red Cross (Comité International de la Croix Rouge), Geneva, Switzerland.

16. New York Dance Festival program, September 5, 6 1970, New York Shakespeare Festival Records, *T-Mss 1993-028, Billy Rose Theatre Division, New York Public Library for the Performing Arts; Don McDonagh, "Dance: Choreographers Have Their Day at Park," *New York Times*, September 7, 1970.

17. For versions of this story, see Stuart Hodes, "Listen Up and Fly Right: Flying, Dancing, & the Meaning of Life," unpub. ms. 2015, 115–16, and Stuart Hodes, *Onstage with Martha Graham* (Gainesville: University Press of Florida, 2021), 249–50.

18. Jennifer Brewer, "The Protegé, the Professor," *Dance Teacher* 25 (January 2003): 50–53; Clay Taliaferro email, April 20, 2019.

19. Murray Sayle, "Confusion as British Reach Hotel," *Sunday Times* (London), September 13, 1970 ("never"); Jesse W. Lewis Jr., "'They Awoke Him . . . and Took Him,'" *Washington Post*, September 13, 1970 ("unlikely"); J. F. S. Phillips "The Dawson Field Hijackings," Diplomatic Report No. 567/70, Jordan, December 22, 1970, pp. 9, 2, Foreign and Commonwealth Office, FCO 17/1374, National Archives of the United Kingdom, Kew, England ("break down"); Bassam Abu-Sharif on-camera interview, "Hijacked," written and directed by Ilan Ziv, *American Experience*, PBS, 2006 ("not to hurt").

20. Jenvizian quoted in Campbell, "TWA Flight 741," 55. Al Kiburis interviewed in "Jordan Hostages," *CBS Evening News*, September 27, 1970, #212445, Vanderbilt Television News Archive, Nashville, TN (hereafter VTNA).

21. United Press International-Cairo, September 7, 1970, folder 2, box 330, Subject Files: Hijacking, National Security Council Files, Nixon Presidential Materials Staff, RNL ("demolition"); Amman to Washington #4372, September 7, 1970, boxes 683–84, RG59, State Department, National Archives and Records Administration, Washington, DC, and College Park, MD (hereafter NARA) ("Time period"); Henry Kissinger to Richard Nixon, "Evening Report on the Hijacking Situation," September [9], 1970, folder marked September 8–14, 1970, 2 of 2, box 971, Alexander M. Haig Chronological Files, National Security Council Files, Nixon Presidential Materials Staff , RNL ("tragedy"); Amman to Washington #4495, September 9, 1970, RG59, State Department, NARA, in *Foreign Relations of the United States*, vol. E-1, Documents on Global Issues (Washington, DC, 2005), document #53, p. 371 ("destroys"); "Contingencies for Hijacking Crisis," September 9, 1970, folder labeled: "Middle East and Hijacking, 9/9/70," box H-077, Meetings Files, Washington Special Actions Group Meetings, National Security Council Institutional "H" Files, Nixon Presidential Materials Staff, RNL ("murdered," "massacre"); Amman to Washington #4521, September 9, 1970, 20:32Z, folder 2, box 330, Subject Files: Hijacking, National Security Council Files, Nixon Presidential Materials Staff, RNL ("rescue"); "Mideast Crisis and American Credibility," *Congressional Record*, September 10, 1970, p. 31180 ("Today"); "Palestinian Hijacks/BOAC/Threats," *NBC Evening News*, September 9, 1970, #453523, VTNA ("Arabs said"); "Ordeal in the Desert," *New York Times*, September 9, 1970 ("cold-bloodedly").

22. Richard White, *Remembering Ahanagran: A History of Stories* (Seattle: University of Washington Press, 1998), 4.

23. Jonathan Scott Holloway, *Jim Crow Wisdom: Memory and Identity in Black America since 1940* (Chapel Hill: University of North Carolina Press, 2013), 8, 9. Of course the archives are suspect too, and both White and Holloway acknowledge this (see White, *Remembering Ahanagran*, 302–3, and Holloway, 10). Interview by Cole and Sullivan, original tape ("wasn't okay").

Chapter Four: Peïra Cava, Hollow Stone

The following abbreviations are used: ADAM (Archives départementales des Alpes-Maritimes, Nice), AHGT (Archives historiques du Groupe Total Énergie, Paris), AMN (Archives municipales de Nice), AOL (Archives de l'Ordre de la Libération, Paris), SHD (Service historique de la Défense, Paris). I am grateful to Alison Gerson, Francine Gerson, Clare Hemmings, and Paula Schwartz for their close readings of this essay.

1. Judith Lyon-Caen, "Les mots et les récits des morts," *Revue d'histoire moderne & contemporaine* 65, no. 2 (2018): 54–67.

2. Mary Jo Maynes, Jennifer Pierce, and Barbara Laslett, *Telling Stories: The Use of Personal Narratives in the Social Sciences and History* (Ithaca, NY: Cornell University Press, 2008). Other scholars of the Second World War have recently made the family a central frame of analysis: Natalia Aleksiun, "A Familial Turn in Holocaust Scholarship?" in *If This Is a Woman: Studies on Women and Gender in the Holocaust*, ed. Denisa Nešťáková et al. (Boston: Academic Studies Press, 2021), 20–42.

3. See Alison Light, *Common People: The History of an English Family* (New York: Penguin/Fig Tree, 2014), 130.

4. Matthew Desmond, "Relational Ethnography," *Theory and Society* 43, no. 5 (2014): 547–79.

5. Kate Brown, *Dispatches from Dystopia: Histories of Places Not Yet Forgotten* (Chicago: University of Chicago Press, 2015), 55.

6. Stéphane F., video conversation with the author, November 14, 2022; marriage certificate between Marie C. and César Louis F., October 4, 1905, online database, ADAM; *Guide annuaire régional de Cannes et de l'arrondissement de Grasse* 16 (1908): 303.

7. Civil tribunal of Nice, audience of January 19, 1919, 3U 1/856, ADAM; César Louis F., conscription record, 1 R 846/243, Archives départementales du Var (Toulon); César Louis F., death certificate, January 5, 1917, French Ministry of War, https://www.memoiredeshommes.sga.defense.gouv.fr; Olivier Faron, *Les enfants du deuil: Orphelins et pupilles de la nation de la première guerre mondiale (1914–1941)* (Paris: La Découverte, 2001), 190–94.

8. Annie B. and Charles B., personnel records, Desmarais frères oil company, 16VA05265, AHGT; Director of the *École pratique de commerce et d'industrie de jeunes filles de Nice* [henceforth: *École pratique*], annual reports for 1919–20 and 1931–32, 5ETP 332, ADAM; Table of pupils admitted into the *École pratique*, June 20, 1921, 1T 233, ADAM; Marianne Thivend, "L'enseignement commercial aux XIXe et XXe siècles approché par le genre. Bilan historiographique et pistes de recherche," *Histoire de l'éducation* 136 (2012): 31; Marie-France Bishop, "Si le Certificat d'études m'était conté," *Le français aujourd'hui* 161, no. 2 (2008): 123.

9. Director of the *École pratique*, annual report for 1922–23, 5ETP 332, ADAM; Marriage certificate of Anaïs B. and Charles B., September 9, 1930, online database, ADAM; Nice census of 1936, 1F 57, AMN. Also: Susan Bachrach, "La féminisation des PTT en France au tournant du siècle," *Le mouvement social* 140 (1987): 83–84; Delphine Gardey, *La dactylographe et l'expéditionnaire. Histoire des employés de bureau (1890–1950)* (Paris: Belin, 2001), 84, 175; Christine Bard, *Les femmes dans la société française au 20e siècle* (Paris: Armand Colin, 2012), 62–64.

10. Monique F., email message to the author, September 17, 2022; Gardey, ibid., 176.

11. Marriage certificate of Anaïs B. and Charles B., op. cit.; Yvan Gastaut and Robert Matthey, *Sant Roc, un quartier niçois* (Nice, France: Ville de Nice, 2016), 22–23, 30; Alain Ruggiero, "Dépôt, ateliers ferroviaires et influences sur l'urbanisation: Le cas niçois," *Revue d'histoire des chemins de fer* 28–29 (2003): 391–402. I am grateful to Yvan Gastaut and Véronique Thuin-Chaudron for sharing their deep knowledge of Nice's neighborhoods.

12. Deed of sale, 21 October, 1940, records of the notary Dumarquez (Nice), 3E 114/1190, ADAM; Michel Massimi, *Cimiez, la banlieue champêtre de Nice* (Nice, France: Campanile, 2021), 194–95; Véronique Thuin-Chaudron, "Cimiez au XIXe siècle: Le phénix qui renaît de ses cendres. Les transformations d'une campagne niçoise en un pôle du tourisme international," *Nice historique* 119, nos. 3–4 (2016): 148–77; Nice census of 1946, 1F 66, AMN; Charles Rocca, building application, November 7, 1929, 2T 583, AMN; Société Riviera Park Hotel housing development, bill of sale, April 3, 1933, 3T 402, AMN.

13. Annie B., personnel record, 16VA05265, AHGT; Miranda Pollard, *Reign of Virtue: Mobilizing Gender in Vichy France* (Chicago: University of Chicago Press, 1998), 150–51.

14. Marguerite Faure, police interrogation, June 21, 1946, 2500W 91, ADAM. On Charles's professional trajectory, see his personnel record as a policeman, 14W 101, Archives départementales des Bouches-du-Rhône (Marseille).

15. Federico Varese and Meir Yaish, "The Importance of Being Asked: The Rescue of Jews in Nazi Europe," *Rationality and Society* 12, no. 3 (2000): 307.

16. *L'Éclaireur du dimanche*, January 4, 1925; Patrick Modiano, *Dimanches d'août* (Paris: Folio, 1986), 66.

17. "École pratique de commerce et d'industrie de jeunes filles de Nice" (Nice, France: Gimello, n.d.), 4, 5ETP 332, ADAM. ·

18. Stéphane F., video conversation with the author, November 14, 2022; Monique F., email message to the author, September 17, 2022; Fortuné Dandreis, Resistance certification request, GR 16 P 156058, SHD.

19. Étienne F., Resistance certification file, GR 16 P 220564, SHD. This discussion also rests on Étienne F., dossier for the Médaille de la Résistance, June 13, 1945, AOL; Jean-Louis Crémieux-Brillhac, *La France libre: De l'appel du 18 juin à la Liberation*, 2 vols. (Paris: Folio, 2001), 1:123.

20. Jean-François Muracciole, *Les Français libres. L'autre Résistance* (Paris: Tallandier, 2009), 176, 230–31; Jean-François Muracciole, "Les Français libres: Les modalités de l'engagement," in *La France Libre: Actes du colloque international*, ed. Francois Broche (Panazol, France: Lavauzelle, 2005), 20–22, 28; Stéphane F., video conversation with the author, November 14, 2022.

21. Patrick Cabanel, *Histoire des Justes en France* (Paris: Armand Colin, 2012).

22. Annette Wieviorka, *Tombeaux. Autobiographie de ma famille* (Paris: Éditions du Seuil, 2022), 239.

23. Anne Boitel, *Le camp de Rivesaltes, 1941–1942: Du centre d'hébergement au "Drancy de la zone libre"* (Perpignan, France: Presses universitaires de Perpignan, 2021), 237–40; Alexandre Doulut, "La déportation des Juifs de France: changement d'échelle" (PhD diss., Université Paris 1 Panthéon Sorbonne, 2021), 245–46, 297.

24. On the historiographical debate regarding Italian occupying forces and Jews, see Alberto Cavaglion, "Juifs étrangers dans l'arc alpin occidental (1939–1945)," in *Le refuge et le piège: Les Juifs dans les Alpes, 1938–1945*, ed. Jean-William Dereymez (Paris: L'Harmattan, 2008), 188–97.

25. Claire Mauss-Copeaux, *À travers le viseur: Images d'appelés en Algérie, 1955–1962* (Lyon, France: Aedelsa, 2003), 78. See also Hadas Zahavi, "The Snap-Witness" (unpublished manuscript); Nancy Martha West, *Kodak and the Lens of Nostalgia* (Charlottesville: University Press of Virginia, 2000). I thank Hadas Zahavi for providing me with a copy of her article-in-progress.

26. Stéphane Audoin-Rouzeau, "A voix nue," episode 2, France Culture, November 15, 2022. On photo albums and affective ties: Doriane Molay, "L'album photographique: Une famille affective?," *Enfances Familles Générations* 40 (2022), https://journals.openedition.org/efg/13797.

27. Director of the *École pratique*, annual report for 1922–23, 5ETP 332, ADAM; "École pratique de commerce et d'industrie de jeunes filles de Nice," op. cit.; Frédérique El Amrani Boisseau, *Filles de la terre: Apprentissages au féminin (Anjou 1920–1950)* (Rennes, France: Presses universitaires de Rennes, 2019), 40, 403. Here and below, my discussion of fashion benefited from exchanges with historian Sophie Kurkdjian.

28. Tables of forenames in France since 1900, https://www.insee.fr/fr/statistiques/3532172.

29. André Gunthert, *Pourquoi sourit-on en photographie?* (Lyon, France: Éditions Deux-Cent-Cinq, 2023).

30. Camille Ménager, "Roundups, Rescue, and Social Networks in Paris (1940–1944)," in *Resisting Genocide: The Multiple Forms of Rescue*, ed. Jacques Sémelin et al. (New York: Columbia University Press, 2013), 415–25; Catherine Masson, "Des femmes et le sauvetage des juifs dans le Nord-Pas-de-Calais," in *Femmes et résistance en Belgique et en zone interdite*, ed. Robert Vandenbussche (Lille France: Publications de l'Institut de recherches historiques du Septentrion, 2007), 105–24; Claire Andrieu, *When Men Fell from the Sky: Civilians and Downed Airmen in Second World War Europe*, trans. Ethan S. Rundell (Cambridge, UK: Cambridge University Press, 2023).

31. Bard, *Femmes dans la société française*, 45; Director of the *École pratique*, annual reports for 1919–20 and 1922–23, 5ETP 332, ADAM.

32. Stéphane F., video conversation with the author, November 14, 2022.

33. Obituary of Jean-Marie Aventini, *Midi Libre*, September 2, 1974, S 3 J, Archives provinciales des franciscains (Strasbourg); Baptism registry, parish of Notre-Dame de Cimiez, Archives de la Chancellerie du diocèse de Nice (Nice); Ralph Schor, "Un diocèse confronté aux crises du XXe siècle, 1926–1963," in *Le diocèse de Nice: Histoire et identités d'une terre de contrastes*, ed. Gilles Bouis (Nice, France: Éditions du Signe, 2015), 227.

34. S. Desmarais, memorandum on the company's wartime damages, August 6, 1945, 1W 312, ADAM; Fiszel Ferdman estate inventory, May 22, 1945, Van Beneden notarial records, Archives de l'État à Bruxelles (Brussels).

35. Annie B., postcard to Zosia Warchiwker, June 20, 1945, Zosia Warchiwker personal papers.

36. Jean-Pierre Vernant, "Weaving Friendship," trans. David Aimes Curtis, *Salmagundi* 130/131 (2001): 76.

37. Jacques Sémelin documents this gratitude in his "The Notion of Social Reactivity: The French Case, 1942–1944," in *Probing the Limits of Categorization: The Bystander in Holocaust History*, ed. Christina Morina and Krijn Thijs (New York: Berghahn Books, 2019), 236.

38. Didier Fassin and Richard Rechtman, *The Empire of Trauma: An Inquiry into the Condition of Victimhood*, trans. Rachel Gomme (Princeton, NJ: Princeton University Press, 2009 [2007]).

39. Emily Bernard, *Black Is the Body: Stories from My Grandmother's Time, My Mother's Time, and Mine* (New York: Knopf, 2019), 103.

40. I borrow these analytical categories from Gunnar S. Paulsson, *Secret City: The Hidden Jews of Warsaw, 1940–1945* (New Haven, CT: Yale University Press, 2002), 247. On the "moral complexities and emotional tangles" that characterized wartime relationships between Jews and those who helped them, see Mark Roseman, *Lives Reclaimed: A Story of Rescue and Resistance in Nazi Germany* (New York: Metropolitan, 2019), 48.

41. El Amrani Boisseau, *Filles de la terre*, 198.

42. Annie B., letter to Zosia Warchiwker, April 18, 1946, Zosia Warchiwker personal papers; Françoise Germain-Musso, "Une étape dans l'urbanisation de la vallée du Paillon-Pasteur et Bon Voyage. La transformation d'une banlieue campagnarde," *Recherches régionales* 1 (1975): 2–45; Annie B., Personnel record, Desmarais frères, 16VA05265, AHGT; Francine Gerson, telephone conversation with the author, July 21, 2021.

43. Camille Lefebvre, *À l'ombre de l'histoire des autres* (Paris: Éditions de l'EHESS, 2022), 112.

44. *Le Soir* (Brussels), July 19, 1947, and April 2, 1948.

45. Like so many other interviewers, I did not ask Zosia to discuss such matters either. See Adelaïde Lachaud, "La maternité chez les femmes juives en France pendant l'Occupation au travers des témoignages" (master's thesis, Université Paris 1 Panthéon-Sorbonne, 2023), 156, 162–64, 177–78.

46. Christopher R. Browning, *Remembering Survival: Inside a Nazi Slave-Labor Camp* (New York: Norton, 2010), 98.

47. *L'Éveil de Nice: La quinzaine religieuse*, September 11, 1943. See also Sarah Fishman. *From Vichy to the Sexual Revolution: Gender and Family Life in Postwar France* (Oxford, UK: Oxford University Press, 2017), xi.

48. Annie B., letter and postcard to Zosia Warchiwker, June 30, 1945 and April 18, 1946, Zosia Warchiwker personal papers.

49. Agnès Fine, *Parrains, marraines: La parenté spirituelle en Europe* (Paris: Fayard, 1994), 39–43, 63, quotation on 63.

50. Marie Richeux, *Sages femmes* (Paris: Sabine Wespieser, 2021), 38.

51. Francine Gerson, conversation with the author, February 18, 2022.

52. Stéphane F., email to the author, October 11, 2022.

53. Stéphane F., email to the author, October 6, 2022; Étienne F., dossier for the Médaille de la Résistance, June 13, 1945, AOL.

54. Josiane Pinto, "Le secrétariat. Un métier très féminin," *Le Mouvement social* 140 (1987): 126–27.

55. Annie B., letter to the administrative director of Desmarais frères, June 11, 1950, 16VA05265, AHGT. Annie's personal file is both too spare and too rich in detail: too spare for us to grasp the accusations made against her, too rich for me to reveal everything while respecting her right to privacy as well as her family's. It is to respect this privacy, and that of Charles's family, that I anonymize their last names.

56. Annette Wieviorka, "'I' in the Plural: A New Writing of History," in *Being Contemporary: French Literature, Culture, and Politics Today*, ed. Lia Brozgal and Sara Kippur, trans. Jane Kuntz (Liverpool, UK: Liverpool University Press, 2016), 224; Bob Moore, "Integrating Self-Help into the History of Jewish Survival in Western Europe," in *Jewish Histories of the Holocaust: New Transnational Approaches*, ed. Norman J.W. Goda (New York: Berghahn, 2014), 193; Marie Moutier-Bitan, "Le sauvetage des Juifs dans les territoires soviétiques occupés," in *Nouvelle histoire de la Shoah*, ed. Alexandre Bande et al. (Paris: Passés composés, 2021), 117.

57. Sarah Fishman makes this point about the wives of prisoners of war: *We Will Wait: Wives of French Prisoners of War, 1940–1945* (New Haven, CT: Yale University Press 1991), 166.

58. Registry of death certificates, Nice, 1970, 1346W 3, ADAM.

Chapter Five : A Child of *Loving*

1. "Marry Whom You Please," *Newsday* (Nassau ed.), June 14, 1967. The paper flatly endorsed the Court's decision, remarking that "antimiscegenation laws were barbaric, vindictive and primitive, and should have been voided long since."

2. For an overview of the US Supreme Court's road to *Loving*, see Peters Wallenstein, "Race, Marriage, and the Supreme Court from *Pace v. Alabama* (1883) to *Loving v. Virginia* (1967)," *Journal of Supreme Court History* 23, no. 2 (1998): 65–86.

3. Jennifer Glaser, *Borrowed Voices: Writing and Racial Ventriloquism in the Jewish American Imagination* (New Brunswick, NJ: Rutgers University Press, 2016).

4. Martha S. Jones, "Who Here Is a Negro?" *Michigan Quarterly Review* 53, no. 1 (Winter 2014): 23–28.

5. "Suzanne Yager," Buffalo, Erie, New York. 1950 Census of Population and Housing. US Department of Commerce. Bureau of the Census. "Paul M. Jones," Boston, Suffolk, Massachusetts. 1950 Census of Population and Housing. US Department of Commerce. Bureau of the Census.

6. *The 1944* (Mount Hermon School: Massachusetts, 1944): 20. On Greensboro in the civil rights era, see William H. Chafe, *Civilities and Civil Rights: Greensboro, North Carolina, and the Black Freedom Struggle* (New York: Oxford University Press, 1980). For Chafe's interview with my grandmother, Susie W. Jones, see "Oral History Interview with Susie Jones with William Chafe (1978)," Civil Rights Digital Archive Project, William Henry Chafe Oral History Collection, University of North Carolina, Greensboro. On my grandparents' decision to send my father and his brothers away to school, see "Black Women Oral History Project: Interview with Susie Jones, July 11, 1977," Schlesinger Library, Radcliffe Institute, Harvard University.

7. On Buffalo's German immigrant community, see Andrew Yox, "The German-American Community as a Nationality, 1880–1940," *Yearbook of German-American Studies* 36 (2001): 181–93.

8. Kelly Hacker Jones, *Lenox Hill Neighborhood House: A History of 125 Years of Service to the Community* (New York: Lenox Hill Neighborhood House, 2019).

9. Arthur Hillman, "Maintaining a Balanced Community: Lenox Hill Neighborhood Association, New York City," *Neighborhood Centers Today: Action Programs for a Rapidly Changing World* (National Federation of Settlements and Neighborhood Centers, 1960); Lenox Hill Neighborhood Scrapbook, vols. 1–3, The Lenox Hill Neighborhood House Collection, 1892–2015, Archives and Special Collections, Hunter College Libraries.

10. "Monday nite," Paul M. Jones to Susie W. Jones, n.d., in possession of author.

11. Paul M. Jones to Susie W. Jones, n.d., in possession of author.

12. Paul M. Jones to Susie W. Jones, n.d., in possession of author.

13. Paul M. Jones to Susie W. Jones, n.d., in possession of author.

14. "Monday nite."

15. Sharon M. Leon, "Tensions Not Unlike That Produced by a Mixed Marriage: Daniel Marshall and Catholic Challenges to Anti-Miscegenation Statutes," *U.S. Catholic Historian* 26, no. 1 (2008): 27–44; Eric Alan Isaacson, "Free Exercise for Whom?—Could the Religious-Liberty Principle that Catholics Established in *Perez v. Sharp* also Protect Same-Sex Couples' Right to Marry?" *University of Detroit Mercy Law Review* 29, no. 1 (June 2015): 29–56.

16. "Monday nite."

17. "Monday nite."

18. "Monday nite."

19. "Apostolic Letter in the Form of Motu Proprio. Matrimonia Mixta. On Mixed Marriages," October 1, 1970, https://www.vatican.va/content/paul-vi/en/motu_proprio/documents/hf_p-vi_motu-proprio_19700331_matrimonia-mixta.html.

20. The New York State Health Department eliminated race from birth certificates eighteen months later, in December 1960. Lawrence O'Kane, "City to Drop Race From Birth Data: Information to Appear Only in Confidential Files," *New York Times*, December 27, 1860. For a general history of the birth certificate in the United States, see Susan J. Pearson, *The Birth Certificate: An American History* (Chapel Hill: University of North Carolina Press, 2021).

21. "New York Will Drop Race in Birth Records: Health Dept. to Keep Facts Confidential," *Chicago Daily Tribune*, December 27, 1960; Pearson, *The Birth Certificate*, 271–73.

22. For a discussion of how courts determined racial identity for purposes of anti-miscegenation laws, see Peggy Pascoe, "Miscegenation Law, Court Cases, and Ideologies of 'Race' in Twentieth-Century America," *Journal of American History* 83, no. 1 (June 1996): 44–69; Peggy Pascoe, *What Comes Naturally: Miscegenation Law and the Making of Race in America* (New York: Oxford University Press, 2010). More generally on trial of racial determination, see Ariela J. Gross, *What Blood Won't Tell: A History of Race on Trial in America* (Cambridge, MA: Harvard University Press, 2009).

23. The trial court ruling was affirmed, and Arizona's anti-miscegenation law was deemed constitutional by the California Court of Appeal in *Estate of Monks*, 48 Cal. App. 2d 603 (1941).

24. Reporter's Transcript, vol. 7, pp. 2543, 2548, *Estate of Monks*.

25. "Many a Man Gets Credit for Paternity and Never Knows," *Daily News* (New York), May 28, 1950.

26. *Physicians' Handbook on Birth and Death Registration*, 9th ed. (Washington, DC: US Government Printing Office, 1939), 7.

27. This phrasing is owed to James Baldwin, who wrote of Americans, including those of German and Irish descent like my mother, as "those who think of themselves as white." James Baldwin, "On Being White . . . and Other Lies," in *The Cross of Redemption: Uncollected Writings* (New York: Pantheon Books, 2010), 135–38. This phase, as an insistence on the socially constructed nature of white identity as a moral choice, was given a twenty-first-century relevance by Ta-Nehisi Coates in *Between the World and Me* (New York: Spiegel & Grau, 2015.) For a general history of US passports, see Craig Robertson, *The Passport in America: The History of a Document* (New York: Oxford University Press, 2012); and on the early history of Black Americans and passports, Elizabeth Stordeur Pryor, *Colored Travelers: Mobility and the Fight for Citizenship before the Civil War* (Chapel Hill: University of North Carolina Press, 2016).

28. "City to Drop Race from Birth Data: Information to Appear Only in Confidential Files," *New York Times*, December 27, 1860.

29. Judith Walzer, *Make Room for Daddy: The Journey from Waiting Room to Birthing Room* (Chapel Hill: University of North Carolina Press, 2009).

30. Gregory Jaynes, "Suit on Race Recalls Lines Drawn Under Slavery," *New York Times*, September 30, 1982; F. James Davis, *Who Is Black? One Nation's Definition* (University Park, PA: Penn State University Press, 2010), 8–11.

31. Gregory Jaynes, "Suit on Race Recalls Lines Drawn Under Slavery," *New York Times*, September 30, 1982; Davis, *Who Is Black?*, 8–11. *Doe v. State*, 479 So. 2d 369 (La. Ct. App. 1985). Phipps lost her appeals to the Louisiana State Supreme Court and the US Supreme Court. "Mrs. Phipps Loses Another Round," *Associated Press*, April 1, 1986; "Woman Loses Battle to Be Declared White," *UPI*, December 8, 1986.

32. Art Harris, "Louisiana Court Sees No Shades of Gray in Woman's Request," *Washington Post*, May 21, 1983.

33. Paul Schor, *Counting Americans: How the U.S. Census Classified the Nation* (New York: Oxford University Press, 2017).

34. Thomas J. Sugrue, *Sweet Land of Liberty: The Forgotten Struggle for Civil Rights in the North* (New York: Random House, 2009).

35. Glenn C. Altschuler and Stuart M. Blumin, *The GI Bill: A New Deal for Veterans* (20009); "White Protestant Sues Club on L.I. over Minority Bias," *New York Times*, November 14, 1979; Richard C. Firstman, "Club Faces a Discrimination Suit," *Newsday*, November 14, 1979; "Leaders Should Blackball Clubs That Discriminate," *Newsday*, September 17, 1979; Lawrence C. Levy and Richard C. Firstman, "A Lonely Fight to Open a Door," *Newsday*, September 9, 1979; Richard C. Fishman, "Private-Club Suit Diminished," *Newsday*, June 25, 1980.

36. "Trying to Conquer, They Stand Divided," *Newsday*, November 24, 1963.

37. Henry Louis Taylor Jr., "Social Transformation Theory, African Americans and the Rise of Buffalo's Post-Industrial City," *Buffalo Law Review* 39, no. 2 (1991): 569–606.

38. "Desegregation and Integration of Greensboro's Public School, 1954–1974," University Libraries of UNC Greensboro, accessed September 19, 2022, https://gateway.uncg.edu/crg/essay greensboroschools.

39. "Manhasset Votes Integration Plan," *New York Times*, March 13, 1964; *Blocker v. Board of Education of Manhasset*, 226 F. Supp. 208 (E.D.N.Y. 1964); Jacob D. Hyman and Wade J. Newhouse Jr., "Desegregation of the Schools: The Present Legal Situation," *Buffalo Law Review* 14, no. 2 (1964): 208–31; Charles F. Howlett, "The Long Island Civil Rights Movement in the 1960s,

Part One: The Struggle to Integrate Public Schools," *Long Island Historical Journal* 8, no. 2 (1996): 145–65.

40. This was not the first time our district became subject to such scrutiny. The NAACP Legal Defense and Educational Fund challenged the district when it proposed to charge tuition to a Black student, newly arrived from Birmingham, Alabama, and the "ward" of a local white family. "Fights L.I. Tuition for Dixie Girl," *Daily News*, January 11, 1967.

41. "Interview with Susie Jones, July 11, 1977," Black Women Oral History Project, Schlesinger Library, Radcliffe College. On Dr. Merze Tate, see Barbara D. Savage, *Merze Tate: The Global Odyssey of a Black Woman Scholar* (New Haven, CT: Yale University Press, 2023).

42. "Interview with Susie Jones, July 11, 1977."

43. Manhattan, New York City (Telephone) Directory (1958), 1064.

44. Derrick Bell, "The Space Traders," in *Faces at the Bottom of the Well: The Permanence of Racism* (New York: Basic Books, 1992): 197–242.

45. "Refusal of Race Identification on Birth Certificate," *Journal of the National Medical Association*, March 1952, 150; "Exit the Race Statistic," *Journal of the National Medical Association*, September 1950, 326; W. Montague Cobb, "Negro Member of Specialty Boards and Fellows of Clinical Colleges," *Journal of the National Medical Association*, July 1956, 273; Pearson, *The Birth Certificate*.

Chapter Six: Who Gave You Permission?

1. Michel-Rolph Trouillot, *Silencing the Past: Power and the Production of History* (Boston: Beacon Press, 1995).

2. Evelyn Nakano Glenn, "Split Household, Small Producer and Dual Wage Earner: An Analysis of Chinese-American Family Strategies," *Journal of Marriage and Family* 45, no. 1 (1983): 35–46.

3. Tao Leigh Goffe, "'The Other Windrush': The Hidden History of Afro-Chinese Families in 1950s London," *gal-dem*, June 30, 2021, https://gal-dem.com/the-other-windrush-the-hidden-history-of-afro-chinese-in-1950s-london/.

4. Tao Leigh Goffe, "The Poetics of Afro-Asian Cuisine," in *Black Food: Stories, Art, and Recipes from across the African Diaspora*, ed. Bryant Terry (New York: 4 Color Books, 2021).

5. Tao Leigh Goffe, "Chop Suey Surplus: Chinese Food, Sex, and the Political Economy of Afro-Asia," *Women & Performance* 30, no. 1 (2020), https://www.womenandperformance.org/bonus-articles-1/category/chop-suey-surplus-chinese-food-sex-and-the-political-economy-of-afro-asia-tao-leigh-goffehtml.

6. Hortense J. Spillers, "Mama's Baby, Papa's Maybe: An American Grammar Book," *Diacritics* 17, no. 2 (1987): 65–81.

7. Toni Morrison, *Beloved* (New York: Knopf, 1987), 248.

8. Ann Laura Stoler, *Carnal Knowledge and Imperial Power: Race and the Intimate in Colonial Rule* (Berkeley: University of California Press, 2010).

9. Toni Morrison, *Sula* (New York: Plume, 1973).

10. Maxine Hong Kingston, *The Woman Warrior: Memoirs of a Girlhood among Ghosts* (New York: Vintage International, 1989 [1975]), 3.

11. Patricia Powell, *The Pagoda: A Novel* (Orlando: Harcourt, 1999); Kerry Young, *Pao* (New York: Bloomsbury, 2011).

12. Tao Leigh Goffe, "Bigger than the Sound: The Jamaican Chinese Infrastructures of Reggae," *Small Axe: A Caribbean Journal of Criticism* 24, no. 3 (2020): 97–127.

13. Anne-Marie Lee-Loy, "Unfinished Synthesis: Georg Simmel's Adventure, Two Chinese Jamaican Migration Narratives, and the Negotiation of Modern Identity," *Caribbean Studies* 38 (2010): 147–67.

14. Burton Holmes, "Hawaiian Islands, Edge of China, Manila," in *Burton Holmes Travelogues* (Chicago: Travelogue Bureau, 1914).

15. Saidiya Hartman, "Venus in Two Acts," *Small Axe: A Caribbean Journal of Criticism* 12, no. 2 (2008): 1–14.

16. Kathleen M. López, *Chinese Cubans: A Transnational History* (Chapel Hill: University of North Carolina Press, 2013); Jason Oliver Chang, *Chino: Anti-Chinese Racism in Mexico, 1880–1940* (Champaign: University of Illinois Press, 2017).

17. Octavia E. Butler, *Kindred* (New York: Doubleday, 1979).

18. Denise Ferreira da Silva explores Butler's question and approach in a powerful interpretation she calls Black feminist poethical reading. Denise Ferreira da Silva, "Toward a Black Feminist Poethics: The Quest(ion) of Blackness toward the End of the World," *Black Scholar* 44, no. 2 (2014): 81–97.

Chapter Seven: Mine

I am deeply grateful to all who contributed to this project, especially my parents and other family members who were willing to generously venture down these uneasy roads with me. Parts of this chapter draw from a video essay in progress called "Oil in Stereo: Ancestry through Infrastructure," with thanks for the relevant permissions. I am deeply appreciative to all participants in the rich discussions at the 2017 "Volatile Futures/Earthly Matters" symposium at Bennington College, where I first presented this essay; the 2019 "Politics of Kinship" Mellon conference at Tufts University; the 2020 "Scholars and Their Kin" symposium at New York University; the 2022 panel "Unsettling the Self: Exploring Autoethnography, Intimate Ethnography, and Ethnographic Memoir" at the American Anthropological Association meetings; and the 2023 "Writing Kinship" panel at the Princeton Department of Anthropology. Special thanks are due to many reviewers and colleagues for helpful comments over the years, including a dear inner circle who gave me more than I have yet been able to fully incorporate.

1. Such fluctuating carbon levels in the planetary atmosphere—plummeting around the year Europeans called 1610—are thought to be the product of forests and vegetation across the Americas growing back over what had previously been residential and agricultural lands, inhabited by the some 55 million Indigenous people who died in those years. See Simon Lewis and Mark Maslin, "Defining the Anthropocene," *Nature* 519 (2015): 171–80; Heather Davis and Zoe Todd, "On the Importance of a Date, or, Decolonizing the Anthropocene," *ACME: An International Journal for Critical Geographies* 16, no. 4 (2017): 761–80; Ned Blackhawk, *The Rediscovery of America: Native Peoples and the Unmaking of U.S. History* (New Haven, CT: Yale University Press, 2023).

2. Lynne Sharon Schwartz, ed., *The Emergence of Memory: Conversations with W.G. Sebald* (New York: Seven Stories Press, 2007).

3. For a more detailed historical account of the formation of the Wabash Confederacy—including how attempts to dismantle it forever shaped US military history and imperial strategy—see William Hogeland, *Autumn of the Black Snake* (New York: FSG, 2017). Strikingly, the heavily armed US military convoys that, led by Anthony Wayne, carried out this systemic military campaign and land dispossession against the Wabash Confederacy in the 1790s came to be

regarded by Indigenous leaders of the time by the name "Black Snake," the same name that was later used to describe oil pipelines such as DAPL during the Standing Rock protests.

4. For a sampling of this local history, see Brian Black, *Petrolia: The Landscape of America's First Oil Boom* (Baltimore: Johns Hopkins University Press, 2003); Colin Jerolmack, *Up to Heaven and Down to Hell: Fracking, Freedom, and Community in an American Town* (Princeton, NJ: Princeton University Press, 2021); Keith Fisher, *A Pipeline Runs Through It: The Story of Oil from Ancient Times to the First World War* (New York: Allen Lane, 2022). Throughout this essay, I try to retain something of how people actually talk about history in the context being described. This includes trying to resist letting more academic language replace certain local expressions and retaining some more conversational turns of phrase (such as second-person voice common in storytelling, and historical events recalled but unpinned to dates). While this sensibility can challenge certain epistemic habits, it seems to me as an anthropologist that this more closely reflects how people in this regional and kin fabric think in history. There are footnotes with dates and details for readers who wish for further context.

5. On themes of infrastructure and repressed memory between anthropology and history, see Michel-Rolph Trouillot, *Silencing the Past: Power and the Production of History* (Boston: Beacon Press, 1997); Teresa Montoya, "Permeable: Diné Politics of Extraction and Exposure" (PhD diss., New York University, 2019); LaToya Ruby Frazier, *The Notion of Family* (New York: Aperture, 2014); Pekka Hämäläinen, *Indigenous Continent: The Epic Contest for North America* (New York: Liveright, 2022).

6. Simon Lewis and Mark Maslin, "Defining the Anthropocene," *Nature* 519 (2015): 171–80.

7. Tao Leigh Goffe, "Scratching the Surface: A Speculative Feminist Visual History of Other Windrush Itineraries," in *The Other Windrush: Legacies of Indenture in Britain's Caribbean Empire*, ed. Maria del Pilar Kaladeen and David Dabydeen (New York: Pluto Press, 2021), 93–111.

8. See, for example, Maude Newton, *Ancestor Trouble: A Reckoning and a Reconciliation* (New York: Random House, 2022); Géraldine Schwarz, *Those Who Forget: My Family's Story in Nazi Europe—A Memoir, A History, A Warning*, trans. Laura Marris (New York: Scribner, 2017); Burkhard Bilger, *Fatherland: A Memoir of War, Conscience, and Family Secrets* (New York: Random House, 2023).

9. Timothy Mitchell, *Carbon Democracy: Political Power in the Age of Oil* (New York: Verso, 2013). For a recent rejoinder anchored in Indigenous histories and present realities, see Andrew Curley, *Carbon Sovereignty: Coal, Development, and Energy Transition in the Navajo Nation* (Tucson: University of Arizona Press, 2023).

10. "PA's Mining Legacy and Abandoned Mine Reclamation," Pennsylvania Department of Environmental Protections, accessed June 20, 2023, https://www.dep.pa.gov/Business/Land /Mining/AbandonedMineReclamation/AMLProgramInformation/Pages/PA's-Mining-Legacy -and-AML.aspx.

11. For a history of emerging fields of "relational ethnography": Stéphane Gerson, "A History from Within: When Historians Write about Their Own Kin," *Journal of Modern History* 94, no. 4 (2022): 898–937. This project draws inspiration from genre experiments in personal and family scales of narration from across the environmental humanities, histories of racialization, anthropologies of labor, and memoirs of landscape and health. See, in particular, Lucas Bessire, *Running Out: In Search of Water on the High Plains* (Princeton, NJ: Princeton University Press, 2020); Kendra Taira Field, *Growing Up With the Country: Family, Race, and Nation after the Civil War* (New Haven, CT: Yale University Press, 2018); Kendra Taira Field and Sarah Pinto, "Defamiliarizing the Family: Genealogy and Kinship as Critical Method" (Andrew W. Mellon

Foundation Seminar, 2019), politicsofkinship.tufts.edu; Frank X. Walker, *Black Box* (Lexington, KY: Old Cove Press, 2005); Frank X. Walker, *About Flight* (New York: Accents, 2015); Natasha Trethewey, *Beyond Katrina: A Meditation on the Mississippi Gulf Coast* (Athens: University of Georgia Press, 2012); Ruth Behar, *Traveling Heavy: A Memoir in Between Journeys* (Durham, NC: Duke University Press, 2013); Hazel Carby, *Imperial Intimacies: A Tale of Two Islands* (New York: Verso, 2019); Christine Walley, *Exit Zero: Family and Class in Chicago* (Chicago: University of Chicago Press, 2013); Susanne Antonetta, *Body Toxic: An Environmental Memoir* (Washington, DC: Counterpoint Perseus, 2001); Sarah Broom, *The Yellow House* (New York: Grove Press, 2019); Elizabeth Chin, *My Life with Things: The Consumer Diaries* (Durham, NC: Duke University Press, 2016); bell hooks, *Belonging: A Culture of Place* (New York: Routledge, 1990); João Biehl, "Insurgent Archivings: Sensing the Spirit of Nature and Reckoning with Traces of Our Dead," *Current Anthropology* 63 (S25) (2022): S2–20; William Vollman, *Carbon Ideologies: No Good Alternative* (New York: Viking, 2018); Christina Sharpe, *Ordinary Notes* (New York: Macmillan, 2023); Christina Sharpe, *In the Wake: On Blackness and Being* (Durham, NC: Duke University Press, 2016); Diane McWhorter, *Carry Me Home: The Climatic Battle of the Civil Rights Revolution* (New York: Simon & Schuster, 2013); Kim Tallbear, "Making Love and Relations Beyond Settler Sex and Family," in *Making Kin Not Population* (Chicago: University of Chicago Press, 2018); Carolyn Kay Steedman, *Landscape for a Good Woman* (New Brunswick, NJ: Rutgers University Press, 1987); Clint Smith, *How the Word Is Passed: A Reckoning with the History of Slavery Across America* (New York: Little, Brown, 2021); Elizabeth Ferry, *La Batea* (Brooklyn, NY: Red Hook Editions, 2017); Kathleen Stewart, *A Space on the Side of the Road: Cultural Poetics in an "Other" America* (Princeton, NJ: Princeton University Press, 1996); Lauret Savoy, *Trace: Memory, History, Race, and the American Landscape* (Berkeley, CA: Counterpoint, 2015).

12. Phil Berardelli, "The Mountains That Froze the World," *Science Magazine*, November 3, 2009.

13. "Grand Ball Given by the Whales," *Vanity Fair*, April 20, 1861. See also David McDermott Hughes, *Energy without Conscience: Oil, Climate Change, and Complicity* (Durham, NC: Duke University Press, 2017).

14. The name "Seneca Oil" was used simultaneously in 1859–60 with "PA Rock Oil Company." For more on how contemporary Seneca Haudenosaunee people themselves view these historical events in Pennsylvania, see Seneca Iroquois National Museum and Onöhsagwë:de' Cultural Center, https://www.senecamuseum.org.

15. "For 13 years now National petroleum Sunday and Petroleum Weekend Retreats have been observed by employees of the Tide Water Associated Oil Company," a newsletter reported at the time of the Seneca oil spring in what became Cuba, New York; *National Catholic Welfare Conference Bulletin* 35, no. 10 (October 1953); see also John P. Herrick, *Empire Oil: The Story of Oil in New York State* (New York: Dodd, Mead, 1949).

16. Paul Giddens, *Pennsylvania Petroleum, 1750–1872: A Documentary History* (Titusville, PA: Drake Well Memorial Park, 1971), 9.

17. Bruce Trigger, *A History of Archaeological Thought* (Cambridge: Cambridge University Press, 2006); Phillip Deloria, *Playing Indian* (New Haven, CT: Yale University Press, 1999).

18. The 1794 Treaty of Canandaigua, affirmed by George Washington, had acknowledged the land rights of the Six Nations. This included the Seneca lands that were wrongfully seized by the US government to build Kinzua Dam in 1965. See *Lake of Betrayal: The Story of Kinzua Dam*, directed by Paul Lamont, produced by Scott Sackett and Caleb Abrams (Seneca Museum, 2017), DVD.

19. For more on this implicit reference to Standing Rock and related associations, see, for example, Nick Estes, *Our History Is the Future: Standing Rock Versus the Dakota Access Pipeline, and the Long Tradition of Indigenous Resistance* (New York: Verso, 2019); Leanne Betasamosake Simpson, *As We Have Always Done: Indigenous Freedom Through Radical Resistance* (Minneapolis: University of Minnesota Press, 2020).

20. Camille von Kaenel, "Fossil Fuel Burning Obscures Radiocarbon Dates," *Scientific American*, July 21, 2015.

21. Indigenous scholars ask us to think of such marine creatures from ancient geological ages as "fossil kin," in the words of Métis scholar Zoe Todd; they point out that it isn't the carbon of their bodies but its colonial extraction that causes harm. I hold this important idea alongside an unwanted relation to marketing I've been consuming all my life, from corporations that also encouraged consumers like me to imagine ties with the ancient plants and marine animals that make up their coal and oil. Companies even published children's books and chemical kinship charts to give a more relatable feeling to their toxic products, which often interact with our own family trees in the form of illnesses. For more on this key literature, see Zoe Todd. "Fish, Kin, and Hope: Tending to Water Violations in Amiskwaciwâskahikan and Treaty Six Territory," *Afterall* (2017): 1, 43, 102–7; [M.] Murphy, "Distributed Reproduction, Chemical Violence, and Latency," *Scholar and Feminist Online* 11, no. 3 (2013): 3, 11; [M.] Murphy, "Chemical Infrastructures of the St. Clair River," in *Toxicants, Health, and Regulation Since 1945*, ed. Soraya Boudia and Nathalie Jas (New York: Routledge, 2015); Max Liboiron, *Pollution Is Colonialism* (Durham, NC: Duke University Press, 2021).

22. Alison Laurence, "Afterlives of Extinction: The Politics of Display in the Modern United States" (Ph.D. diss, MIT, 2019); Martin Rudwick, *Scenes from Deep Time: Early Pictorial Representations of the Prehistoric World* (Chicago: University of Chicago Press, 1992).

23. Naomi Yuval-Naeh, "Cultivating the Carboniferous: Coal as Botanical Curiosity in Victorian Culture," *Victorian Studies* 61, no. 3 (2019): 419–45.

24. Thomas Trautmann, *Lewis Henry Morgan and the Invention of Kinship* (Lincoln: University of Nebraska, 1987), vi. See Lewis Henry Morgan, *Systems of Consanguinity and Affinity in the Human Family* (Washington, DC: Smithsonian Press, 1871). For crucial historical context, see Audra Simpson, *Mohawk Interruptus: Political Life Across the Borders of Settler States* (Durham, NC: Duke University Press, 2014); Patrick Wolfe, "Settler Colonialism and the Elimination of the Native," *Journal of Genocide Research* 8, no. 4 (2006): 387–409; Aileen Moreton-Robinson, *The White Possessive: Property, Power, and Indigenous Sovereignty* (Minneapolis: University of Minnesota Press, 2015); Anand Pandian, Donald Moore, and Jake Kosek, *Race, Nature, and the Politics of Difference* (Durham, NC: Duke University Press, 2003).

25. Lewis Henry Morgan, "Essay on Geology," Morgan papers (Special Collections, University of Rochester, 1841), series IV, box 21, folder 2.

26. Ralph Stone and Frederick Clapp, *Oil and Gas Fields of Greene County, PA* (Washington, DC: US Geological Survey and Department of the Interior, 1907), 56.

27. Stone and Clapp, *Oil and Gas Fields*, 62, 35.

28. Sung Tieu, *Infra-Spector* (Brooklyn, NY: Amant, 2023); Abdou Maliq Simone, "People as Infrastructure: Intersecting Fragments in Johannesburg," *Public Culture* 13, no. 3 (2004): 407–29.

29. "The two time scales–the one human and emotional, the other geologic—are so disparate. . . . A million years is a small number on the geologic time scale, while human experience is truly fleeting—all human experience, from its beginning, not just one lifetime. Only occasionally do the two time scales coincide. When they do, the effects can be as lasting as they are

pronounced." John McPhee, "Book Four: Assembling California," in *Annals of the Former World* (New York: FSG, 2000), 458. For a moving ethnographic engagement with geology, family, and grief, see Hugh Raffles, *The Book of Unconformities: Speculations on Lost Time* (New York: Pantheon, 2020).

30. Claude Lévi-Strauss, *Tristes Tropiques*, trans. John and Doreen Weightman (New York: Penguin Books, 1955).

Chapter Eight: The Genre of Inheritance

1. All quotations from my short story "Grandma Was a Dancer" are from the unpublished July 2020 version and appear in italics.

2. Queer readings of conventional narrative form have long sought to challenge its heteronormativity by proposing other kinds of longing as both interrupting of its smooth arc, and as telling a different story. De Lauretis brilliantly insists that *desire* is at the heart of narrative success and failure. For de Lauretis, this allows a queer reframing of the visual, while for Roof queer narration interrupts the flow of heteronormative *story* as well as offering alternative subjects and objects. Teresa de Lauretis, *Alice Doesn't: Feminism, Semiotics, Cinema* (Bloomington: Indiana University Press, 1984); Judith Roof, *Come as You Are: Sexuality and Narrative* (New York: Columbia University Press, 1996).

3. Freccero thus argues for queering as a radical rethinking of heteronormative temporality at an epochal level, and Keeling thinks in queer decolonial vein to highlight the heteronormativity of colonial history and the racism of reproductive time. Carla Freccero, "Queer Times," *South Atlantic Quarterly* 106, no. 3 (2007): 485–94; Kara Keeling, *Queer Times, Black Futures* (New York: New York University Press, 2019).

4. I thus follow in the footsteps of feminist cultural historians Kuhn and Steedman, who insist histories of class and nation require grappling with gendered stories that dominant history typically obscures. Annette Kuhn, *Family Secrets: Acts of Memory and Imagination* (London: Verso, 1995); Carolyn Steedman, *Landscape for a Good Woman: A Story of Two Lives* (New Brunswick, NJ: Rutgers University Press, 1987).

5. Clare Hemmings, *Why Stories Matter: The Political Grammar of Feminist Theory* (Durham, NC: Duke University Press, 2011).

6. Clare Hemmings, *Considering Emma Goldman: Feminist Political Ambivalence and the Imaginative Archive* (Durham, NC: Duke University Press, 2018).

7. Marianne Hirsch, "The Generation of Postmemory," *Poetics Today* 29, no. 1 (2008): 103–28; Marianne Hirsch, *Family Frames: Photography, Narrative, and Postmemory* (Cambridge, MA: Harvard University Press, 1997).

8. Saidiya Hartman, *Wayward Lives, Beautiful Experiments: Intimate Histories of Social Upheaval* (New York: Norton, 2019).

9. Saidiya Hartman, "Venus in Two Acts," *Small Axe: A Caribbean Journal of Criticism* 12, no. 2 (2008): 1–14.

10. Nancy K. Miller, "The Entangled Self: Genre Bondage in the Age of the Memoir," *PMLS* 122, no. 2 (2007): 432.

11. I am influenced in my framing of genre as a question of *readership* by Delany, whose engagement with science fiction leads him to think of all genre less in terms of formal content (or its breaching), but as a "reading protocol." Samuel Delany, "Some Reflections on Science Fiction Criticism," *Science Fiction Studies* 8, no. 3 (November 1981): 235.

12. Delany, "Some Reflections," 235.

13. Mikhail Bakhtin, "Characteristics of Genre and Plot Composition in Dostoevsky's Works," in *Problems of Dostoevsky's Poetics*, ed. and trans. Caryl Emerson (Minneapolis: University of Minnesota Press, 1984), 106.

Chapter Nine: Beyond Taboo, Worship, and Irony

1. Marnix Beyen, "Laat die hele IJzerbedevaart maar achterwege," *De Morgen*, November 3, 2012.

2. The most famous examples are Bruno De Wever, the most important historian of the Flemish Nationalist collaboration during the Second World War (see his *Greep naar de macht: Vlaams-nationalisme en Nieuwe Orde. Het VNV 1933–1945* [Tielt: Uitgeverij Lannoo, 1994]), and Pieter Lagrou, who became an expert on the history of the Resistance and its legacy in postwar Europe: *The Legacy of Nazi Occupation. Patriotic Memory and National Recovery in Western Europe, 1945–1965* (Cambridge, UK: Cambridge University Press, 1999).

3. I described these developments in "'Zwart wordt van langsom meer de zwartgezinde massa.' De Vlaamse beeldvorming over bezetting en repressie, 1945–2000," in *Het gewicht van het oorlogsverleden*, ed. José Gotovitch and Chantal Kesteloot (Ghent, Belgium: Academia Press, 2003), 105–20.

4. Karel Van Isacker, *Irma Laplasse. Haar gevangenisdagboek. De kritiek van haar strafdossier* (Kapellen, Belgium: De Nederlandsche Boekhandel, 1995).

5. On the history of this series, see Veerle Vanden Daelen, "Lou de Jong en Maurice de Wilde: twee oorlogsmonumenten," *Bijdragen tot de Eigentijdse Geschiedenis* 10 (1982): 161–96.

6. See Evert Peeters and Bruno Benvindo, *Scherven van de oorlog. De strijd om de herinnering aan WOII* (Amsterdam: De Bezige Bij, 2011), 7.

7. See also his recently published memoir: *Pour en finir avec De Ghelderode* (Paris: Edilivre, 2023).

8. My father obtained his PhD in 1968 with a biography of De Ghelderode, which he published in 1971 (the year I was born) as *Michel de Ghelderode ou la hantise du masque*. In 1987, he published *Bibliographie de Michel de Ghelderode*, and between 1990 and 2012 a ten-volume annotated *Correspondance de Michel de Ghelderode*.

9. The theoretical "bible" for this postmodern position was the essay *De vreugden van Houssaye. Apologie van de historische interesse* by the Leuven historians Tom Verschaffel and Jo Tollebeek (Amsterdam: Wereldbibliotheek, 1992).

10. J. C. H. Blom, 'In de ban van goed of fout? Wetenschappelijke geschiedschrijving over de bezettingstijd in Nederland," in his *Crisis, bezetting en herstel. Tien studies over Nederland 1930–1950* (Rotterdam, Netherlands: HB uitgevers, 1989), 102–20.

11. Nadia Nsayi, *Dochter van de dekolonisatie* (Antwerp, Belgium: EPO, 2020).

12. Suze Zijlstra, *De voormoeders. Een verborgen Nederlands-Indische familiegeschiedenis* (Amsterdam: Ambo Anthos, 2021).

13. See, for example, the blog by Roschanack Shaery-Yazdi, professor in the History Department of the University of Antwerp, about her youth in Tehran: https://blog.uantwerpen.be/power-in-history/remembering-st-martins-day-in-tehran/.

14. Sarah Wagner, "Srebrenica in Court," in *Srebrenica in the Aftermath of Genocide*, ed. Laura Nettelfield and Sarah Wagner (Cambridge, UK: Cambridge University Press, 2014), 217–49, esp. 222.

15. On the history of this party, see De Wever, *Greep naar de macht*.

16. See Frank Seberechts, *Geschiedenis van de DeVlag. Van cultuurbeweging tot politieke partij (1935–1945)* (Ghent, Belgium: Perspectief Uitgaven, 1991).

17. See Advisory Committee for the Interned, section Veurne, to the Minister of Justice, March 24, 1945, Brussels, Belgium State Archives (BSA), nr. 10.770.

18. Report of the Inspector of the Security of the State to the services of the Military Justice, June 5, 1945, BSA, Files Military Court August Beyen, 611/47. All the archival sources mentioned below stem from this same file.

19. "Verzoekschrift om genade. Verslag en voorstellen" [*Request for grace. Report and proposals*], April 25, 1946, BSA, 611/47.

20. Military Justice Bruges to the President of the Sequester, September 26, 1946, BSA, 611/47.

21. Testimony of Alphonse Dumon, June 4, 1945, BSA, 611/47.

22. In any case, my father did not recognize his mother's handwriting in the letters she signed.

23. August Beyen to the military judge of Bruges, August 1, 1946, BSA, 611/47; Marie-Louise Coulier to the military judge of Bruges, December 27, 1946, BSA, 611/47.

24. Most elaborately so in August Beyen to the military judge [of Veurne], March 25, 1945, BSA, 611/47.

25. Beyen, *Oorlog en verleden*, 414.

26. Rudolf Dekker, *Plagiarism, Fraud, and Whitewashing: The Grey Turn in the History of the German Occupation of the Netherlands* (Amsterdam: Panchaud, 2020). This is the English-language translation of an essay Dekker published in 2019 under the title *Plagiaat en nivellering: nieuwe trends in de Nederlandse geschiedschrijving over de Tweede Wereldoorlog*.

27. These criticisms were most notably directed at Chris van der Heijden, *Grijs verleden. Nederland en de Tweede Wereldoorlog* (Amsterdam: Boom, 2001), and Bart van der Boom, '*Wij wisten niets van hun lot'. Gewone Nederlanders en de Holocaust* (Amsterdam: Boom, 2012). Hans Blom, the aforementioned pioneer of the "beyond right and wrong" paradigm, has recently revealed the collaborationist past of his own family (to which his father was a partial exception). He did so in a documentary series broadcast on Dutch public television in 2024.

28. See my "Ideologisch engagement, lokale padafhankelijkheid en individuele keuzen. Het verzet in Wijgmaal tijdens de Tweede Wereldoorlog," *Belgisch Tijdschrift voor Nieuwste Geschiedenis* 52, nos. 1–2 (2022): 120–39.

29. See Joris Smets, "Jeanne Dormaels krijgt eigen plein aan station van Wijgmaal," *Het Laatste Nieuws*, July 7, 2020. See also my "Een monument voor Jeanne Dormaels," *De Standaard*, November 24, 2018.

30. I wrote more general reflections on this in my "Een stap terug, voor het te laat is. Bekentenissen van een halfslachtige Tweede Wereldoorlog-historicus," *Belgisch Tijdschrift voor Nieuwste Geschiedenis* 49, nos. 2–3 (2019): 202–9.

31. Michael Rothberg, *The Implicated Subject: Beyond Survivors and Perpetrators* (Stanford, CA: Stanford University Press, 2019). For an application of Rothberg's view to the current Dutch debates, see Barbara Henkes, "De historicus als *implicated subject*. Het aandeel van historici bij het vorm en betekenis geven aan een gewelddadig verleden," *BMGN-Low Countries Historical Review* 137 (2022): 68–83.

Chapter Ten: Jack in the Fog

1. Annie Ernaux, *L'Atelier noir* (Paris: Gallimard, 2022), 143.

2. Christine Bard, *L'histoire traverse nos peaux douces. Jack* (Donnemarie-Dontilly, France: Éditions iXe, 2022).

3. This title situates me in the "literary tradition" of *returns*—*Returning to Reims* (Didier Eribon, trans. Michael Lucey), *Retour à Yvetot* (Annie Ernaux)—while distinguishing myself through the plural form, the regularity of my visits to my parents, and the affectionate and emotional tone of my story. Maubeuge is the small town in the north of France where I grew up, not far from Jeumont, on the Franco-Belgian border, where I was born. It is located about a hundred kilometers south of Lille. It had 36,000 residents in the 1970s. The town was fortified at the end of the seventeenth century; two-thirds of the ramparts have been preserved, creating a green and slightly natural space in the town that favors discreet encounters.

4. I am not implying that the search for and transmission of knowledge lack emotion: see Françoise Waquet, *Une histoire émotionnelle du savoir. XVIIe-XXIe siècle* (Paris: CNRS, 2019).

5. As I told the volunteers at the parish in Maubeuge who were preparing the religious ceremony for my mother's burial with us, her three children, this was a difficult constraint concerning my mother, that saint. The ceremony took place on July 26, 2022.

6. Translator's note: Poujadism was a right-wing populist movement led by Pierre Poujade in the 1950s. Its objective was to defend small business interests in France.

7. The sociologist Anne Muxel notes "the extreme individual specificity in the description and recall of a memory" in the material she gathered for her work: *Individu et mémoire familiale* (Paris: Nathan, 1996), 13.

8. Muxel, *Individu et mémoire familiale*, 13.

9. Among others, Alain de Mijola, *Préhistoires de famille* (Paris: PUF, 2004).

10. This is a subject on which I elaborated in *Mon genre d'histoire*, with Jean-Marie Durand (Paris: PUF, 2021).

11. Chantal Jacquet, *Les transclasses ou la non-reproduction* (Paris: PUF, 2014). Vincent de Gaulejac's work on class neurosis and shame is very inspiring.

12. That is why writer Daniel Mendelsohn turned himself into a historian: *The Lost: A Search for Six of Six Million* (London: Harper, 2008 [2007]).

13. Mona Ozouf, *Composition française. Retour sur une enfance bretonne* (Paris: Gallimard, 2009); Ivan Jablonka, *A History of the Grandparents I Never Had*, trans. Jane Kuntz (Stanford, CA: Stanford University Press, 2016 [2012]); Camille Lefebvre, *À l'ombre de l'histoire des autres* (Paris: EHESS, 2022); Claire Zalc, *Z ou souvenirs d'historienne* (Paris: Éditions de la Sorbonne, 2021); Stéphane Audoin-Rouzeau, *Quelle histoire: un récit de filiation (1914–2014)* (Paris: Gallimard/Seuil, 2013) (a later version includes an added section on the women in his family: "Du côté des femmes").

14. Danièle Sallenave, *L'églantine et le muguet* (Paris: Gallimard, 2018). This blurring phenomenon has been analyzed in several works, including Ivan Jablonka's *History Is a Contemporary Literature: Manifesto for the Social Sciences*, trans. Nathan Bracher (Ithaca, NY: Cornell University Press, 2018 [2014]).

15. Ernaux, *L'atelier noir*, 143.

16. Annie Ernaux, *A Man's Place*, trans. Tanya Leslie (New York: Seven Stories Press, 2012 [1983]), 13.

17. It is not possible to elaborate on this fundamental aspect of my work here. Mourning clearly pushes people to write a large variety of literary memorials. I wanted to pay homage to my father in the style of Albert Cohen's *Book of My Mother*, trans. Bella Cohen (New York: Archipelago, 2012 [1954]).

18. Philippe Lejeune, *Le pacte autobiographique* (Paris: Éditions du Seuil, 1975).

19. Vincent de Gaulejac, *L'histoire en héritage. Roman familial et trajectoire sociale* (Paris: Payot, 2012), 11.

20. Translator's note: In French, the masculine noun "père" (father) must be accompanied by a masculine possessive, "mon" (my). Here, the author uses the feminine possessive "ma" in its place. Also, the original text plays with the double meaning of the word *genre*, which in French means both gender and literary category.

21. Translator's note: A reference to the motto of the Vichy government.

22. That can produce a raw gaze on the maternal figure. See Gay Block's photographic biography of her mother: *Bertha Alyce: Mother exPosed* (Albuquerque: University of New Mexico Press, 2003).

23. See, among others, Sophie Chauveau, *La fabrique des pervers* (Paris: Gallimard, 2016); and, published in a post-MeToo context, jurist Camille Kouchner's *La familia grande*, trans. Adriana Hunter (New York: Other Press, 2022 [2021]).

24. Rose-Marie Lagrave recently used the qualifier "feminist" in the very title of her autobiography: *Se ressaisir. Enquête autobiographique d'une transfuge de classe féministe* (Paris: La Découverte, 2021).

25. Marguerite Yourcenar, *Dear Departed*, trans. Maria Louise Ascher (New York: FSG, 1991 [1974]); Marguerite Yourcenar, *How Many Years: A Memoir*, trans. Maria Louise Ascher (New York: FSG, 1995) [1977]).

26. This notion of "emptying" one late parent's home is now associated with psychoanalyst Lydia Flem's wonderful *The Final Reminder: How I Emptied My Parents's House*, trans. Elfreda Powell (London: Souvenir, 2015 [2004]).

27. And so I reproduced the excess that had characterized the inside of my parents' home, intended to appear "bourgeois."

28. Novelist Marie-Aude Murail wrote her family saga after her parents' deaths, waiting until her later years to satisfy her desire "to be a historian": *En nous beaucoup d'hommes respirent* (Paris: L'Iconoclaste, 2018).

29. Michelle Perrot, "L'air du temps," in *Essais d'ego-histoire*, ed. Pierre Nora (Paris: Gallimard: 1987), 241–92.

30. Olivier Schwarz, *Le monde privé des ouvriers. Hommes et femmes du Nord* (Paris: PUF, 1990).

31. Translator's note: The original text contained an untranslatable play on words between the homophones "cher" (dear, treasured) and "chair" (flesh) to emphasize the importance of Jack's body in the author's memories.

32. In 1978, Georges Perec published *Je me souviens* (*I Remember* [2014]), in which he listed his memories related to the minute aspects of daily life that characterized his childhood and youth in postwar France. He seemed to have been inspired by the autobiographical work of the American artist and writer Joe Brainard, author of *I Remember* (London: Noting Hill Editions, 2012 [1970]).

33. Translator's note: *Paperoles*, an invented word, blends *paperasse* (papers, paperwork) and *paroles* (words, speech) to mean approximately "paper speech."

34. Patrice Marcilloux, *Les ego-archives. Traces documentaires et recherche de soi* (Rennes, France: PUR, 2013).

35. To use the category created by Violette Morin in a foundational article, "L'objet biographique," *Communications* 13 (1969), taken up by Thierry Bonnot in *L'attachement aux choses* (Paris: CNRS Éditions, 2014), 84.

36. This passage can be contextualized by several books dealing with family memory of the Algerian War and the documentative benefit of family photos. The most recent is Raphaëlle Branche, *"Papa, qu'as-tu fait en Algérie?"* (Paris: La Découverte, 2020).

37. The *Régiment de Corée*, literally the Korea Regiment, fought as a battalion in Korea and French Indochina before arriving in Algiers in 1955.

38. Martine Sonnet, *Atelier 62* (Mazères, France: Le temps qu'il fait, 2008), 229.

39. I also included three of his other texts: a children's tale, a retirement speech, and a recipe for regional cuisine.

40. I have been steeped in Annie Ernaux's legacy for such a long time! Roland Barthes: what poetical and analytical wonders. A memory of the shock of reading Didier Eribon's *Returning to Reims*. But also my classics: Albert Cohen, Romain Gary, Georges Pérec, Hélène Cixous, Colette, Anaïs Nin.

41. As I write these lines, I feel as though I am joining Camille de Toledo and Alice Zeniter, writers born in the 1980s. See Camille de Toledo, *Thésée, sa vie nouvelle* (Paris: Verdier, 2020); Alice Zeniter, *The Art of Losing*, trans. Frank Wynne (New York: FSG, 2021 [2017]).

42. Delphine Horvilleur, *Vivre avec nos morts* (Paris: Grasset, 2021), 66.

43. Most of the readings that struck me are collected in Aurore Turbiau, Margot Lachkar, Camille Islert, Manon Berthier, and Alexandre Antolin, eds., *Écrire à l'encre violette. Littératures lesbiennes en France de 1900 à nos jours* (Paris: Le Cavalier bleu, 2022).

44. Paule du Bouchet, *Emportée* (Paris: Actes Sud, 2011); *Debout sur le ciel* (Paris: Gallimard, 2018); Marie Nimier, *La reine du silence* (Paris: Gallimard, 2004); Anne Pauly, *Avant que j'oublie* (Lagrasse, France: Verdier, 2019); Virginie Linhart, *Le jour où mon père s'est tu* (Paris: Seuil, 2008); Yaël Pachet, *Le peuple de mon père* (Paris: Fayard, 2019); Colombe Schneck, *Les guerres de mon père* (Paris: Stock, 2018); *Voies de pères voix de filles*, fifteen women writers' texts collected by Adine Sagalyn (Paris: Maren Sell & Cie, 1988); Leïla Sebbar, ed., *Mon père* (Montpellier, France: Chèvre-feuille étoilée, 2007).

45. Ernaux, *L'atelier noir*, 16.

46. We had spoken about it beginning at the end of the 1990s in a double context: the fight for civil unions, in which I participated (a law authorizing these unions was passed in 1999), and major publications regarding homosexuality, particularly those of Didier Eribon, who helped introduce queer theory in France. I think I shared impressions from my readings of his *Réflexions sur la question gay* (Paris: Fayard, 1999). I participated in the *Dictionnaire des cultures gays et lesbiennes* (Paris: Larousse, 2003), edited by Eribon; and entered into a civil union in 2001. There were thus many opportunities to talk about homosexuality, but my father never allowed himself to say "I."

47. Cited by Ernaux. Translator's note: The English translation quoted here is from Marcel Proust, *The Captive*, trans. C. K. Scott Moncrieff (New York, 2022 [1923]), 87.

48. Alison Bechdel, *Fun Home: A Family Tragicomic* (Boston: Houghton Mifflin, 2006); Alison Bechdel, *Are You My Mother? A Comic Drama* (Boston: Houghton Mifflin Harcourt, 2012); Alysia Abbott, *Fairyland* (New York: Norton, 2013); Isabelle Carré, *Les rêveurs* (Paris: Grasset, 2018); Constance Joly, *Over the Rainbow* (Paris: Flammarion, 2021). Two of these gay fathers died from AIDS in the 1990s.

49. Sébastien Lifshitz's documentary film *Les invisibles* (2012) is very precious in this regard. He provided homosexual men and lesbians between the ages of seventy-five and eighty-five with an opportunity to speak.

50. Michel Larivière, *Femmes d'homosexuels célèbres* (Paris: La Musardine, 2016).

51. In addition to my activism, associative work, and research, I have, for example, overseen a research program on "Gender and Sexist and Homophobic Discriminations."

52. The word returns incessantly as I write. While using a camera, I am also irresistibly attracted to all that veils. For example, I took a series of photos of Maubeuge through the curtains (made of netting) of the windows in my parents' apartment.

53. As Lionnette Arnodin demonstrates in "Imaginaires du brouillard," *Ethnologie française* 39, no. 4 (2009): 609–22.

54. For example, in the production of *Dictionnaire des féministes*, ed. Christine Bard with Sylvie Chaperon (Paris: PUF, 2017).

55. And while reading Ludivine Bantigny, *L'œuvre du temps* (Paris: Éditions de la Sorbonne, 2019).

56. I wrote this text immersed in Ernaux's *Atelier noir*. The following sentence echoes my title: "And what if History only existed by passing through beings?" (41).

Afterword

1. Martha Minow, *Between Vengeance and Forgiveness: Facing History After Genocide and Mass Violence* (Boston: Beacon Press, 1999), 58.

2. Ariella Azoulay, *Potential History: Unlearning Imperialism* (New York: Verso, 2019).